SAVING SPORT

In memory of my mother
Mary F. (Ciss) O'Gorman

Kevin O'Gorman SMA

Saving Sport

SPORT, SOCIETY AND SPIRITUALITY

the columba press

First published in 2010 by
the columba press
55A Spruce Avenue, Stillorgan Industrial Park,
Blackrock, Co Dublin

Cover by Bill Bolger
Origination by The Columba Press
Printed in Ireland by ColourBooks Ltd, Dublin

ISBN 978 1 85607 670 8

Table of Contents

Introduction

I spent the decade of the 1990s in South Africa, one of the most beautiful countries on the planet, blessed with an abundance of human and natural resources but also blighted and broken by the brutal laws and legacy of apartheid which for decades had forcibly separated and subjugated people on the grounds of colour. The fault lines of that state were formed around and along the contours of race. Sport played a significant part in the life and leisure of that society but it also reflected and reinforced the divisions which were political, racial and economic. Soccer was mainly the preserve of the black and coloured communities, while rugby was the pride and property – the famed and feared Springboks – of white South Africa, both Afrikaans and English speaking. By 1990 cricket had quietly commenced a policy of inclusion and integration.

I remember seeing an interview on television in which Nelson Mandela related the delight he and his fellow-prisoners on Robben Island took whenever they heard of the Springboks' defeat, particularly during the 1974 British and Irish Lions rugby tour, a defeat that assumed almost apocalyptic proportions in the local media and which even reverberated in the state parliament. This made his visit – in the year after his inauguration as President of the newly democratic South Africa – at the team's training ground in Cape Town prior to the opening game of the 1995 World Cup tournament against Australia, all the more incredible. After South Africa had defeated their arch-rivals the New Zealand All-Blacks in the final, as he presented the Webb Ellis trophy to Francois Pienaar he sported a number 7 jersey similar to the won worn by the victorious captain throughout the competition.[1] The euphoria of that event rivalled the excite-

---

1. For an account of the events leading up to and around the final itself see John Carlin, *Playing the Enemy – Nelson Mandela and the game that made a nation*, London: Atlantic Books, 2008.

ment of his own inauguration, engendering the possibility that sport could sow precious seeds of healing and reconciliation. Sport, one of the most spontaneous activities of human beings, was seen as symbolic of both the need for and possibility of transformation. As the whole of South Africa seemed to rejoice at the team's success (their first participation in the Rugby World Cup) there was a sense in the country that sport was no longer a force for division but rather a factor in unification. A sign of this was the offer made subsequently by the South African Rugby Football Union to make its superb stadia throughout the country available for the bid to host the 2006 soccer World Cup, which will be held there in 2010.

Returning to Ireland at the end of 2001, I was surprised to see and hear the extensive media coverage of sport in Ireland and Britain on radio, television and in the press. The prevalence of sport and its coverage is highlighted by the fact that on Saturday 23 February 2008 BBC1 showed twelve hours of almost continuous sport coverage, prompting journalist Barney Ronay to state that 'even to a veteran armchair sports omnivore like me there was something vaguely appalling about the experience, comparable only to having a funnel wedged into your trachea and being forcibly engorged with multiple helpings of live and exclusive top-flight international super-sporting action'.[2] Commenting on this amount of television coverage, Irish media analyst Terry Prone states that 'the BBC apologised for broadcasting too much sport last weekend; they browbeat viewers with sport, whether they wanted it or not'.[3] The importance of sport in this part of the world is highlighted by a statement of Professor Joe Lee of University College Cork: 'For many people, sport isn't just the icing on the cake of life. It is life. Next to sex, it is what makes the world go round for a large proportion of the western world, now with plenty of time on its hands and not a notion of what to do with it. That is why sport has become far too important to be left to the sports pages.'[4] In this context the remark of television presenter and journalist Michael Parkinson that 'the importance

---

2. 'The BBC's sports coverage can be a real test of stamina', *The Guardian*, 26 February 2008.

3. *Sunday Tribune*, 2 March 2008.

4. Quoted in *Village*, 22-28 April, 2005, p 12

of sport is that it doesn't matter, except as an antidote to things that do'[5] raises interesting questions.

Reading English and Irish newspapers for some time made me realise that another dynamic was being played out in the descriptions and deliberations of players and teams, games, venues and events delivered by sport fans and journalists. The association of the language of faith and worship, spirituality and salvation with these activities and arenas alerted me to the articulation of what appears as an alternative theology. Crowds, commentators and columnists regularly have recourse to the language of religious faith – particularly the traditional terms and themes of Christianity – to express and enthuse over the efforts and results of teams and individuals competing at club, county and country levels. This was especially evident in relation to the 'Big Three' of Gaelic games, rugby and soccer, but elements were also discernible in relation to sports such as golf and even horseracing. A number of examples illustrated my growing interest in this development and the need to interpret it. Firstly, 'Limerick resist changes and keep faith'; 'Red road to redemption'. The former referred to the decision of the Limerick selectors to retain the same team for the replay of their first round Munster hurling championship game against Tipperary, while the latter looked at the prospects of the so-called Red Hands, Tyrone, for whom 'the road to redemption begins in Omagh on Sunday against Down'.[6] Secondly, the reference made by the presenter of BBC *Match of the Day Two* to 'this football Sabbath' and his statement that 'the good Lord giveth Van de Saar but taketh Keane'. Thirdly, *The Sunday Times* sports section which carried both the caption 'Maradona's Road to Redemption' and the headline 'Given the saviour as Ireland sneak home', references to the former Argentinian captain and the contribution of goalkeeper Shay Given to Ireland's 1-0 win over Cyprus in a critical World Cup qualifier.[7] Fourthly, in an article on the fate of Mayo's Gaelic footballers over the decades (with a phototgraphic insert of the headline *Mayo – God Help Us!* following a 16-point defeat by Galway in 1982) the sportswriter

5. *The Daily Telegraph*, 5 September 2005
6. *Irish Examiner*, 19 May 2005
7. 9 October 2005

included references to faith, redemption and forgiveness.[8] Fifthly, Munster's progress to the 'Holy Grail' of Rugby's European cup was often presented in the media as a crusade. Biblical and religious images abounded in attempts to articulate what was considered as much a spiritual matter as a sports match. The 'Promised Land' was reached in 2006 after a (biblical) seven years in the wilderness. Writing in *The Sunday Telegraph* the day after, Rupert Holmes declared that after this victory 'there is only heaven itself to play for', while decrying the claim of Captain Anthony Foley that no team had a divine right to winning the tournament: 'Rubbish. No side deserve it more. "Irish by birth, Munster by grace of God" read one of the banners. In which case God yesterday was a little man with a huge heart, Peter Stringer.'[9]

In 1988 Sean Kealy had already adverted to 'the real danger of sport becoming a religion for the many, with its quasi-religious terminology: spirit, ritual, dedication, sacrifice, ultimate, commitment, not to mention the colourful banners and signs, the fanatic supporters and mini-skirted vestal virgins'.[10] Twenty years later the 'quasi-religious' terminology has given way to and been replaced by a religious register with the symbols of Christian spirituality and the language of its liturgy devoted to the depiction and description of the deeds of (mostly) professional sports players and managers. Increasingly, words like faith, cross, redemption, salvation, worship, messianic, sacred, resurrection and their associated symbols of worship are employed to express the efforts of players, managers and promoters of sport. This is the 'scripture' of sport, the type – and hype – of language used by journalists (and increasingly by their audiences) to articulate and analyse events on and around the field(s) of play. It is ironic that, in the context of the current debate about religious advertising in the media, at many major games which are shown on Irish television there is (free) space for such advertising in the form of a placard (3:16) held up directly behind one of the goalposts. This refers to the gospel of

---

8. 'Fall Guys', *The Sunday Times*, 7 August 2005
9. 21 May, 2006
10. 'Towards a Theology of Sport', *Doctrine & Life*, 38 (September 1988), 348.

John: 'For God so loved the world that he gave his only Son, so that everyone who believes in him may not perish but may have eternal life.'[11]

A study of the relationship between the sport and Christian faith suggests three distinct stages: Discovery, Discernment, Development. The first stage of discovery demands a survey, both historical and contemporary, of the connections between the world(s) of sport and the witness of Christianity in the context of its community of belief (faith), understanding (theology) and worship (prayer). This process of discovery delineates how the scriptures and subsequent teaching have seen and stated links between faith and sporting activity, how the church, both in terms of individual interest and institutional involvement has interacted with the socio-cultural performance, and promotion of sport. This leads to looking at how media (and advertising) have adopted the language and logic of the Christian creed and code to both communicate and comment on the world of sport at local, national and international levels. This descriptive probing necessarily leads to a process of discernment where central and critical questions are asked about the image of God (theology), interpretation of hope (redemption) and implications for morality and spirituality being conveyed in the activity, articulation and analysis of sport. In the context of contemporary culture and conspicuous coverage of sport, this course of discernment calls for the following questions to be considered: Does the assumption of the vocabulary and symbols of Christian faith by the sporting media amount to a collapse of transcendent truth into profane and mundane terms that are merely relics without any religious significance, witnessing to a loss of the sense of the sacred? How is sport, as one of the substantive 'signs of the times', to be interpreted theologically? If sport is often seen and stated in terms of salvation, in what sense is it meaningful to speak of saving sport?

Over eighty years ago the philosopher Max Scheler stated that 'sport has grown immeasurably in scope and in social importance, but the meaning of sport has received little in the way

---

11. *The Holy Bible – New Revised Standard Version*, (Oxford: Oxford University Press, 1989).

of serious attention'.[12] While this work is mainly devoted to the description of the relation between sport and religious faith and the theological discernment of its representation in the sporting press, it suggests avenues both of inquiry and interpretation where the meaning of sport may be developed, particularly in the light of Christian revelation and redemption. This development would deal with the meaning of sport in philosophical terms, focusing on areas such as aesthetics (the game as a form of art, 'the beautiful game'), ethics (sport seen as welfare and not warfare) and metaphysics (sport in terms of time, tragedy and transcendence). Such a trajectory would traverse sport in terms of the beautiful, the good and the true as a positive threshold to a theological measure of its meaning in the context of the Christian mystery. Key areas for such an interpretation of sport would include theological anthropology with its issues of human embodiment, exercise and expression, and moral theology which investigates the historical implications of the Incarnation.[13] A dialogical imagination which deals with the fundamental issue of faith and culture could inspire and inform such a development of the meaning of sport.

The style of this work aims to be an amalgam of both the anecdotal and analytical. 'Anecdotal' because it aims to recount events and experiences of sport in its many forms and fields of play and among its many fans. If sport is essentially part of the human story in an embodied form it needs the element of narrative to express it. The anecdotal articulates the initial (and often lasting) impressions of people who participate in sport as players, spectators and commentators. 'Analytical' because it is the connection between sport and Christianity that has developed from the time of Saint Paul to the teaching of Pope John Paul II, where sport is seen both in terms of a metaphor for and measure of the moral and spiritual life of its members. 'Analytical' also because it attempts to assess and address theologically the activity and aim of adopting the traditional language and symbols used to conceptualise, command and celebrate that moral and

12. Quoted in 'Editorial – Sport, Society and Religion', *Concilium* 205 (1989), 4
13. See my 'Theology's Four Quartets', *Doctrine & Life*, 57 (April 2007) 31-49

spiritual life. If sport is a new form of spirituality which has no need for Christianity, and the texts of sporting journalists tell of an alternative theology, the church(es) need urgently to address this alienation in its many aspects.

Sport is here understood in the sense of the definition given by Robert J. Higgs: 'Competitive games that are bound by rules in space and time, thus differing from other forms of play in this regard, and requiring strain or agony, both mental and physical, on the part of contestants.'[14] These contests involve both individuals and teams, amateur and professional. Success in many such games was summarised simply, though not simplistically, by the legendary American football coach Vince Lombardi: "Here are the basics. This thing in my hand is called a football. And these are your legs and arms. Now our aim is to get that ball, using your legs and arms, in spite of those who will try to stop us, from one end of the field to the other.'[15]

As the many references indicate, this book has been in gestation for several years. I am grateful to my friends Joe Egan SMA and Michael McCabe SMA for their reading and commenting on the text at different stages. Parts of chapters 6 and 8 previously appeared as articles in *Doctrine & Life* and *The Furrow* and are reproduced here with kind permission.

---

14. Quoted by John Coleman in 'Sport and the Contradictions of Society', *Concilium* 205 (1989): 21-31 at 21
15. Quoted in Daniel O'Leary, 'Begin with the Heart', *The Furrow*, 58 (April 2007) 212

CHAPTER ONE

Saint Paul and Pope John Paul II on Sport

'Let us run with perseverance the race that is set before us, looking to Jesus the pioneer and perfecter of our faith, who for the sake of the joy that was set before him endured the cross, disregarding its shame, and has taken his seat at the right hand of the throne of God.' *(Hebrews 12:1-2)*

'How can the church not be interested in sport?'[1]

Scripting Sport

On 11 May 2002 the then three Irish broadsheets – *Examiner, Independent* and *Times* – all carried photographs on their front pages of the Republic of Ireland and Manchester United captain Roy Keane who had been conferred with an honorary Doctorate in Law at University College Cork the previous day. The *Examiner* editorialised: 'It was fitting that the football genius of Roy Keane should be acknowledged by University College Cork yesterday, an institution where outstanding achievement is a goal pursued to the same degree as he pursues perfection on the field.' Considering him to be, on the eve of the soccer World Cup, 'probably the best player in the world' the leader lauded him 'as the epitome of what the spirit of sport is all about'. In the light of events that unfolded in and around the Irish training camp in Saipan a few weeks later, which convulsed the country and its media, the irony of both *The Examiner*'s heading 'Keano has the law on his side' and *The Independent*'s caption 'Now Roy can really lay down the law' was, in hindsight at least, remark-able, if not indeed risible. The pursuit of perfection provided its own cost, for both the Corkman and the country. To be even handed to 'Doctor Roy', as some subsequently dubbed him, he

1. Pope Pius XII, *Address to Roman Athletes*, 20 May 1945. Quoted by Carlo Mazza, 'Sport as viewed from the Church's Magisterium' in *The World of Sport Today – A Field of Christian Mission*, Pontifical Council for the Laity, Libreria Editrice Vaticana, 2006, 55-73 at 61

acknowledged his embarrassment at being alongside the other recipients of honorary degrees, amongst whom were the Dominican scripture scholar Jerome Murphy-O'Connor whose citation included reference to both his native Cork and Corinth which acknowledged his expertise on the life and letters of Saint Paul. A fitting footnote perhaps to Keane's citation could have referred to the fact that the Corinthians of Paul's concern and correspondence hosted the biennial Isthmian Games for professional athletes who 'competed for monetary prizes, either a sum of money or reduction of taxes ... Sometimes the reward for a victorious race came from the winner's home town, honoured as it was by the fame and glory that resulted from the victory.'[2]

Playing Paul

There are a number of sporting connotations in the correspondence of Paul to different Christian communities:

'Do you not know that in a race the runners all compete, but only one receives the prize? Run in such a way that you may win it. Athletes exercise self-control in all things; they do it to receive a perishable garland, but we an imperishable one. So I do not run aimlessly, nor do I box as though beating the air; but I punish my body and enslave it, so that after proclaiming to others, I myself should not be disqualified.' (1 Cor 9:24-27)

'I went up in response to a revelation. Then I laid before him the gospel that I proclaim among the Gentiles, in order to make sure that I was not running or had not run, in vain.' (Gal 2:2)

'Beloved, I do not consider that I have made it my own; but this one thing I do: forgetting what lies behind and straining to what lies ahead, I press on towards the goal for the prize of the heavenly call of God in Jesus Christ. Let those of us then who are mature be of the same mind.' (Phil 3:13-15)

In his encyclical *Redemptoris Missio* Pope John Paul II employs the example of Paul preaching to the Athenians in the

---

2. Quoted by Timothy A. Friedrichsen in 'Disciple as Athlete', *The Living Light*, 39(Winter 2002), 15

Aeropagus 'in language appropriate to and understandable in those surroundings'[3] as an instance of inculturation of the gospel and initiation of the church. Connie Lasher notes that 'in nearly every discussion of the topic, John Paul II proffers St Paul's First Letter to the Corinthians as one that illustrates the papal philosophy and theology of sport' and illustrates this with his homily at the Olympic Stadium in Rome: 'The Apostle to the Gentiles, in order to bring the message of Christ to all peoples, drew from the concepts, images, terminologies, modes of expression, and philosophical and literary references not only of the Jewish tradition but also of Hellenistic culture. And he did not hesitate to include sport among the human values which he used as points of support and reference for dialogue with the people of his time. Thus he recognised the fundamental validity of sport, considering it not just as a term of comparison to illustrate a higher ethical and aesthetic ideal but also in its intrinsic reality.'[4] Both in his missionary preaching and penmanship Paul consciously uses the metaphor of sport(s) for communities familiar with both the gymnasium and games in their (Greek) culture. Thus he is in continuity with the Greek philosophical tradition which portrayed athletic struggle as a symbol of the search for meaning and morality. His First Letter to the Corinthians was written between AD52 and 57, with 54 preferred as the most probable date. This correspondence was occasioned by problems and questions in the community and also by Paul's concern, as Murphy-O' Connor commented, 'to bring them a true appreciation of authentic life in Christ'.[5]

The Imperishable Prize
Paul's reference to both running and boxing in 1 Corinthians occurs at the end of chapter nine where he has stated his renunciation of the rights of an apostle in order to (more) freely announce the gospel to the community. In renouncing such rights

---

3. *Catholic International*, 2 (March 15-31, 1991) par.37(c), 269
4. 'A Hymn to Life: The Sports Theology of Pope John Paul II', *The Living Light*, 39 (Winter 2002), 6
5. Raymond E. Brown, Joseph A. Fitzmyer and Roland E. Murphy, eds, *The New Jerome Biblical Commentary*, Englewood Cliffs, NJ: Prentice Hall, 1990, 799

and reward, the prize he receives is highlighted all the more. (The Corinthians hosted the Isthmian games for professional athletes in contrast to the amateur contests at Olympia.) In verse 24 Paul states that he does 'it all for the sake of the gospel, so that I might share in its blessings'. As Lincoln E. Galloway notes, Paul 'invites the Corinthians to understand his apostolic freedom that requires him to be constantly exhibited to the world as an example, and marked by the athlete's hardship, toil and self-control'.[6] However, his employment of the metaphor of running a race for evangelisation – with its emphasis on individual effort and achievement – seems initially to undermine the communal sharing and responsibility he is concerned to communicate to his readers and hearers. He does not resolve this apparent antimony but enthusiastically endorses running and winning, exhorting them to engage likewise. Perhaps the encouragement of 'competition' is an example of evangelical exaggeration. At any rate, he emphasises the necessity for self-control as an ethical imperative intended to integrate this element of Stoic virtue and value into the Christian moral life. His reference to the body recapitulates the teaching of chapters five and six where he rejected the influence of the so-called Spirit-people who so stressed the significance of the mind, soul and knowledge that they devalued the importance of the human body. Paul clearly knew how to mine the various veins and values of a metaphor.

Paul's argument and appeal to his audience appears as another instance of acknowledging the activity of God and of asking them to accept the assistance of the Holy Spirit, thereby overcoming alienation and division in the community. It is the grace of God in Christ which has made him into an apostle, 'and his grace towards me has not been in vain' (15:10). The goal of the 'imperishable garland' is the same prize for both the proclaimer of the gospel and for those who persevere in its grace, prompting Paul to give thanks to God 'who gives us the victory through our Lord Jesus Christ' (15:57). With the prospect of a common goal Paul promotes the essentially communal nature of Christian competition.

---

6. *Freedom in the Gospel*, Leuven: Peeters, 2004, 196

Running Heavenwards

> 'I want you to compare faith with running in a race. It's hard, requires concentration of will, energy of soul … Everyone runs in his or her own way. But where does the power come from to finish the race? From within … commit yourself to the Lord and he'll see you through to the end.' (Eric Liddle in *Chariots of Fire*)[7]

On several occasions Paul refers to his life of itinerant preaching and follow-up letter writing as a race that he is running. (There is an independent recourse to this image in relation to Paul, in Acts of the Apostles, where he is interpreted as telling the Ephesians that he is about to leave them for the last time: 'I do not count my life of any value to myself, if only I may finish my course and the ministry that I received from the Lord Jesus, to testify to the good new of God's grace.' 20:24.) It is in the Letter to the Philippians that Paul, almost literally, pushes the metaphor of running a race to its limits. This epistle was addressed to the first church Paul established in Europe, in the Roman colony of Philippi. Written probably in or around AD55, in this letter from prison (the first of a long list in this genre of Christian communication), Paul presents many of the paradoxes he delighted in by being 'a prisoner of the Lord', for example, the feeling of freedom in captivity and the delight of joy in detention. In chapter 3 he presents a resume of his life, the result of his conversion from relying on righteousness and merit by his own efforts to the mercy and reconciliation gained by Christ through his death and resurrection, the 'righteousness from God based on faith'(3:9). Describing himself in the manner of an athlete struggling to finish the race, Paul considers his present plight as suffering that is sharing in the passion of Christ so that he may eventually reach the destiny of 'citizenship in heaven' (3:20) through his resurrection from the dead. 'This one thing I do: forgetting what lies behind and straining to what lies ahead, I press on towards the goal for the prize of the heavenly call of God in Christ Jesus.' (3:13-14)

Sean Kealy describes how Paul draws on five phrases from the culture of Greek games to clarify the meaning of maturity in Christ:

---

7. Quoted in 'Towards a Theology of Sport', 339

a) *'I press on'*. Here Paul proclaims the pursuit of striving towards resurrection-destiny, salvation in and through Christ.

b) *'Forgetting what lies behind'*. This is the attitude adopted from the athlete who is absolutely dedicated and driven to attain the finishing line.

c) *'Straining to what lies ahead'*. This conveys the almost palpable sense of the athlete stretching every sinew to succeed.

d) *'Towards the goal'*. In running, this was represented by the pillar at the completion of the racecourse.

e) *'For the prize'*. Used only here (and earlier in 1 Corinthians), this signifies the perishable crown or garland given to winning athletes. For Paul the prize that does not perish is to be given a place in and with Christ in the resurrection from the dead, that is, eternal life.[8]

Paul's intention is not individualistic. In exhorting the Philippians to imitate him, he invites them to persevere and attain their goal, and thus avoid the fate of some of the Galatians who gave up ('You were running well; who prevented you from obeying the truth?' Gal 5:7). It is this concern for the communities he has converted to the gospel of Jesus Christ that will consume him until he has completed his apostolic course and received his reward: 'The time of my departure has come. I have fought the good fight, I have finished the race, I have kept the faith. From now on there is reserved for me the crown of righteousness, which the Lord, the righteous judge, will give to me on that day'. (2 Tim 4:6-7)

The Team Player
As Timothy Friedrichsen has noted, the 'athlete-as-disciple metaphor limps a bit. In a footrace or a boxing match there can be only one winner.'[9] In a lecture given a few days after receiving his honorary doctorate in UCC, Murphy-O'Connor spoke of how Paul had to overcome the insecurity of individualism, as instanced by the need to look out for himself and take care of his possessions, particularly his leather-working tools: 'Such experiences were also to lead Paul to an understanding of the import-

---

8. *Scripture in Church*, 34 (October-December 2004), 127
9. 'Disciple as Athlete', 19

ance of community. To travel in a group solved his problems. His companions looked out for him, as he looked out for them. The demands of charity and security were both met. Eventually, he thought of the church as having the organic unity of a living body, the antithesis of a divided world.'[10] However, the strain of Christian realism that runs through Paul's letters (and presumably his ministry) exempts him from any charge of naïvete. Paul's perception of the 'power of sin' at play in the world covered the sporting arena as well as other areas of society. As Murphy-O'Connor remarks: 'The most radical societal value of fallen nature for Paul was "covetousness" which is but the obverse of "selfishness" ... with a realism and consistency that is not shared by our contemporaries, Paul saw the false value system of society as an overwhelming power.'[11] Like other areas of human life and history, the sporting sector shows its own spectrum ranging from selfishness to solidarity.

On Easter Sunday (2005), six days before his death, RAI (the Italian state television) broadcast a documentary depicting the life and work of Pope John Paul II. (One correspondent characterised it as 'almost in obituary style'.) The programme contrasted the ailing and failing condition of the Pope, unable for the first time in twenty-seven years to celebrate or even participate in the Holy Week ceremonies, with the dashing, dynamic image of the man known in earlier years as 'God's Athlete'. Like the French existentialist philosopher Albert Camus, Karol Woijtyla had been a keen goalkeeper in soccer in his youth, a sport he continued to keep an interest in throughout his life. The Polish midfield player Zibi Boniek recounts an encounter with his fellow countryman after their country's loss to Italy in the semi-final of the 1982 World Cup when the Pope reportedly said, 'I don't normally pray for a football match but I did for this one. I tried to give you all a hand. You played well, okay, but not well enough.'[12] Notwithstanding the Polish pontiff's partiality on that occasion, the Italian Football Federation cancelled the full programme of *Serie A* games in anticipation of his death.

---

10. 'Paul Challenges the Celtic Tiger', *Doctrine & Life*, 52 (November 2002), 520
11. 'Paul Challenges the Celtic Tiger', 521-522
12. Quoted in *The Irish Times*, 4 April 2005

Throughout the world various sporting associations paid tribute to him by observing times of silence during sporting events and draped flags at half mast. The Italian soccer club Juventus, whose colours are black and white, edged their website home page tribute to him with a black border. Photographic memoirs of his life included images of him boating and skiing, both in the Tatra mountains of his native Poland and in the Italian Appennines. Various members of the Irish squad who had participated in the 1990 soccer World Cup in Italy recalled in media interviews their meeting with Pope John Paul II prior to their quarter-final game againt Italy.[13]

A Papal Theology of Sport
Connie Lasher gives an account and analysis of the purpose and value of sport as a human activity within the framework of the theological anthropology of John Paul II. This theological vision is the golden thread that runs from his first encyclical *Redemptor Hominis* (*The Redeemer of Humanity*, 1979), which takes its inspiration from the Christocentric interpretation of humanity and its history. Addressing athletes from all over the world gathered in Rome to celebrate the Jubilee for the World of Sport, John Paul II ends with these words: 'We have offered sports to God as a human activity aimed at the full development of the human person and at fraternal social relations. This altar, placed in Rome's great Olympic Stadium, has reminded us that sports too are above all God's gift. This gift now asks to become mission and witness.'[14]

The Pope considers sport to be a 'human activity' alongside others in the composition of culture, interpreting its autonomy as an earthly reality which carries an ethical dimension. Referring to 'an attitude of redemption, of Christianity accepting and adopting, perfecting and elevating human values' he positively

13. A pamphlet by Joseph Brennan SJ on the papacy and the church, including reference to issues of primacy/infallibility, pictures a robust pontiff clad in rugby boots attempting a penalty kick/conversion with the papal triple tiara as the ball. Its title is *The Triple Crown*, Dublin: Irish Messenger Publications, 1989.
14. Quoted in 'A Hymn to Life: The Sports Theology of Pope John Paul II', 11

evaluates sport, even to the point of being effusive, and celebrates it in the evocation of 'a hymn to life'.[15] Theologically he
situates sport as a human activity/cultural artifact alongside
work, art, and scientific research as arenas of evangelisation according to the age old principle of his mentor Thomas Aquinas,
gratia naturam presupponit et eam perficit (grace presupposes nature
and perfects it).[16] The Pope's reference to 'an attitude of redemption' highlights the awareness that sport, with all aspects of
human culture, stands in need of redemption. John Paul II interprets the activity and validity of sport as involving a series of
interlocking relationships which include the individual, interpersonal and international dimensions of human existence. On
the personal level he perceives sport as providing the possibility
of self-awareness, discipline and sacrifice through an acceptance
of the individual's strengths and weaknesses. This view is supported by Paul Hayward, the chief sports writer for *The Daily
Telegraph:* 'Sport's only real point is to help people find out
about themselves, and to show how good life can be when
human potential is fulfilled.'[17] The profoundly moral dimension
of sporting activity is seen in the social values it both fosters and
furthers, such as fair play, loyalty, solidarity (a key term in the
thought and policy of the Polish Pope), even generosity and
friendship. Adverting to an ethical affinity between sports and
Christian faith he once asked rhetorically, 'Are not these athletic
values the deepest aspirations and requirements of the gospel
message?'[18] While appreciating the elements of moral obligation
and aspiration attached to sport, Pope John Paul was not unaware that a realistic appraisal of sport involves a recognition of
the element of competition as well as that of recreation. However,
victory is not to be prized as the ultimate value of sport but must
be set alongside the virtues of respect and solidarity which serve

15. Quoted in 'A Hymn to Life: The Sports Theology of Pope John Paul
II', 8
16. A variation, and aberration, of this theological thought pattern and
terminology is the portrait of Jim Williams in a Munster rugby jersey
with the caption 'Aussie by birth, Munster by grace of God', *Village*, 15-
21 January 2005
17. 27 May 2005
18. Quoted in 'Towards a Theology of Sport', 347

to humanise sport in what John Paul called 'the effective school of human and social maturity'.

Sporting Solidarity

In his second social encyclical, *Sollicitudo Rei Socialis*, John Paul II defined 'solidarity' in the following terms: '[It] is not a feeling of vague compassion or shallow distress at the misfortunes of so many people, both near and far. On the contrary, it is a firm and persevering determination to commit oneself to the common good; that is to say, to the good of all and of each individual, because we are all really responsible for all'.[19] 'Solidarity' was the cornerstone and fundamental concept of his social ethics, rooted in and springing from the essential sociality of human nature, the source of a universal moral standard which transcended (particular and partial) perspectives of nationality, gender, race and culture. He saw solidarity as the means to foster fraternal and friendly relations in the international arena, furthering the promotion of the global common good and world peace. As Lasher comments, this is a great responsibility 'which pertains to everyone involved in sports [and] has been a central theme in John Paul II's many allocutions to international athletic gatherings over the course of his pontificate'.[20] She notes that he has continually and consistently called on all those involved in the field of sporting activity – contestants and coaches, administrators and audiences, commentators and columnists – 'to make sports an opportunity for meeting and dialogue, over and above every barrier of language, race or culture'.[21]

An example of this spirit of solidarity enabled and engendered by sporting competition is evident in the letter by Russ Turner from Wales in the wake of his country's victory over Ireland in the RBS Six Nations rugby championship of 2005, when Wales won both the Triple Crown and Grand Slam titles: 'Wales won the game but Ireland contributed far more than sport commentators seem willing to acknowledge ... Amid the cacophony that followed the final whistle, the cheering, singing, slightly delirious Welsh fans stood shoulder to shoulder with

---

19. Libreria Editrice Vaticana, Rome: 1987, par 38
20. 'A Hymn to Life: The Sports Theology of Pope John Paul', 8
21. Quoted in 'A Hymn to Life: The Sports Theology of Pope John Paul', 8

their Irish friends. Very few left the stadium during the present-ation ceremony and the men in green, despite being hugely dis-appointed, were gloriously magnanimous in defeat, still smiling and offering handshakes and congratulations. We partied well into the next day, the strains of *Cwm Rhondda* and *The Fields of Athenry* being heard in equal measure. This was an occasion never to be forgotten. The game is consigned to history but the memory of the sportsmanship shown by the Irish supporters will stay with me forever.'[22] While clearly this communication is a case of 'Celtic solidarity', the spirit of the occasion showed the general goodwill that sport can generate and contribute to the common good.

The visit of Team Ferrari to the Vatican in autumn 2004, after their fifth successive championship success in Formula One motor racing is a memorable event, occurring towards the end of his pontificate. After presenting him with a one-fifth scale model of the season's winning vehicle the team President Luca di Montezemolo addresses him using the description of a com-pany as a 'community of people', culled from the Pope's own encyclical *Centesimus Annus* (Centenary of Rerum Novarum, 1991): 'Community is the key word, the formula one of our suc-cess. Victory is born from a mechanism made of many gears but one soul.'[23] He praises the Pope for his promotion and defence of human rights, adding that it placed him 'in pole position on the highway of humanity'. While the mixing of metaphors, me-chanical and moral, may seem somewhat manipulated, the occa-sion clearly moved the Pope deeply. In response he reiterates the importance of sport in the education of young people, espe-cially when it is exercised 'with full respect for the rules'.

Training for Transcendence
The transcendent dimension of sporting and athletic activity has been a constant theme of the Pope's teaching on the topic, which has been rooted in his own personal (and also pastoral) experi-ence of mountain climbing and skiing. Saint Thomas Aquinas

---

22. *The Irish Times*, 26 March 2005
23. Quoted in Damian McNiece, 'The Horsepower and the Glory', *The Word* 54 (April 2005)

considered beauty as one of the transcendental properties of being and Pope John Paul connects the appreciation of beauty in nature with contemplation. He calls on mountaineers to make their sport a signal for the experience of transcendence and the expression of spirituality: 'Help your members also to be contemplatives, to enjoy ever more deeply in their mind the message of creation. In contact with the beauties of the mountains, in the face of the spectacular grandeur of the peaks, the fields of snow and the immense landscapes, man enters into himself and discovers that the beauty of the universe shines not only in the framework of the exterior heavens, but also that of the soul that allows itself to be enlightened, and seeks to give meaning to life. From the things that it contemplates, in fact, the spirit is lifting up to God on the breath of prayer and gratitude towards the Creator.'[24]

A focus for Pope John Paul's evangelising papacy was furnished by the series of World Youth Days. Set against the spectacular backdrop of the Rocky Mountains for the Denver Day, the patron designated by the Pope for these events had particular significance. The Italian mountaineer and athlete Pier Giorgio Frassati (beatified in 1990) combined a love for the outdoor life with a passion to serve the sick and poor of Turin. At an opening of an exhibition on Frassati (who died at the age of 24 after contracting polio) in the Pope's former diocese of Krakow, his influence and inspiration were interpreted in the following terms: 'A "modern" young man, open to the problems of culture, sport – a tremendous mountaineer – to social questions, to the real values of life … A deep believer, nourished on the gospel message, passionately eager to serve and consumed by charity, which led him to approach, in an order of absolute precedence, the poor and the sick.'[25]

Anxious to avoid the interpretation of sport as a purely immanent affair, Pope John Paul II does not perceive its enjoyment as solely an experience of the 'passionate transitory' (to borrow a phrase from the poet Patrick Kavanagh). His ideas on the social and spiritual dimensions and demands of sport clearly go

---

24. Quoted in 'A Hymn to Life: The Sports Theology of Pope John Paul', 9
25. Idem

against the grain of a culture of individualism and an excess of consumerism which is often communicated and contributed to by the media 'colossus'. To borrow a concept from the first of his social encyclicals (*Laborem Exercens – On Work*, 1981) sport has a 'social mortgage'. This cost elevates an ethic of teamwork over trophies, participation above prizes, taking part and not victory at any costs as the true testimony of a common humanity rather than the humiliation of rivals. He considers sport to be 'a means of effacing intolerance and constructing a world of fraternity and solidarity [where] good sportsmanship demands teamwork, an attitude of respect, recognition of a rival's qualities, honesty in play and the humility to recognise one's limitations.'[26] The words of Michael Schumacher (who donated $10 million to the Asian tsunami appeal fund) are worth reflecting on, especially as they were expressed after meeting the Pope, not after one of his many race or championship victories: 'It is an enormous emotion, it is difficult to explain what one feels, it has been something truly special.'[27]

Pope John Paul II often spoke of the 'world' of modern communications as a 'new Aeropagus' for the proclamation of the gospel. Closely associated to this phenomenon are the arenas, stadia and venues that contribute to the 'new Coliseum'. Sport is one of the 'signs of the times', where seeds of the Word can be sown, signs of the Spirit discerned, dialogue between peoples of different cultures and religions (and none) developed and authentic human values promoted. While evangelisation does not 'fix upon the errors, confusions and defects ... of sin and human weakness',[28] a moral-theological evaluation of the world of sport and its evangelisation are effective epitaphs to the memory of the Pope who lauded sport and loved sportspeople.

A Vatican initiative prior to the 2004 Olympic Games showed that John Paul II's interest in sport would continue with the announcement of the creation of an office for 'Church and Sport', situated within the Pontifical Council for the Laity. In

---

26. Quoted in 'Editorial', *The Word* 54 (April 2005)
27. Quoted in Damian McNiece, 'The Horsepower and the Glory', *The Word* 54 (April 2005)
28. *Message of [1985] Synod to the People of God*, Nairobi: St Paul Publications, 1986, p 26

November 2005 its first seminar was organised around the theme of 'The Christian mission in the field of sport today' with the following five aims:

1) To carry out an initial examination of the world of sports to highlight the 'most critical questions and challenges directly concerning this new office;

2) To present an integrated synthesis of the teaching(s) of the Magisterium of the church to provide a basis for both reflection and research;

3) To explore the means of fostering a Christian presence in the world of sport and examine the structures/resources of the church to respond to this challenge;

4) To facilitate an initial exchange of ideas and information;

5) To bring together those with expertise in the various arenas of sporting activity such as scholars, professional athletes and administrators to assist the office of Church and Sport in outlining and achieving its goals.[29]

The seminar reflected on the global role of sport with its repercussions in the areas of education and ethics in the contemporary world and in line with the teaching of Pope John Paul II to promote a culture of sport contributing to the wellbeing of persons and the welfare of communities both nationally and internationally. Its proceedings were published as *The World of Sport Today – A Field of Christian Mission*.[30]

Commentators contrast the Polish Pope's passion for and knowledge of sport with an incident where his successor seemed to be unaware of the identity of the Brazilian soccer player Pele.[31] However, this interpretation ignores his radio

---

29. 'Report', *L'Osservatore Romano* (Weekly English edition), n 46 (1919), 16 November 2005, 9
30. Pontifical Council for the Laity, Libreria Editrice Vaticana, 2006.
31. 'Pope Benedict XVI was introduced to Pele, the world's most famous footballer, but had no idea who he was, it was reported yesterday. They met at the World Youth Day event in Cologne last week and Pele, according to press reports, told the Pope: "I bring you greetings from all the footballers in the world." The Pope asked him where he was from, and when Pele replied Brazil, the pontiff asked again: "You're from Brazil?" An aide then told the Pope: "Holy Father, Pele was the world's greatest footballer".' *The Daily Telegraph*, 25 August 2005

broadcast when, as Cardinal Joseph Ratzinger, he addressed the value of football and asked about its attraction for so many people: 'Football has become a global event which unites people the world over in their hopes, fears, passions and joys. Hardly any other event has such a widespread impact. This shows that it must appeal to something primordially human and the question is what is this powerful attraction based on.' Speaking on the eve of the 1978 soccer World Cup he stated that games 'symbolise life itself , an attempt to return to Paradise, to get away from the enslaving seriousness of everyday life and enjoy what does not have to be and is therefore wonderful'.[32] As Benedict XVI he spoke of sport shortly after his election in terms similar to his predecessor: 'The Day of Sport is being celebrated in Italy today for everyone; it was established to keep alive the authentic values of sports ... I hope that sport practised in a healthy and harmonious way at all levels will encourage brotherhood and solidarity between people as well as respect and an appreciation of the natural environment.'[33]

---

32. Quoted in *The Tablet*, 7 June 2008, 18
33. 'After the Angelus', *L'Osservatore Romano* (Weekly edition in English), n 23 (1897) 8 June 2005

CHAPTER TWO

Situating Sport

'What has religion got to do with football?' is a question I have often been asked by quizzical and bemused radio commentators. This is an understandable question because the church has moved over the years from being at the centre of public life, which was the case a few generations ago, to the reality today where it is very often viewed as being peripheral in community life and, indeed, is generally regarded by many people as being irrelevant and outdated. However, I often reverse the question by responding with the robust rejoinder, 'What has football got to do with religion?' And the answer is a great deal.[1]

I love reading the sports pages. At least you know what's in them is true, unlike the rest of the papers.[2]

Sociology and Sport

Eric Dunning entitles his sociological study of sport *Sport Matters* 'because it implies something about the book's subject matter while simultaneously conveying the idea that this subject matter is important'.[3] To indicate the social significance of sport he selects the following factors and features: massive media interest and the involvement of large sums of money, both public and private (one need only think of the investment and involvement of international financiers in the fortunes, literal and metaphorical, of major teams in the English Premiership); business advertising in and around the area and arena of sport (e.g.

---

1. Arthur Cunningham in Jeffrey Heskins and Matt Baker, eds, *Footballing Lives – As seen by chaplains in the beautiful game*, (Norwich: Canterbury Press, 2006), xiii
2. Former Taoiseach Bertie Ahern, *Irish Independent*, 3 February 2005. (Quoted in *De Bertie Book*, Dublin: Merlin Press, 2007)
3. London: Routledge, 1999, 1

Guinness sponsorship of the Gaelic Athletic Association, Heineken sponsorship of the European Rugby Cup); increasing state involvement to, on the one hand, positively promote public health and national pride and, on the other hand, to negatively curb and counter violence by fans; involvement/participation of large numbers of people – players, supporters/ spectators, administrators, employees serving both catering and communication industries; the formation of a *lingua franca* to foster friendship and forge ties between people participating in the sporting sector; the widespread use of sporting metaphors in political/industrial/military sectors, indicating the symbolic superstructure that sport generates throughout society; the consequences of worldwide tournaments and events such as the Olympic Games, Rugby and Soccer World Cups. (Interestingly, the Rugby World Cup anthem is entitled 'World in Union'.)

However, Dunning decries the neglect of sport(s) in sociology. Given that sport seems a ready-made subject for sociological research, for the study of human leisure and treatment of such key themes as socialisation, education, gender, class and deviance, this lacuna looks surprising. He locates the reason for this lack of interest in the ideological impetus that lay behind the development of the discipline rather than its status as a science. He asserts that 'as a result, despite its manifest importance as indicated by the various measures [above], sport is not seen as posing sociological problems of economic, political and domestic life or even with such aspects of leisure as "the arts". That is, the value of sport even tends to be downgraded as a leisure activity because it is perceived as being 'physical' in character and not engaging with the supposedly higher 'mental' and 'aesthetic' functions'.[4] Perhaps the difficulty in dealing with sport(s) in an adequate sociological analysis lies in a narrow and restrictive conception of what constitutes 'culture'.

Notwithstanding his negative assessment of the treatment of sport in sociology, Dunning states that the past three decades have seen a significant growth in the sub-discipline of what he terms the 'sociology of sport'. This growth has been generated by the expansion of the leisure and pleasure sectors within soci-

---

4. *Sport Matters*, 11

ety, with their economic effects explaining this phenomenon. This interest is best interpreted as a 'specialism', situated in and springing from the study of physical education. Despite neglect by the parent subject of mainstream sociology Dunning depicts how this specialism or subdiscipline 'has become a terrain contested by protagonists of all the main sociological paradigms ... functionalist, symbolic interactionist, Weberian, figurational and varieties of feminist and Marxist approaches. Latterly, post-structuralism and post-modernism have been added to what, paraphrasing William James, one might call the "blooming, buzzing confusion".'[5] Perhaps it is the 'blooming, buzzing confusion' caused by the vast array of sporting activities and arena that has contributed to this spectrum of such approaches, both analytical and descriptive. An excellent example of the sociology of sport and the 'blooming, buzzing confusion' it examines is Jay Coakley's *Sports in Society – Issues and Controversies* wherein he comments that 'Continued growth of the sociology of sport depends primarily on whether scholars in the field do research and produce knowledge that makes meaningful contributions to people's lives.'[6]

Klaus Heinemann identifies national concerns and concentrations in fields of empirical research such as the link between sport, economy and politics in France, between sport and cultural value systems in Finland, and the connections between sport and violent crowd behaviour (centred on soccer) in England.[7] Issues of embodiment in sport raise interesting empirical and even ethical questions, with wider gender implications. Examination of the theme of embodiment in sport embraces and is extended into the question of time employed in engaging in sporting activity as this embraces issues of leisure and recreation, enjoyment and (self)expression. The marketing of sport for both entertainment and education, for healthcare and wellbeing, for example, the question of growing obesity in children and society at large (pun not intended!) has certain economic benefits and costs for the state and sectors such as the so-called leisure industry.

---

5. Ibid., p 13
6. Boston: McGraw-Hill, 9th ed, 28
7. 'Sport and Society: The Major Questions', *Concilium*, 205(5/1989): 11-20

The role of sport in the processes of socialisation and accult-uration, the internalisation of value systems, the organisation and co-ordination of sporting bodies and associations, the rela-tion between particular sports and educational/religious instit-utions/groups are critical areas for the study of sport(s) in soci-ety. The development of golf in the so-called television era, with its gradual move from the elitist quasi-country club set to popular status, is a subject that would benefit from research and reflec-tion. Furthermore, the decline of competitive sport[8] and of phys-ical play by children in particular raises questions that run the spectrum of cultural attitudes and analysis. A preference among the population for various forms of technological entertainment is a development in recent decades that demands longitudinal studies of attitudes and issues involved and an analysis of their implications. Surrogate sport, that is sport sacrificed as an out-door activity in favour of forms of armchair and couch viewing, creates the risk of seeing sport becoming a virtual reality. A re-lated issue may be the reluctance of adults and even parents to mentor and monitor team and training activities by children and adults, given the dangers attendant on sexual abuse and allega-tions around the same. The voluntary contribution and particip-ation of coaches and organisers may be compromised by risks involved in areas of travel, transport and training, especially where issues of physical contact may be involved.

Interpreting sport

Sport is an invariable feature of human living and constitutes part of the social construction of reality and its transmission through processes of socialisation and enculturation. Boyle and Haynes indicate the cultural contribution of sport: 'It has mat-tered to thousands of players and fans across the globe, with dif-fering sports playing a particularly important role in the cultural life of countries and people. While football is the global game, other sports such as baseball occupy a central position in

---

8. A study of 2,000 adults, commissioned by the Buxton Natural Mineral Water Company, compared rates of participation in sport which point to both a long term decline in team games and lower rates of involvement in competitive sport among middle class children. 'Competitive sport in decline', *The Irish Times*, 3 June 2005

American popular culture; cricket and Aussie Rules in Australian life; Gaelic games and football in Ireland; cricket and baseball in Caribbean culture, while rugby union is important in constructions of Welsh and New Zealand national identities.'[9] As a segment of the construction and communication of meaning in society, sport is both of value in itself and also a vehicle of value. Notions such as 'fair play' and being a 'good loser' have their normative origins in the realm of sport. The social status and significance that sport enjoys varies considerably from culture to culture, even from continent to continent. However, John Huizinza, in his classic study *Homo Ludens – A Study of the Play Element in Culture,* decries the interpretation of sport that includes it as an item in the definition of culture: 'The ability of modern social techniques to stage mass demonstrations with the maximum of outward show in the field of athletics does not alter the fact that neither the Olympiads nor the organised sports of American universities nor the loudly trumpeted international contests have, in the smallest degree, raised sport to the level of a culture-creating activity. However important it may be for the players or spectators, it remains sterile.'[10] Huizinga's complaint against the inclusion of sport in the concept of culture ignores the fact that sport is 'an anthropological universal found in almost every known human society',[11] which qualifies it eminently as an element in both the description and definition of culture in anthropological and cultural categories. His reluctance, even refusal, to allow sport enter the portals portrayed as 'culture' may represent a hierarchical, hallowed notion of the same which bears little reference or relevance to life in the twenty first century (or indeed throughout the twentieth century). In his centenary assessment of the Gaelic Athletic Association (founded in 1884) Liam Ryan employs T. S. Eliot's notion of culture as comprising the preferences and pursuits that are characteristic of a particular people.[12] While debate about sport and art, their respective

9. *Power Play – Sport, the Media & Popular Culture,* London: Longman, 2000, 1
10. Boston: The Beacon Press, 1955, 198
11. 'Editorial: Sport, Society and Religion', in Gregory Baum and John Coleman eds, *Concilium,* 205 (5/1989), 5
12. Liam Ryan, 'The GAA – "Part of What We Are",' *The Furrow,* 35 (December 1984), 753

role in society and the value of provision of public funding for their pursuit is a legitimate concern, the status of sport in 'popular culture' is beyond dispute. The complete separation of aesthetic and athletic activity carries a risk of cultural elitism ('high' versus 'low') and more than a hint of social snobbery.

Political considerations may also be involved in interpreting sport, not least historically. Cricket as an instrument of ideological imperialism was a factor in the expansion of the British Empire in the late nineteenth and early twentieth centuries. While cricket occupies a level playing field today in relation to race, class can still be an index of not only involvement but interest in the game. The development of games and insistence on amateurism was an organ of colonial socio-cultural control. In *Empire Games,* Roger Hutchinson states that 'the Victorian British did not introduce cricket to their empire solely because they enjoyed the game … Just as it taught discipline and honour to their own young officer cadets, so those qualities might rub off on some of the subject peoples, [that] as it delivered a moral lesson to Englishmen, so might it have a missionary effect upon Asians, native Australians and Polynesian islanders.'[13] (There is a lovely tale told about two Irish missionaries taking refuge from the rain in a college far from home: while one lamented the loss of a day's play in cricket the other responded that it would be a good opportunity to mend tackle for horses.) The fascination that cricket furnishes in the Indian sub-continent stands in marked contrast to Ireland. This divide represents issues of conflict as much as class, nationalism as much as as elitism. Mark Tierney, the biographer of Archbishop Croke (after whom Croke Park is named), commented that, in seeking to avoid the imposition of a foreign cultural and minority sport on the Irish, the Gaelic Athletic Association 'unwittingly established one elitist sports system in direct opposition to another ('West British').'[14] However, one wonders how cricket would have developed (and rugby in relation to Gaelic football) in the dexterous and disciplined hands of Irish hurlers with their array of skilful, sometimes silken strokes. The development of Gaelic games in

13. Quoted in Sean Moran, 'Much more than just a spectator sport', *The Irish Times,* 18 May 2005
14. Quoted in 'The GAA – "Part of What We Are",' 753

Ireland as an expression of national 'personality' and protest originated in the late nineteenth century. Though it resisted a takeover bid by the Irish Republican Brotherhood in its early years, the connection between the Association's codes and the cause of Irish nationalism has historically been a cultural given, a fact celebrated in many forms and fields over the years and more recently in the context of Northern Ireland. Asking whether sport was the medium or the message, *The Irish Times* sports journalist Sean Moran ironically notes the comment of the self-styled iconoclast Conor Cruise O' Brien on the impact of the GAA in initiating and sustaining Irish Republican nationalism: 'More than the Gaelic League, more than Arthur Griffith's Sinn Féin, more even than the Transport and General Workers' Union and, of course, far more than the movement which created the Abbey Theatre; more than any of these, the Gaelic Athletic movement aroused the interest of large numbers of ordinary people throughout Ireland. One of the most successful and original mass movements of its day, its importance has perhaps not even yet been fully recognised.'[15] Debate at the 2005 Congress of the Association about the possibility of making its showpiece stadium available for soccer and rugby internationals drew attention to this involvement, if not identification between nationhood and the need to preserve a sense of purity on its playing fields. While rugby and soccer in Ireland cannot be said in any sense to represent a 'foreign field that is forever England', some people would prefer to see the 'national stadium' reserved for homegrown, Gaelic games. The lingering feeling of hurt, if not quite hostility, to the hosting of such codes at Croke Park, is ironically indicated by the former Irish soccer international player, writer and television pundit Eamon Dunphy: 'It is not a rational approach, I know, but a relative of mine was killed [by Crown forces] in Croke Park on Bloody Sunday in 1920 and therefore I'd have problems with people playing soccer there.'[16]

Belonging versus Bowling Alone
In the nineteenth century the German sociologist Max Weber used the terms *gemeinschaft* and *gesellschaft* to indicate the shift

15. Quoted in Moran, 'Much more than just a spectator sport'.
16. Quoted in *Magill*, 18 May-14 June 2005, p 7

from forms of social intimacy found in agrarian communities to the sense of increasing isolation found in the towns and cities created by and in industrial societies. His French counterpart Emile Durkheim developed a theory of *anomie* which in part accounted for the growing sense of alienation of people in urban, industrial centres. More recently the American writer Robert Putnam has explored the question of the cohesion of society and the collapse of community involvement, particularly in the context of the United States. Putnam has pursued the notion of 'social capital' which 'refers to dense networks of connections between individuals, including norms of reciprocity and trust, which arise from community involvement. Social networks have value, affecting the happiness and productivity of both individuals and groups ... It can be traced back separately to classical theorists like Marx, Marshall, Durkheim and Dewey.'[17] The question of involvement raises deeper questions of identity and integration in society, that is, issues of bonding with others and belonging rather than being on one's own and 'bowling alone', the title of Putnam's book which has provoked much discussion and debate. The social benefit and brokerage brought by sport, bringing together both participation and play, is well stated by Dunning: 'In modern societies, sport has come to be important in the identification of individuals with the collectivities to which they belong; that is, in the formation and expression of their "we-feelings" and "we-I" balance. Through their identification with a sports team, people can express their identification with the city that it represents or perhaps with a particular subgroup within it such as a class or ethnic group. There is even reason to believe that, in the context of a complex, fluid and relatively impersonal modern industrial society, membership of or identification with a sports team can provide people with an important identity-prop, a source of "we-feelings" and a sense of belonging in what would otherwise be an isolated existence within what Reisman called the "lonely crowd" ... Sport today provides a context in countries all over the world where people can meet and bond if sometimes only fleetingly, and it can help to give people a sense of continuity and purpose in contexts

17. Paul Gillespie, 'Halting the erosion of social capital', *The Irish Times*, 10 September 2005

which are highly impersonal and beset by what many experience as a bewildering pace of change.'[18] The implications of the question identified by Liam Delaney and Tony Fahey are wider than the Irish context: 'Whether the social presence and community benefits of sport might be most effectively extended in the future through those sports which are already strong but which may be reaching the limits of maturity, or through those which are underdeveloped but could be judged to have an untapped potential for the future.'[19]

Issues of identity and involvement with sporting clubs are well illustrated in the events surrounding the takeover of Manchester United by the American businessman Malcolm Glazer in May 2005. Under a provocative headline of 'Life as PLC could end in RIP for United' Paul Hayward, Chief Sports Writer for *The Daily Telegraph,* comments that 'English football is being ripped away from its moorings in the community.'[20] He links this loss of nineteenth century origins and traditions to the moment when 'the big Premiership clubs mutated from sporting and community organisations into corporations'.[21] In the same issue his colleague Henry Winter is more caustic, calling Glazer a 'carpetbagger', who had converted the Theatre of Dreams into Sold Trafford! Moreover, he wonders whether the American tycoon would be capable of distinguishing soccer from other games involving round balls. Jeff Lewis notes that the shift needs to be interpreted in more than geographical terms: 'Manchester United is no longer located in the urban centre but is a spectator commodity available for community formation and consumption all over the globe'.[22] Ironically the club's success, both on the field of play and in the marketplace of merchandise and image rights, sowed the seeds for its sale to the man Winter described as an 'American predator' who 'does not understand that English clubs are about dreams as well as dollars',[23] a fate that the famous club developed in the past fifty

18. *Sport Matters,* 6
19. *Social and Economic Value of Sport in Ireland*, (Dublin: The Economic and Social Research Institute, 2005, 73
20. 13 May, 2005
21. Idem.
22. *Cultural Studies – The Basics,* London: Sage Publications, 332
23. *The Daily Telegraph*, 13 May, 2005

years by Matt Busby and Alex Ferguson does not deserve. Jim White laconically lists some of the options for supporters.[24] In the course of this controversy, quoting the author Richard Kurt, Mary Hannigan notes the connection between the famous football club and the Catholic Church: 'Thirty years ago, when the Main Stand (at Old Trafford) was thick with clerical cloth and the faint whiff of incense, the Roman domination (of Manchester United) was taken for granted. If the Church of England was the Tory party at prayer, then Man United was the Catholic Church at play. Much of United's early support was, of course, built upon Catholic Celtic (Irish) immigrants – indeed, Newton Heath almost became Manchester Celtic in 1902.'[25] Today the characterisation of English soccer clubs as denominational is outdated, though the terms and titles Catholic/Protestant still retain sociocultural, if not quite ecclesial and theological, significance in the soccer turf (and other) wars in the city of Glasgow.

'The GAA: too important to be left to the sports pages'[26]

The 'trinity' of community, club and county is particularly revealed in the context of Gaelic games in Ireland. Historically this connection was created by the fact that the parish furnished the foundation and focus for both the Catholic Church and the Gaelic Athletic Association. (Keith Duggan dismisses this dovetailing, albeit in the urban context of Dublin: 'You listen and see the glossy advertisements promoting the great cultural institu-

---

24. 'United fans are faced with a choice. Most of those of my acquaintance seem torn between defiance and surrender. For many, this is the final straw. After years of seeing the link between community and club steadily eroded by commerce, their reservoirs of affection are drained.' 'United have lost their soul but at least I got £1.73 dividend on my PLC shares', *The Daily Telegraph*, May 14, 2005
25. 'Weekend Review', *The Irish Times*, 14 May 2005
26. Paul Rouse, *Village*, 22-28 April, 2005. Rouse refers to Diarmaid Ferriter's *The Transformation of Ireland 1900-2000* to reject the revisionist caricature and carping of Oxford academic Roy Foster: 'It is the first broad survey of Irish history to deal with sport as a vital element of modern Ireland, presenting sport as a central part of people's lives, rather than as a mere emblem of political or cultural identity ... And, significantly, he documented the importance of GAA clubs as the focal point for communities across Ireland.'

tion of Gaelic games and the accompanying homily about the mysticism of the parish and you wonder to whom they are reaching out. It is a tired and outdated yarn, particularly for the children of Dublin city who play *Cumann na mBunscol*. The parish is an alien concept to many children and becoming the town or village warrior, wearing the fabled jersey, no longer holds the same weight.'[27]) Theologian D. Vincent Twomey inter-prets the incorporation of the GAA into parish life as fortuitous, 'with the result that (probably without any conscious reflection) the powerful quasi-religious practice that is sport was (once again) "christianised". It is thus not surprising that from its ranks came its finest priests, to such an extent that it was no ex-aggeration to say that, in rural areas at least, the Irish Catholic Church was the GAA at prayer.'[28] The memorable saying of Matt the Thresher in Charles Kickham's nineteenth century novel *Knocknagow* – 'for the honour of the little village' – capt-ures the sense of pride in place which has been the historical hallmark of the GAA in Ireland (and indeed of other codes in countries throughout the world). Club competition can rightly be called the seedbed for both talent and triumph at county, provincial and international levels. The cornerstone upon which the GAA was constructed was the connection between club and community, praying in and playing for a particular place. This 'local habitation and a name'[29] formed an inseparable nexus of individuality, social insertion and cultural identity which has persisted over the years even in the face of exile. The export of Gaelic Games is evidence of both the social expression and effect of sport, even in contexts that historically would have been con-sidered completely foreign to the code and its culture. Thus

---

27. *The Lifelong Season: At the Heart of Gaelic Games*, Dublin: Town House, 2004, p 237. Compare this claim with his chapter four which covers the history of St Jarlath's, Tuam, quest for Gaelic football glory and his comment that 'GAA players are unique in their fastidious and almost religious devotion to the cause of playing for their county', *The Irish Times*, 8 October, 2005
28. *The End of Irish Catholicism?* Dublin: Veritas, 2003, 84
29. William Shakespeare, *A Midsummer Night's Dream*, Act V, Scene 1 in *The Arden Shakespeare*, Ed. Harold F. Brooks, London: Methuen, 2004, 104

Clifford Coonan states that 'the Asian GAA has been given county-board status by the organisation's headquarters'.[30]

Liam Ryan lists as one of the greatest successes of the GAA its capacity to create for the Irish people a medium through which they could, for the first time, express their national identity in a socially routinised and culturally recognised manner. This helped to heal the disruptions and divisions that developed historically in the course of the nationalist and Republican struggle. Common membership of *Cumann Lúthcleas Gael* created bonds which brokered bitter battles and brought people together: 'Men who were deeply divided over Parnell, neighbours who had shot at one another in the Civil War, families who had squabbled over grievances great and small, real or imagined, all soon displayed a greater willingness to forgive and forget when gathered round the goalposts than when gathered around the altar.'[31] Another priest prominently associated with the GAA, Fr Harry Bohan, praises the Association as a powerful force for integrating and uniting people: 'I was asked just the other day if the church could learn anything from the GAA. And straight away, I said "Belonging". Much of what has happened in this country has been for the good and parts of Clare have enjoyed phenomenal growth, really extraordinary development. But all that fluctuation and change has left a vacuum too and I think that the very fact of people gathering together in Cusack Park [county ground], from urban estates and country farms, from hills and valleys is something special in itself. It is a connection to a way of life that some people find hard to locate now'.[32] Writing against a background of comment on the decline of social capital and decay of community, Déaglán de Bréadúin celebrates the spirit of GAA headquarters Croke Park in the summer season. In the context of the collapse of religious observance and decline of the moral authority of the Catholic Church, he discerns a hint of hope in the help that sport in general and the GAA in particular could provide: 'We may not have great temples of faith and the humbler ones we do possess may not attract the same level

30. 'Gael Force', *The Irish Times* – Magazine, 8 November, 2008
31. Ryan, 'The GAA – "Part of What We Are"',' 757-758
32. 'Belonging in the Banner', *The Irish Times*, 16 April, 2005

of devotion, but we do have at least one marvellous edifice which enshrines important values and provides hope that all is not entirely lost. I refer to that Temple of sport, Croke Park. A place of major importance in sporting terms, it also plays an almost invisible role in the formation of our young people and their outlook on life.'[33] De Bréadúin locates this inspiration in the lack of corruption, absence of drug-taking and exemplary behaviour of the players with their *esprit de corps* and commitment to high standards of sportsmanship. However, his extolling of exemplarism is tempered by evidence of indiscipline by individuals and teams on and off the field of play and the on-off saga of the battle of will and words between players and management/administration involved in Cork's county hurling setup.

The importance of sport is indicated by high levels of interest and involvement throughout society. In the twelve month period up to the end of September 2005 forty six per cent of the adult population in Ireland attended a sports event within the country, with six per cent attending a fixture outside. The 'triumvirate' of Gaelic games, rugby and soccer took the lion's share with eighty one per cent of the total, with hurling and football together capturing fifty seven per cent.[34] Eoghan Rice put the worldwide fascination with soccer more catchingly than columns of statistics could by commenting that 'with the exception of praying and procreation, football is now humanity's favourite pastime. The sport has more followers than any single church, more believers than any system of government and commands more loyalty tan any nation. Football has penetrated every culture on earth, from China to Africa to the Americas. Across the globe, literally billions of people play the game, watch the game and obsess about the game.'[35] Quoting David Winner's book on the history of soccer, *Those Feet*, Rice refers to the need to reflect on the meaning of sport: 'What is its place in society? I don't know. But it's a question we need to be thinking about. Two thousand years from now, anyone looking at our

33. 'Spirit of Croke Park gives us all hope and inspiration', *The Irish Times*, 26 September, 2005
34. 'GAA dominate attendance figures', *The Irish Times*, 6 October 2005.
35. 'More than just a game', *Sunday Tribune* – Magazine, 17 April 2005.

culture will want to explain how sport became such a huge cultural phenomenon. I don't think we understand what we're dealing with. It must be of great significance but we're only just beginning to realise what is going on'.[36]

'Situating sport' operates on three levels, on the actual playing fields, in the media and the academy. The primary situation of sport is found locally, regionally (county/province), nationally, internationally. There are hybrid formations such as the British and Irish Lions in rugby, America versus Europe in the Ryder Cup in golf and occasional configurations such as contests between the northern and southern hemispheres. The facility of travel enables fans to follow their teams and clubs literally to the ends of the earth, while the 'global village' of social communications allows them to stay at home and follow events from afar. In this context sport carries a spectrum of meanings ranging from explicitly religious associations through cultural and political connotations to the merely enjoyable and ephemeral.

The secondary location of sport, in the audio-visual and print media, has led to a burgeoning industry and its identification as a 'big business' in its own right. The critical and sometimes controversial role it plays in the mediation and interpretation of sport to a huge audience of listeners, readers and viewers calls for research and reflection. The third 'venue' for sport is situated in the accounts and analyses that academics advance around the plurality of meaning(s) that sport carries socially and culturally. Here the task of theology is to identify how sport increasingly articulates its message and meaning in religious terms and interrogate the extent to which these are evidence of a misrepresentation of faith and its manipulation for mercantile and ideological purposes.

36. 'More than just a game'.

CHAPTER THREE

Faith in Sport

'Billy Graham spoke up in favour of sport as a suitable activity for Christians, keeping them busy with healthy pursuits. In the USA many winners thank God for their achievements in prize-winning speeches. In the American university, the enormous status of sport was something their churches and chaplaincies could not ignore. C. S. Prebish argues that religion and sport each have a body of beliefs, accepted in faith by large numbers of people. In both the tradition is maintained essentially by men. Sport has saints and ruling patriarchs, high councils and scribes who report it. Like religion, sport has shrines – Halls of Fame and the like – and emotive symbols. Both sport and religion are the subject of merchandising. They use a common language of dedication, sacrifice and commitment.'[1]

'Sporting his faith.'[2]

Emerging from Exodus
In Judaeo-Christian tradition faith is both found in and formed through the narratives that have normatively become known as the Bible. In the Hebrew scriptures the Exodus-event (liberation from Egypt) emerges as the original and originating experience that engendered a covenant between Yahweh and the people elected to become Israel. The faith of Israel was formed by and formulated the sacred and salvific nature of a relationship with the living God who was recognised as both Redeemer and Creator. The Christian scriptures situate the emergence of the

---

1. Terence Copley, *Indoctrination, Education and God*, London: SPCK, 2005, 49
2. Heading for profile of former GAA president Sean Kelly, *The Voice Today*, 11 August 2006

church in the story that is both a record of and a reflection on the totality of the life, death and resurrection of Jesus of Nazareth. The Exodus and Christ events are connected in a chain of promise and fulfilment, whereby Christianity considers the latter to be the definitive self-disclosure of God and deliverance of humanity from evil, sin and death. Thus the Christ-event is expressed as the eschatological Exodus. Both of these defining acts of God have been taken to describe a spectrum of events ranging from the political to sporting arenas. The key Old Testament symbols of Exodus and Covenant have historically been hijacked and held up as purely inner-worldly states of affairs in various political contexts, ranging from (modern day) Israel to Northern Ireland and South Africa. More recently 'Exodus' has exercised the fertile (if not quite faithful) imagination of journalists who have presupposed at least a nodding acquaintance with the Bible among their own readers. Taking liberty with looking at sporting events through the lens of biblical faith, Exodus has been employed as a metaphor of sporting escape.

The 50th European Cup Final between A.C. Milan and Liverpool in May 2005 represented for many fans and commentators the greatest sporting comeback in history. 3-0 down at half-time against a team thought to have the best club defenders in the world, with the midfield craft of the Brazilian maestro Kaka and the powerful strike force of Crespo and Shevchenko, in the eyes of spectators and commentators alike Liverpool looked like the proverbial 'dead and buried'. Their best option for the second half seemed to be one of damage limitation, to avoid a humiliating defeat for the once proud masters of Europe. In six minutes in the second half Liverpool scored three times. Suddenly level, the Milanese seemed punch drunk. The game drifted into extra time, requiring two marvellous saves from the Liverpool goalkeeper Dudek to guarantee that the contest would require a penalty shoot out to settle it. The tide stayed in Liverpool's favour and they won their fifth European Cup. The tale of those dramatic hours is told graphically by John Williams and Stephen Hopkins in *The Miracle Of Istanbul*.[3] In *The Times* souvenir supplement two days after the game Simon

---

3. Edinburgh: Mainstream Publishing, 2005

Barnes proclaimed: 'There is a phrase from exodus that has always haunted me. It comes from the Red Sea crossing: 'and the angel of the Lord changed station'. For a start, I like the way the angel of the Lord is considered a completely unremarkable part of a retreating army and therefore fully capable of doing a mundane thing like changing station, almost as if it were going from Liverpool Street to Waterloo. But I especially love that matter-of-fact acceptance of a miraculous momentum, a decisive change of events that none of the participants can control.'[4] (Subsequently *The Sunday Independent* conflated and confused biblical symbols in its caption 'How a Sea of Red Reached the Promised Land'.[5]) Barnes' prose may be perceived as prophetic, though to judge from his exegesis of the book of Exodus this characterisation could not be considered in terms of canonical categories of the Bible and its interpretation. While his mention of the miraculous suggests divine intervention, Barnes mixes this with reference to magic and the mass intensity and influence of the Liverpool supporters. In the end the basic biblical metaphor of Exodus emerges somehow strangely stranded between the shores of religious belief and bewilderment at the impossibility of causal explanation. His conclusion is both confused and confusing: 'Putting this turnaround down to one thing is to miss the point. It is the crazy inspired mixture of things that matters.'[6] Thus irrational interpretation, despite the possibility of inspiration, collapses the divine intervention involved in the Exodus (and Easter) event to the category of a journalistic cliché. This is drama but not divinely inspired. Moreover, the presupposition that many of Barnes' readers would know or understand the reference to Exodus cannot simply be presumed as a positive fact. His accompanying piece on the Liverpool Polish keeper Jerzy Dudek, depicting how 'a maverick goalkeeper drained the belief from Milan,'[7] only serves to show the

---

4. *The Times* – 'Champions', 27 May, 2005
5. 29 May, 2005
6. *The Times* – 'Champions', 27 May, 2005
7. 'Dudek's Wild Side a Saving Grace', *The Times* – 'Champions', 27 May, 2005

extent to which he evacuates the biblical symbol.

'Thine is the Kingdom'

> Now after John was arrested, Jesus came to Galilee, pro-
> claiming the good news of God, and saying, 'The Time is
> fulfilled, and the kingdom of God has come near; repent,
> and believe in the good news.' (Mark 1:14-15)

The so-called synoptic gospels of Mark, Matthew, and Luke all agree that the central message and meaning of Jesus of Nazareth's mission and ministry are contained in the symbol 'kingdom of God'. This was the determining vision and driving passion of his life. Jesus lived his life (and death) as a sign and instrument of God's definitive irruption into and involvement with human history. He intended his ministry as a revelation and realisation of the rule or Reign of God.[8] The Reign of God was the constant reference point of Jesus' healing and liberating activity, the point and purpose of his preaching. While never defining this 'Reign of God', Jesus described it indirectly (some-times obliquely) in his parables, inviting his hearers to exercise their imagination and thus extend their image of God and his relation to them beyond their familiar concepts and categories. His failure to succeed in this teaching partly contributed to his experience of rejection which ultimately resulted in his crucifix-ion and death. However, the horizon of the gospels and their purpose of narrating/forming faith extend through the life and death of Jesus to his resurrection and reflection on the relation between Jesus and God, between the proclaimer of the kingdom message and the One proclaimed as the Christ, Lord, Saviour, Son of God. In the later words of Origen, Jesus is 'the kingdom-in-person'.

On Saturday 28 May 2005 the cover of the sports section of *The Irish Independent* carried a caption of 'The Kingdom Gospel' with colour inserts of five senior county Gaelic football man-agers against a backdrop of Croke Park. The Kingdom's (Kerry's) sporting and social soubriquet) high 'five' of Mick O' Dwyer (Laois), Jack O' Connor (Kerry), Páidí Ó Sé (Westmeath), Liam Kearns (Limerick) and John Kennedy (Clare) were seen as mis-

---

8. For an overview of the biblical-theological understanding see John Fuellenbach, *The Kingdom of God*, Maryknoll: Orbis Books, 1995

sionaries spreading the message of Kerry's dominance at both provincial and national levels. The statistics of 'Kingdom Spreading' were presented like the figures on a financial spreadsheet and the article assumed the air of a business statement (with the sub-text of 'business as usual'). The conjunction of 'kingdom' and 'gospel' is a clear conflation of the foundational concept and formative genre of Christian faith. In the context of football it represents a caricature of the content of this creed and connotes a surrogate spirituality and liturgy. The emphasis on honours and success, with the comparison of the managers concerned, carries a message that failure cannot be countenanced. The 'Kingdom Gospel' is a clever play on words, particularly when they are portrayed against the background of the new Croke Park stadium which sportswriter Keith Duggan has called the 'cathedral': 'And when Irish people gather on the dedicated Sundays of All-Ireland finals, they expect to see nothing less than the great, sweeping curve of cold grey as surely as the risen saints expect to see Heaven's Gate'.[9] Sacred time and space are synthesised in this image which symbolises the intersection of time and eternity, earth and heaven. This type of writing also sees a transposition of biblical personalities such as 'David and Goliath', as in a reference to the relative fortunes of the Everton soccer manager David Moyes and Chelsea prior to their Premiership clash in October 2005.[10] Also, an article arrayed with the heading 'Daniel slays Lions' describes the role of the New Zealand outhalf Daniel Carter in the 48-18 defeat of the British and Irish Lions in the second test of their 2005 tour.[11] A profile of the Welsh rugby captain Gareth Thomas plays on his surname in speaking about proving 'the doubting Thomases wrong'.[12] Other examples of borrowing from the Bible are 'Jeremiah the Cork Messiah'[13] (referring to Cork hurler Jerry O' Connor), 'the gospel according to St John'[14] in a piece entitled

9. *The Lifelong Season*, 31
10. *The Sunday Times*, 23 October, 2005
11. *The Sunday Times*, 3 July, 2005
12. *The Daily Telegraph*, 26 October, 2005
13. *Sunday Tribune*, 1 January, 2006
14. *Irish Examiner*, 30 November, 2005

'Saint or Sinner?' which profiles the former Liverpool striker Ian St John, 'Gospel according to Matty'[15] which looks at the life and career of Wexford footballer Matty Forde.

Forms of Faith

Faith in Christian experience and the church's expression is not a human religious construct reaching heavenwards from earth. It is a situated, sincerely personal and profound response in the grace of the Holy Spirit to the invitation of communion with God, the Father of the Lord Jesus Christ. This invitation, commencing in creation and continuing through covenant(s) in the course of Israel's history, culminates in the Christ-event. The close connection between Christian faith and certain events of history is clearly brought out by the Australian theologian John Thornhill: 'God's self-disclosure – the essential concern of faith – is realised through the unfolding of a story of a people and, in particular, in the events with which that story comes to its climax: the life, death and resurrection of Jesus of Nazareth. In other words, the truth which we are called to accept in faith is a truth embodied in a history.'[16] Traditionally theology has both thought of itself and taught in terms of revealed faith and its relation to human reception/reason as in St Anselm of Canterbury's classic description *fides quaerens intellectum*/faith seeking understanding. Thornhill offers a fuller definition: 'An interpretation of faith in God revealed in Jesus Christ: faith rendering an account of itself in various human and cultural contexts',[17] while the French theologian Yves Congar followed Anselm and simply formulated theology's function as the thinking out of faith. In his encyclical *Veritatis Splendor* (*The Splendour of Truth*) Pope John Paul II describes the relation of faith and reason and the latter's restriction before the mystery of God: 'By its nature, faith appeals to reason because it reveals to man the truth of his destiny and the way to attain it. Revealed truth, to be sure, surpasses our telling. All our concepts fall short of its ultimately unfathomable grandeur. Nonetheless, revealed truth beckons reason –

---

15. *The Sunday Times*, 19 June, 2005
16. *Christian Mystery in the Secular Age – The Foundation and Task of Theology*, Westminster, MD: Christian Classics, 1991, 49-50
17. *Christian Mystery in the Secular Age*, 37

God's gift fashioned for the assimilation of truth – to enter into its light and thereby come to understand in a certain measure what it has believed.'[18]

The depth, diversity and even difficulty of understanding the term 'faith' is underscored by Denis Billy in his description of 'a more developed presentation' of faith in distinct models: propositional – transcendental – fiducial – affective –experiential – obediential – praxis – personalist.[19] The complexity of faith cannot be captured in captions, however 'catchy' or 'cool' they may seem. The commonplace is the catalyst for conversion to the cliché. In the tradition a distinction developed between the experience of faith and its expression, between *fides qua*, the faith by which/the act of believing faith and *fides quae*, the faith which is believed/content of faith. A danger exists of dividing and separating these dual dimensions of faith, such that faith becomes, on the one hand, purely interior and perhaps ultimately irrational and, on the other hand, intellectual assent to a series of scholarly propositions which ignores the nature of faith as a personal response which is professed and practised in the integration of mind and heart, imagination and intellect. Christian faith is finally trust that, in the words of the poet Patrick Kavanagh, 'God's truth is life.'[20]

Terence Copley notes that religion and sport both exhibit a body of beliefs which are accepted by those who belong to their communities and/or codes and that they share a similar language of commitment, devotion and sacrifice.[21] Sports writers and commentators, players and fans are increasingly availing of the traditional terminology and symbols of religious faith to express this sporting 'belief system', as the following selection shows:

'Sport restores faith. It determines who walks into history as

---

18. Vatican City: Libreria Editrice Vaticana, 1993, 163, par 109
19. 'The Role of Theology in the Ministry of Spiritual Direction', *Studia Moralia*, 43 (Luglio-Dicembre 2005), 432
20. 'The Great Hunger' in *Collected Poems*, London: Martin Brian & O'Keefe, 1975, 36
21. *Indoctrination, Education and God*, London: SPCK, 2005, 49
22. Sue Mott, *The Daily Telegraph*, 12 April, 2005

a champion.'[22]

'A complacent congregation of United fans once shared that faith.'[23]

'BELIEVE. The boys are back and they want it all.'[24]

'He [Brian O' Driscoll] remembers as a symbol of his faith buying the season video for 1987-8, a year when [Man] United finished 11th. His special devotion was to Mark Hughes.'[25]

'Liverpool will put their faith in the spiritual ways of Rafael Benitez.'[26]

'Liverpool kept defying, kept believing. As the red and white banner draped over one railing declared: "Our faith is the weapon most feared by our enemies".'[27]

'I've [Pádraig Harrington] been in the top 10 for quite a while now and I'm very comfortable with that. I think it requires a leap of faith rather than an improvement in ability to move up there.'[28]

'Revitalised Harrington putts faith in St Jude.'[29]

'But God, they were in an All-Ireland final. The county, he was told, was one big mad carnival. In GAA terms for [Leslie] McGettigan, that fact was like the Second Coming. And he had just renounced his faith.'[30]

'Punters put faith in the Geordie saviour.'[31]

23. Kevin McCarra, *The Guardian*, 12 November, 2002
24. Cover title of *United*, official magazine of Manchester United, n 124, January 2003
25. Tom Humphries, Lions 2005 Supplement, *The Irish Times*, 1 June, 2005
26. Dion Fanning, *Sunday Independent*, 1 May, 2005
27. *The Daily Telegraph*, 28 February, 2005
28. Quoted in *The Observer*, 29 May, 2005
29. *Irish Examiner*, 5 June, 2007
30. *The Lifelong Season*, p 191
31. Report on transfer of footballer Michael Owen from Real Madrid to Newcastle United in *The Racing Post*, 31 August, 2005
32. Headline of article analysing the goalkeepers' performances in the All-Ireland hurling final in *Irish Examiner*, 12 September, 2005

'Keepers of the faith.'[32]

'Glorious profession of faith.'[33]

'Holy Orders rewards faith of punters.'[34]

'Kauto's gold standard has the edge on Denman's leap of faith.'[35]

'Faithful.'[36]

'Faithful flock in search of messiah.'[37]

Here references to religious faith and belief range from sport in general through soccer and Gaelic games to golf and horseracing. The first statement sees faith solely in earthly, inner-worldly terms of success and achievement without any transcendent or eschatological reference, entry into history and not heaven. The relation of Manchester United and faith/devotion are interesting in the light of the purchase of the club by Malcolm Glazer. Prior to this 'successful' takeover Keith Duggan mixed the sacred and the profane in lamenting the loss of belief: 'At its truest level – on the field – Man United is something quite sacred, even for those of us left cold by its contemporary representation. And to see it teeter on the whim of legal and financial mind-games makes a mockery of the previous generation of men for whom Man United meant a credo.'[38] The references to Liverpool FC are remarkable in the light of the club's much vaunted 'return from the dead' in the 2005 European Cup final. At the other end of the soccer scale, Mark Hodkinson's *Believe in the Sign* is a book dedic-

---

33. Headline of article by Eamonn Sweeney in *Sunday Independent*, 2 October 2005, on Tyrone's victory over Kerry in the previous Sunday's All-Ireland football final

34. Report on victory of nine-year-old's victory at the Curragh racecourse, *Sunday Tribune*, 25 September, 2005

35. *The Independent*, 14 March, 2008

36. Title of book by Boston Red Sox fans Stewart O'Nan & Stephen King chronicling their baseball team's progress to World Series victory in 2004

37. Caption for review of book by Pete McParlin, *Standing in the Corner – Watching Newcastle United in the Wilderness Years*, Parrs Wood Press, 2005 in *The Independent* on Sunday 8 January, 2006

38. *The Irish Times*, 31 January, 2004

39. *The Daily Telegraph*, 11 January, 2007

ated to the floundering fortune of Rochdale football club where 'bits keep falling off their dilapidated Spotland stadium'.[39] Harrington's 'leap of faith' is future-oriented, focusing on the winning of the 'holy grail' of a golfing major. The possibility of such a victory is placed in his performance in the St Jude Championship prior to the 2007 US Open, despite the event being named after the patron of hopeless cases. The link between faith and salvation is seen in secular and not sacred terms in the case of striker Michael Owen's move to Newcastle United. While 'Holy Orders' victory at the Curragh is seen in terms of vindication, both Chris McGrath in *The Independent* and Sue Mott in *The Daily Telegraph* use the existential 'leap of faith' to characterise the chances and conquest of Denman over stable mate Kauto Star in the 2008 Cheltenham Gold Cup.

Variations of the 'faith' theme are found in reference to a number of popular phrases. 'Keepers of the faith' also finds an echo in two pieces playing on the father-and-son theme in two pieces featuring well-known soccer goalkeepers and their fathers. A profile of Seamus Given, father of Shay (Newcastle United and Republic of Ireland goalkeeper) was published under the caption of 'Faith of the Father'.[40] The doyen of soccer writers Brian Glanville devotes a piece to Chelsea goalkeeper Carlo Cudicini with the caption 'Cudicini keeps the faith'.[41] This recalls the exploits of his famous father, Fabio, who kept goal for A.C. Milan for many years. Following the faith of their father is taken literally, that is, onto the field of play and between the goalposts. James Lawton profiles Chelsea and erstwhile England captain John Terry as 'Defender of the faith',[42] while Stuart Barnes rests the fate of England in their 2007 Rugby World Cup game against South Africa on the 'Supreme Believer', Lawrence Dallaglio.[43] 'Blind Faith' is the caption for cricket columnist Mike Atherton to consider the fortune (and fate) of England in the 2007 World Cup.[44] Loss of faith is not left out, as in Ian O'Riordan's dogmatic statement that 'since retiring in 2003

40. *Sunday Tribune*, 3 March, 2002
41. *The Sunday Times*, 19 January, 2003
42. *The Independent*, 19 August, 2006
43. *The Sunday Times*, 3 June, 2007
44. *The Sunday Telegraph*, 15 April, 2007

[Jonathan] Edwards found himself taking a leap of faith in the other direction, and has recently been describing his conversion to devout atheist'.[45] The relation of faith and doubt is referred to in '[Lewis] Hamilton's faith washes away doubt'.[46] A clever caption, 'Faith in pitch is growing',[47] captures the growing confidence of Croke Park groundstaff in the quality and durability of the new surface of the playing field for the summer season ahead. In this context veneration of 'holy ground' assumes a variable meaning.

Lex orandi, lex credendi

The first document of the Second Vatican Council (1962-65) was devoted to the reform and promotion of the liturgy of the Catholic Church. The document declares that: 'It is through the liturgy, especially, that the faithful are enabled to express in their lives and manifest to others the mystery of Christ and the real nature of the true church'.[48] Both the worship and witness of faith are inextricably linked in and to the liturgical life of the church which is seen as the most important work of the faithful, the People of God, on their pilgrim journey to the Reign of God in its fullness. While admitting that 'the sacred liturgy does not exhaust the entire activity of the church', the document also asserts that 'nevertheless the liturgy is the summit toward which the activity of the church is directed' and 'also the font from which all her power flows'.[49] This affirms the priority of prayer – public prayer – in the life of the faith community. Liturgy is the *locus* where the Word of God is addressed, in season and out of season, to the audience of faith which, in turn and in time, acknowledges the reception of this Word in a loving and hopeful response that ranges from doxology to devotion, through praise to petition. Liturgy is the focal point where the Christian faithful gather so that God's grace may be conferred upon them and

---

45. 'Edwards' loss of faith no godsend', *The Irish Times*, 7 July, 2007
46. *The Daily Telegraph*, 9 October, 2007
47. *The Irish Times*, 26 April, 2005
48. Ed. Austin Flannery, Vatican Council II – The Conciliar and Post Conciliar Documents, Dublin: Dominican Publications, 1987, 1, par 1
49. Ibid, 6, pars 9, 10

multiplied among them. This is a cause for celebration which both enables thanksgiving and empowers the translation of this word of life in terms of service and solidarity both within and without the boundaries of belief.

With the Holy Spirit as the primary agent in the assembly of the faithful, the liturgy looks primarily to the sanctification of the People of God and the salvation of humanity. The liturgy is the earthly crossroads where divine grace and human response intersect in the true centre of history. It also represents the point of departure for a faithful people to take up the task of consciously witnessing to and working for the transformation of the world. Proclamation, profession, praise and petition are performative elements of this liturgical process. A foundational principle of this is contained in the Latin axiom *lex orandi lex credendi*, which asserts that the law of prayer is the law of belief, that the creed of the community comes from its celebration of word and sacrament. Cult and creed are considered two sides of the coinage of the church.

The Sacred Council (title of the Council's Constitution on the liturgy) desires 'that the faithful should be led to that full, conscious, and active participation in liturgical celebrations which is demanded by the very nature of the liturgy.'[50] The three criteria of 'full, conscious and active' constitute the norm for both participating in and understanding the nature of the liturgical assembly, particularly in the promotion of inculturation in the diaspora that determines the catholicity of the church. The nature of Christian communal worship covers a spectrum of human expression extending from joy and gladness through gratitude and intercession to grief and sadness. Nothing that is authentically human is alien to the action of the liturgy in giving glory and gratitude to God and asking for the assistance of God's grace. To paraphrase the words of Joe Lee quoted in the introduction, liturgy is too important to be left lying in documents. The truth of *lex orandi, lex credendi* – that the nature of prayer is the norm of the profession of faith – is the touchstone for testing the credibility and currency of the sacramental economy of the

---

50. Ibid, 7, par 14
51. Ibid, 1, par 2

church which is 'visible, but endowed with invisible realities'.[51]

Lex orandi, lex ludendi?

John Coleman comments that 'frequently, sports spectacles are called, today, new liturgies, replacing Christian liturgies as a bond of community'.[52] In this context the traditional theological formula is transposed to *lex orandi, lex ludendi,* 'the law of prayer is the law of play', that the spectacle of sport functions as a surrogate liturgy. In this perspective assembly and adoration become focused on the arena and stadium, not on the sanctuary and altar. Variations on this theme are found in the portrait of two families in 'Costly family devotions' which characterises their commitment to club and county teams in the course of a Gaelic football season, calling the fixture list their bible and claiming that their faith is tested by the rising cost of admission to games.[53] In a play on words, former soccer player turned pundit Liam Brady dismissed the impact of Roy Keane's return to international duty for the Republic of Ireland as being of 'no benefit to idle worship'.[54]

In summer 2004, in its treatment of the theme of pilgrimage in Europe, *Time* notes that the phenomenon has taken a secular turn. Alongside the ancient pilgrimage route to Santiago De Compostela and the trail of James Joyce in Dublin, Simon Kuper inquires in an article on Glasgow – 'Faith in Football' – whether soccer stadia have become the new spiritual centres, acting as modern-day cathedrals where 'congregations' of fans celebrate and confess football rather than faith: 'In the flowery language of the sporting press, football grounds are "temples", "cathedrals" or "meccas". Comparing football to religion is a soft-headed cliché. The truth is more extreme: Western Europe may have reached the point where football passion outstrips religion, class warfare, nationalism, even ethnic hatred. It now just borrows some of the language to make matches more fun.'[55] The association of religious devotion and its ability to draw diverse peoples together with forces and factors of division and even

---

52. 'Sport and the Contradictions of Society', *Concilium* 205 (5/1989), 31.
53. *Sunday Independent,* 2 May, 2005
54. *Sunday Tribune,* 2 October, 2005
55. 5 July, 2004

destruction displays a naïve if not sceptical attitude, while the reference to 'fun' in the context is facile, if not facetious. Developing the stadium/cathedral analogy, Kuper sees both venues as vehicles where crowds and congregations – increasingly interchangeable terms in media commentaries – sense something that is larger than themselves, a greater beauty. His reference to Newcastle rates comparison with a comment by Henry Winter about Newcastle United's Lee Bowyer, after a serious on the field clash with team-mate Kieron Dyer: 'St James' [soccer stadium] press room will soon rival Durham Cathedral and Lindisfarne [ancient monastic site] on the North-East tourist trail'.[56] Asserting that soccer stadia were constructed with concerns for aesthetics as much as the ancient cathedrals, Kuper imagines tourists in future centuries, as they survey the ruins of these sites, 'trying to understand what it was that got twenty-first century Europeans so worked up'.[57] However, the analogy between cathedrals and stadia fails at the point of perceiving them equally as 'aesthetic 'events', given that the cathedrals were constructed primarily for adoration rather than for aesthetics, and that the beauty of such buildings is an expression and enjoyment of blessedness rather than a place where one team beats another. Sue Mott sees the bodies of sportsmen such as rugby union's Jonny Wilkinson, golf's Tiger Woods and horseracing's Tony McCoy as 'the temple that we, the congregation, worship'.[58] The great Brazilian soccer player Pele once called Wembley stadium the church of football, which may be interpreted as a form of homage to the so-called home of association football. Writing about the revamped Thomond Park in Limerick, Tony Ward states that 'The quaint little church is now a mighty cathedral.'[59]

The difficulty with depicting sporting stadia as 'cathedrals' is twofold. Firstly, there is a question of meaning, that is, of the extent to which the metaphor is intelligible and interpretative today. Secondly, cathedrals were constructed as centres of spiritual worship and as places where liturgy could be celebrated.

56. *The Daily Telegraph*, 4 April, 2005
57. *Time*, 5 July, 2005
58. *The Daily Telegraph*, 12 April, 2005
59. *Irish Independent*, 20 November, 2008

Their architecture and accompanying aesthetic were statements and symbols of the sacred, of God's overture to humanity and its offering in response.[60] In an era evidently estranged from the epoch of explicit religious and ecclesiastical architectural expression, marked by a more fragmented and functional worldview, the equation of macro-cosmic order and micro-cosmic observation of that reality is seriously reduced, if not almost effectively removed. Nevertheless, the employment of sporting venues for explicit religious events, such as papal Masses and meetings with young people especially, furnishes a fascinating counter example to trends of taking the sacred out of postmodern space(s). The symbolic and strategic importance of sporting stadia is shown in the video presentation of the successful New Zealand bid to stage the 2111 Rugby World Cup, as noted by Paul Ackford: 'A long shot of New Zealand's glorious coastline ... closed in on the cliffs and then moved upwards to dwell on what appeared to be a stadium which had emerged from the geography of the country. One stadium of four million people was the theme of the bid. It did the trick.'[61] A promotion for whiling away weekends in wintertime offered the memory (if not quite the hope) of 'heaven on a Saturday afternoon' through a visit to the National Football Stadium at Preston North End's Deepdale Stadium advertised as 'the world's largest temple to football'.[62]

The association of sport and the sacred is articulated not only in terms of places but also of people. A 'worshipful throng' welcomed Roy Keane on his return to Cork to sign copies of his autobiography.[63] On the eve of the 2002 All-Ireland hurling final *The Irish Times* magazine cover carried a photograph of Dublin fans in Croke Park's Hill 16 with the caption 'A People At

---

60. See Philip Sheldrake, 'Space and the Sacred: Cathedrals and Cities', *Contact*, 147(2005): 8-17

61. *The Sunday Telegraph*, 20 November, 2005. His closing comment is also worth considering: 'Now all they have to do is to add substance to the image'. Gerry Thornley links ethics and evangelisation in adavancing the case for Japan to host the event: 'There will be a moral argument for spreading the gospel by having the 2011 finals in Japan', *The Irish Times*, 9 July, 2005. He re-echoed this call a month later with a headline 'Aim is to spread the gospel'.

62; *The Observer Sport Monthly*, January 2006

63. *Sunday Tribune*, 10 November, 2002

Worship'.[64] Given these associations, it is right and fitting to ask if *lex ludendi* – the law of play – has become the law of prayer and belief? Dunning explains the tendency to transpose the language and symbols of faith, the subjects and spaces of worship into sporting terms and themes: 'For the most committed fans, and perhaps for others besides, sport can be said to function as a "surrogate religion" … To the extent that sports fans can be said, through their involvement in and identification with a particular club, to "celebrate" or "worship" one or more of the collectivities to which they belong, sport can be said to possess some of the characteristics of a religion in Durkheim's sense…[His] analysis of the "collective effervescence" generated in the religious rituals of the Australian aborigines which he saw as the root of the experience and concept of "the sacred" can be transferred, *mutatis mutandis*, to the feelings of excitement and communal celebration that constitute a peak experience in the context of a modern sport. It may even be the case that part of the explanation for the growing significance of sport in modern societies lies in the fact that it has come to perform some of the functions performed earlier by religion. That is, it may in part be catering for a type of need which, for increasing numbers of people, is not met elsewhere in the increasingly secular and scientific societies of our age.'[65]

Brannon Hancock considers the possibility of envisaging the Eucharist outside the explicit categories and confines of the church.[66] In the context of a 'post-ecclesial' world he imagines incarnations of this sacramental presence and praxis through the spirit bringing people together in various contexts and thereby creating bonds of community through sharing in different forms of celebration and communion. This perspective lays to rest pre-

---

64. The following day the *Sunday Independent* 'sported' a half page advertisement for the final with an image of the Tomas McCarthy Cup being thrust into the waters of Glendalough [St Kevin] with the Round Tower in the background. The front right corner carried the word 'Believe' with the harp logo of the competition's sponsors Guinness replacing the letter 'V'. Comparison with the rite of Christian baptism was clearly intended.
65. *Sport Matters*, 6-7.
66. 'Pluralism and Sacrament: Eucharistic Possibility in a Post-Ecclesial World', *Literature & Theology*, 19 (September 2005) 265-277

vious separations of sacred and profane places and sees 'spaces previously thought profane, from the dance-club to the shopping mall, and their accompanying practices being identified for their quasi-religious character'.[67] Sports stadia and arenas would obviously be such spaces. Intending the Eucharist as the sacrament promoting pluralism and inclusivity and performing the church, Hancock seeks 'to place the Christian Church and its practices, in constructive, redemptive (which is to say loving) engagement with the culture, which the Church so often seems to desire to convert but also, paradoxically, holds contemptuously and defensively at bay'.[68] He investigates two examples of so-called 'interpretive communities' as possibilities for presenting and perceiving sacramental practice. The first example of literary incarnation imagines a community of readers which is not confined to book clubs of various designations but which draws in the invisible community of those who meet in a mode of mystical communion as they seek meaning from the text which offers itself sacrificially in order to transform its audience. Analogy with the liturgy's table of the Word of God is intended in this exposition of encounter with literature. However, criteria for choosing which texts are to be taken, broken and given in eucharistic mimesis, what counts as a classic corpus of literature are not considered. The second example of cinematic community compares the 'ritual' of cinema-going to church gathering. In common with the ecclesial elements of space set apart and seating situated to face the sanctuary (and screen) the cinema creates community, however transitory and illusory this may be. On such terms comparison with attendance at sporting events and consideration of the question posed by Clive Marsh, whether one could classify the liturgy of football as a substitute religion,[69] are inevitable. The criterion for considering which texts to take and what films to give in initiating eucharistic anamnesis and assembly is its capacity for *kenosis*, that is, the mimetic measure of self-emptying. Application of this account of sacramental practice and communal performance to sport could include elements of entertainment, enjoyment, even a certain ecstasy.

---

67. Ibid., 267
68. Ibid., 268
69. *Christianity in a Post-Atheist Age*, London: SCM Press, 2004

However, the estimation of escapism, of *fuga mundi* (abandonment of the world) and the fictional nature of such exercises cannot be eliminated. In evaluating such environments the criterion statement of Philip Sheldrake that, for a 'place to be sacred, it must affirm the sacredness of people and the human capacity for transcendence',[70] must be considered. Can libraries, cinemas and sports stadia affirm such sacredness and actualise such transcendence? If such venues are to be places where, in the words of Peter Berger, 'rumours of angels' are capable of being heard and heralded, how is the Sacred Council's call for full and conscious participation of the faithful to be catered for without explicit commitment and evangelical celebration? While there are references to the Christian narrative and resonances with its normative self-understanding in Hancock's account of literary and cinematic communities, his analysis ultimately renders a reduction of both the mystery and mission which the church proclaims and to a certain extent realises. In his last encyclical *Ecclesia de Eucharistia* Pope John Paul II referred to the privilege of celebrating the sacrament in places ranging from the Cenacle in Jerusalem to cathedrals and country churches, 'on altars built in stadiums and in city squares'.[71] Announcing his intention to awaken amazement for its universal and cosmic significance (while not losing awareness of its local and historical situation) he asserted that 'the church is anxious to hand on to future generations of Christians, without loss, her faith and teaching with regard to the mystery of the Eucharist ... for "in this sacrament is recapitulated the whole mystery of our salvation".'[72] In these terms occasional gatherings of literary, cinematic and sporting 'communities' are not forms of Christian congregations assembled in the amazement and articulation of faith in the Incarnate Word and his eucharistic presence. 'There can be no danger of excess in our care for this mystery.'[73] If the church exists through the Eucharist, it embodies the mission of Christ in extending bonds of faith and communion by holding out hope that the horizon of human and historical consciousness is a barrier to be both blessed and where it befits, broken.

---

70. 'Space and the Sacred', p 11
71. Dublin: Veritas, 2003, 10, par 8
72. Ibid., 54, par 61
73. Idem

CHAPTER FOUR

Spirituality and Sport

'Man is a sporting as well as a praying animal.'[1]

'Many people in the United States are beginning to think about and discuss sports in relationship to the spiritual life.'[2]

'The Spirituality Sprawl'

Michael Downey coined this phrase and devotes the first chapter of his book *Understanding Christian Spirituality*[3] to describing the array of spiritualities available for human perception, practise and even purchase. His survey of this 'sprawl' ranges from explicit relation and reference to the Absolute through processes of self-realisation to typical patterns of handling the human situation. In 2003 *Cosmopolitan* appointed a new 'Spirituality Editor' and *The Economist* also appointed a Religion Correspondent (its first) Bruce Clarke, who stated that 'there was an assumption that religion was being relegated to the margins of human life and ultimately would disappear altogether, which has proved wrong'.[4] Such innovations represent the widespread interest in spirituality both as a significant commodity for the market and as a factor in the mores of society. The increase in interest in spirituality seems ironically linked to an accompanying decline in formal church involvement and institutional religious adherence. Reviewing a book entitled *The Spirituality Revolution*, David Hay remarks on the paradox that while there is a serious crisis of

1. Oliver Wendell Holmes, quoted in David Pickering ed, *Cassell's Sports Quotations*, London: Cassell & Co, 2002, 333
2. Patrick Kelly, 'Experiencong Life's Flow – Sports and the Spiritual Life', *America*, 20 October 2008, 19
3. New York: Paulist Press, 1997
4. *The Irish Catholic*, 29 January 2004

plausibility for Christianity in Australia and the wider Western world there is a concomitant increase in the credibility of spirituality as a social phenomenon.[5] Quoting the French sociologist Yves Lambert, he notes the statistic of young people surveyed across nine countries in the European Study of Values who, while happy to hold themselves as being spiritual/religious persons, are simultaneously anxious to deny formal church attendance and adherence. Against this background, the comment of C. A. Barron is worth considering: 'Many Catholics, reflecting their American culture, use a combination of personal beliefs and experiences as norms to justify practices, moral positions and theological interpretations that are at odds with Rome but seem reasonable to them. Moreover, this situation among Catholics seems to confirm the findings of Paul Heelas about the general New Age movement's influence on American religion (and Western Europe): there is a shift towards detraditionalised, individualised, eclectic spiritualities in service of personal enhancement, outside and inside of conventional religious institutions and continuous with contemporary consumerist life industries'.[6] Downey's *caveat* concerning the need for discretion and discernment in the face of this vast array of spiritualities, some of which are not authentic and even personally and humanly alienating, is apposite and asks questions about the interpretation of spirituality.

The concept of 'spirituality' in contemporary Western culture(s) is notoriously vague. Some commentators, especially from the confines of the Christian churches, complain that it is vacuous. Its valence ranges from policies, practices and programmes stretching from Tarot through Reiki to yoga, through self-help and solidarity with various causes of liberation, preoccupation with philosophies of Western and Eastern origin to private/public performance of traditional religious beliefs and worship, to esoteric and erotic experiences, the paranormal and the supernatural culminating in fascination with the occult. A glance at the 'Spirituality' shelves in bookshops gives a sense of

---

5. *The Tablet*, 21 August 2004, 19
6. 'Postmodern Theology of Marriage' in J. Haers and P. De Mey, eds, *Theology and Conversation*, Leuven: University Press Uit Peeters, 2003, 581

the vast spectrum subsumed under the general subject heading. From Celtic spirituality through New Age to Zen Buddhism the choice of reading material and ready-to-go and do topics is confusing, if not indeed conflictual. In November 2004 an article in *Time*,[7] treating attempts to trace the genetic roots of spirituality, quotes a professor of Buddhist studies who states that such a discovery would be 'amusing and fun'. (The background of belief in reincarnation and resultant genetic inheritance makes such a position more plausible.) A twenty question quiz queried the degree of spirituality individuals subscribe to, though the content was more interested in intuition and psychology oriented than in intellectual and theological insights. There was no explicit reference to Divinity, the Almighty or an Absolute. David Quinn, Religious & Social Affairs correspondent for *The Irish Independent*, explores the theme of the search for spirituality and separation from God and the church. He quotes Professor Patricia Casey on the divide between spirituality and religion: 'People now tend to describe themselves as spiritual rather than religious. They think spirituality allows them to look to something greater than themselves, but without the challenging moral requirements of religion. So they feel spirituality gives them the benefits of religion without the perceived downside.'[8] The separation of spirituality and morality and the option for religious benefits which omits a willingness to bear any burdens represents a most serious challenge for mainstream religious traditions. In particular the threat to the gospel and Christian theology/spirituality from Gnosticism remains a perennial problem.[9]

Christian Spirituality

According to Joann Wolski Conn, spirituality refers to 'both a lived experience and an academic discipline. For Christians, it means one's entire life as understood, felt, imagined and decided upon in relationship to God in Jesus Christ, empowered by the [Holy] Spirit. It also indicates the interdisciplinary study of this

7. 'Is God in Our Genes?', 29 November, 2004
8. *Irish Independent*, 16 July, 2005
9. See Luke Timothy Johnson, 'A New Gnosticism – An Old Threat to the Church', *Doctrine & Life*, 55 (November 2005), 2-12

religious experience, including the attempt to promote its mature development.'[10] (A lacuna of Conn's definition lies in the lack of reference to and rooting of Christian spirituality in the life of the church, in the communion of faith which is both the cradle of its formation and the circle of its celebration.) The experience of Christian spirituality was classically expressed by St Augustine in his *Confessions* with his concept of the *cor inquietum*, 'our heart is restless until it rests in you', which confesses the horizon where the human heart hopes to enjoy the Beatific Vision of God in heaven. The awakening, articulation and actualisation of this spiritual potential on earth is the perception that, in the phrase of Patrick Kavanagh, 'God is in the bits and pieces of everyday.'[11] This is the economy where divine grace and human freedom encounter and exchange, the realm of human response to the gratuitous invitation of God issued in creation, intensified in covenant(s), incarnated in the absolute involvement of God with humanity and its history in Jesus Christ and, through the Holy Spirit, intended for resurrection-destiny and eternal communion. In the Christian context spirituality is explicitly thematised in Trinitarian terms, in reference to God the Father of the Lord Jesus Christ and the Holy Spirit. The history of Christian spirituality, however, suffered at times from a certain doctrinal deficit which saw the life of faith in general and prayer in particular only in relation to one of the persons of the Holy Trinity. Karl Rahner once complained that the Trinity was not really taken seriously in Christian spirituality, that people effectively related to God or Christ or the Spirit but not to God as Father and Son and the Spirit as the sign and gift of their love. (Here I am reminded of a remark of a former student who unwittingly wrote that 'There are some people who don't believe in even one person of the Trinity' and the reality that two decades after the Second Vatican Council a local church considered reference to the Trinity too complicated to be included in its particular catechism.) Downey describes this deficit and divorce

---

10. J. Komonchak, M. Collins and D. Lane, eds, *The New Dictionary of Theology*, Delaware: Michael Glazier, 1989, 972. (It is interesting that there is no entry for 'Theology' in the corresponding dictionary of Spirituality.)

11. 'The Great Hunger', in *Collected Poems*, 42

of spirituality from doctrine (and theology) in the following terms: 'The connection between the Trinity and the spiritual life has not always been clear, or clearly drawn. Because the Trinity has by and large been viewed as an abstraction since the fifth century, this eminently practical doctrine has lost its footing as the central and unifying Christian mystery. This has resulted in an impoverished Christian spirituality, as well as an under-standing of God cut off from the wellsprings of spirituality'.[12]

References to the Trinity are frequent in recent sportswriting. Four examples, taken from Gaelic games, rugby and soccer reveal this tendency:

'For a little while this summer we thought all the talk of Gaelic football having a Big Three might just have been a little too pat and a tad too premature. Then, in the space of eight days, Armagh destroyed Laois, Tyrone smote Dublin and finally, Kerry razes Cork. There is a trinity. We believe. Sorry, if we strayed from orthodoxy.'[13] (When the annual All-Star football awards were announced in November 2005 only players from Armagh, Kerry and Tyrone were represented among the recipients.)

'Between them, New Zealand's Holy Trinity [Graham Henry, Steve Hansen and Wayne Smith] have hardly missed a trick and with their extensive experience in Europe, they realised immediately that [the All Blacks] had to act immediately to build a world class front five if they are to achieve their stated objectives.'[14]

In the 1960s the Manchester United strikeforce of George Best, Bobby Charlton and Denis Law were often likened to the Trinity. In the 2007-8 season when Manchester United won both the English Premiership and the European Champions League their 'Trinity' was repre-

12. *Understanding Christian Spirituality*, 44. See also his *Altogether Gift – A Trinitarian Spirituality*, Maryknoll: Orbis Books, 2000, where he develops the Christian grounding of spirituality through the Trinitarian grammar of 'Giver, Given, Gift/ing'.
13. Tom Humphries, *The Irish Times*, 29 August, 2005
14. Brendan Gallagher, *The Daily Telegraph*, 28 November, 2005

sented by Cristiano Ronaldo, Wayne Rooney and Carlos Tevez.

"Holy trinity' keeps Barca believing'.[15] This headlines hails the three goalscorers for Barcelona in their 5-0 'demolition' of Deportivo La Coruna, described in the following terms: 'God exists and he plays for Barcelona', read one banner in honour of Leo Messi, who scored another improbable goal for the first. 'With two goals for [Thierry] Henry and two for Samuel Eto'o, Deportivo felt the full force of the holy trinity'. (Ironically Messi's score is seen as improbable, despite his 'divine' status.)

These sporting references treat the distinct but related triple categories of teams, players and coaches. (One of the writers expressly acknowledges the deviation involved in such word games.) The Triune God of Christian faith (notwithstanding the problems of understanding how this Trinitarian revelation occurs in and through the two missions of the Word/Son and Holy Spirit and how the traditional theological language of persons, processions and relations within the Trinity can be presented today) is converted into clichéd and stock phrases as if it were a commonplace mode of communication. This seems to create, as it were, a level playing field of language where the deployment of doctrinal and devotional thought patterns and terminology has the same currency and value as advertising slogans and symbols which adorn the continually changing hoardings around pitches. If the name of the Holy Trinity can be reduced to commonly connote (changing) constellations of counties, clubmates and coaches there is a need for the Christian churches to cry foul in some appropriate form. However, the difficulty of finding a forum where double-edged protest and profession finds a voice presents a major problem, particularly as this also includes the involvement and influence of the media and mass communications.

Important elements of Christian spirituality are its ethical and experiential dimensions. As well as academic (and analytical) aspects, Christian spirituality is also applied, that is, concerned

15. Pete Jenson, *The Independent*, 19 January, 2009

with a process of practice and performance which touches and transforms the person's relation(s) to both God and neighbour. As Karl Rahner emphasised, 'The human person is not only a hearer of the Word but a doer of the Word as well. Christian spirituality is not merely an 'experiencing' but a 'doing', an activity, necessarily involving a 'praxis' of solidarity with one's neighbour.'[16] Imitation of the Incarnate Word, Jesus Christ, involves a discipleship of deeds as well as of devotion. Christian faith seeks a way of integrating contemplation and action, body and soul. The wisdom of such integration is ultimately seen in the witness to what the Australian theologian Neil Brown called the 'quality of life' revealed in Jesus Christ. The experiential element of spirituality in general, and Christian spirituality in particular, seems self-evident and suggests a self-fulfilling prophecy, especially in an age when experience has become for many the hallmark of what it means to be human. A famous remark of Rahner brings this element to the fore: 'The devout Christian of the future will either be a 'mystic', one who has 'experienced' something, or he will cease to be anything at all.'[17] While the dimension of experience cannot be denied, the reference to 'something' requires reflection and discernment. Appeal to experience is unavoidable but the form of its apprehension and articulation needs to be analysed and understood. Margaret Farley's definition, 'the actual living of events and relationships, along with the sensations, feelings, images, emotions, insights and understandings that are part of this lived reality',[18] displays both the depth of and difficulty in exploring experience. Religious experience refers to the realm of what Paul Tillich terms 'ultimate concern', that is, the revelation that there is more to human existence than encountering the 'sensible and merely 'understandable' world'.[19] As Elizabeth Dreyer and Mark Burrows note, 'de-

16. Declan Marmion, 'Rahner and his Critics', *Irish Theological Quarterly*, 68 (Autumn 2003), 200
17. 'Christian Living Formerly and Today', *Theological Investigations*, London: DLT, 1971, vol 7, 15
18. 'The Role of Experience in Moral Discernment' in Lisa S. Cahill and James F. Childress, eds, *Christian Ethics*, Cleveland: Pilgrim Press, 1996, 135
19. William James, quoted in R. Studzinski, 'Experience, Religious', *The New Dictionary of Theology*, p 370

finitions of Christian spirituality may contain diverse elements, but they are also bordered by key concepts such as belief in a tri-une God, commitment to live a gospel life of love with justice and active concern for the world, and the means of self-transcendence that might lead us toward both personal and social transformation'.[20] Since Christian spirituality is ultimately concerned with the experience of the revelation of the Triune God in the scriptural record, the church remains a vital arena for its verification and valuation.

Seeking Spirituality

A tour through bookshops bearing 'Mind, Body, Spirit' and similar sections, combined with a trawl of the Internet, disclose the variety and diversity of avenues and approaches open to those who seek spirituality. In his study of the so-called 'Generation X', Gordon Lynch quotes the statement of Mike Starkey that 'spirituality is on sale at a High Street and shopping mall near you'.[21] As a symbol of the longing and hunger at the heart of the human person, there is a danger that this sense of itemised appeal and immediate answer may sink spirituality to the level of a mere slogan, a commodity to be located on the shelves alongside so many other products, goods and services. Starkey starkly calls this phenomenon a product of Western capitalism, consumer spirituality.[22] In a world of globalising markets, forces and trends this spirituality can all too easily and often seem to be simply one substance among many in the search for meaning and hope, mystery and the holy. From acquisition to activity (one American actress called surfing 'spirituality'), through consumption to cinema spirituality has become both a buzzword and a business. By way of response, the eight annual Céifin conference, called 'Filling the Vacuum', commends the quest for spiritual values as an answer and antidote to a culture which President Mary McAleese warns could become 'a cul de sac of complacent consumerism'.[23]

20. *Minding the Spirit: The Study of Christian Spirituality*, Baltimore: John Hopkins University Press, 2005, xiii
21. *After Religion – 'Generation X' and the search for meaning*, London: DLT, 2002, 105
22. Ibid., 106
23. *The Irish Times*, 9 November, 2005

Sandra Schneiders offers a general definition of spirituality as 'the experience of conscious involvement in the project of life-integration through self-transcendence toward the ultimate value one perceives'.[24] This links issues of integration and transcendence in relation to the self within a horizon of hope, purpose and meaning. Ruling out any belief-systems or behaviours which are reductive and conducive to dysfunctionality, addiction or narcissism, it highlights the need for integration as integral to the quest for identity. In the (cultural) context of postmodernism, with its characteristics of fluidity and particularity, there is a clear challenge for spirituality considered as the inner search for such identity and integration to fly 'in the face of forces of fragmentation and depersonalisation'.[25] The thrust to transcendence is not understood in an individualist sense but seeks the intersection of moral and spiritual truth beyond the barriers of self-absorption and isolation. The *summum bonum* of this experience is explicated in trans-empirical terms of ultimate concern, commitment and possibly communion. However, the cultural matrix in which socialisation and individuation occurs (or not) needs to be considered. Anthropological analysis attends to questions of worldview, value and belief systems, lifestyles and leisure pursuits and practices. The link between sport and spirituality explores the human composite and complex of body and spirit, time and space, individual and society. In his Foreword to a recent study of this link, Professor Shirl James Hoffman states the spiritual substratum of sport: 'The fascinating aspects of the hyper-kinetic world of sports – the acrobatics of the goalkeeper, the ballet moves of the basketball player, or the golfer's precision shot to the green – have the regrettable tendency of diverting our attention from what may be the most important thing about them. Statistics may precisely denote all of the athletes' accomplishments, photos may underscore their aesthetic brilliance, and science may clarify their biological concomitants, but none is able to capture sport's essence: its capacity for touching us in deep, mysterious and difficult-to-explain ways.'[26]

24. 'The Study of Christian Spirituality' in *Minding the Spirit*, 6
25. *Understanding Christian Spirituality*, p. 14
26. Jim Parry, Simon Robinson, Nick J. Watson and Mark Nesti, *Sport and Spirituality – an introduction*, London: Routledge, 2007, xi

In the context of considering the relationship between spirit-uality and sport, between recreation and religion, the remark of Lynch raises significant questions: 'The kind of physical activi-ties mentioned above [including sport and football fandom] may have a 'religious' element for some people if they offer them an occasional experience of something greater than their individual lives that can give them a sense of peace, meaning, joy or value.'[27] The extent to which such experiences engender a passage to transcendence and process of integration needs philosophical and theological exploration. Is 'an occasional ex-perience of something greater' an adequate answer to the human spiritual quest? An interesting example of the linking of spirituality and sport emerged from the decision, in November 2005, by the International Rugby Board to award the 2011 World Cup to New Zealand. Having hosted (and won) the original event in 1987, the contest between venues came down to a ques-tion of a vehicle of consolidation (New Zealand or South Africa) or of expansion (Japan). Several commentators argue the case for the latter, employing the language of evangelisation.[28] Eddie Butler articulates the need to approach the presentation not in terms of statistics but rather spirituality (though in seemingly contradictory terms): 'New Zealand is the only bidder that must put aside facts and figures and offer spirituality as the magnet ... with less spiritual generosity [they] have never sent the All Blacks to play in Fiji, Tonga or Samoa.'[29] This synthesis of sport and spirituality, not only in the cauldron of match competition but also in the context of market commercialism, is both striking and suggestive of the need for further ethical and theological re-flection.

Sporting spirituality

Edward Hastings argues that the disconnection between sports

---

27. *After Religion*, 119
28. Paul Ackford comments that 'spreading the gospel [to Japan] is one thing, but there is nothing worse than attending big matches in the company of corporate hospitality happy-clappers with the visceral commitment and knowledge that all New Zealanders possess'. *The Sunday Telegraph*, 13 November, 2005
29. *The Observer*, 13 November, 2005

and spirituality (only) developed in the last four centuries and that the (re)discovery of God's presence and involvement in the world needs to overcome a false dichotomy between altar and arena, competition and contemplation.[30] Moreover, Hastings holds that 'if Jesus was living his earthly life presently, he would have chosen the venue of sports to articulate and present his message to his followers'.[31] The popularity of sports presents an invaluable avenue for announcing the gospel. In the course of teaching modules such as 'Sports and Spirituality', 'The Soul of Athletics', 'Moral and Spiritual Dimensions of Athletics' he tries to help students trace the hand of God in their lives through a process of identifying and interpreting significant experiences in sporting events. This 'incarnational' methodology involves the discernment of God in the events and experiences of (ordinary) life. Another approach involves the broadening of the idea of 'spirituality' and its application to sporting activity via the acronym CARBS – community, awareness, reflection, balance, self-knowledge/transcendence, social justice. Here Hastings highlights the importance of community in both the spiritual and liturgical tradition(s) of Christianity and in the context of sport, illustrating this with the example of the New England Patriots preferring to be introduced as a team rather than individually prior to a Super Bowl final, which they won. He links Anthony de Mello's description of spirituality in terms of awakening to awareness with the need for attentiveness to what is happening all around on the field or floor of play. The role of reflection in relation to spirituality and sport is seen as critical for learning, not least in regard to errors and failures. The need for a holistic perspective to pursue self-integration is balanced by concerns to contribute to the common good of a team in the course of competition. Referring to Schneider's definition of spirituality, he emphasises the priority of self-transcendence and its connection in Christian terms with the Paschal Mystery. Engagement with issues of social justice emerges and is empowered, as in the example of Mississippi State championship basketball team defying segregationist and racist policies of exclus-

---

30. 'Spirituality and Sport', *Spirituality*, 10 (May/June 2004), 160-166
31. Ibid., 160

ion. In conclusion he states that while the ancient connection between sport and spirituality has often been forgotten, he hopes for 'the day when coaches are looked upon as ministers and players looked upon as actually "playing" or re-creating for God'.[32]

However, while Hastings' hermeneutic of sport holds some of the elements expressed traditionally in Christian spirituality such as asceticism and community, his perspective appears to emphasise more the psychological conditions necessary for success and victory in a manner somewhat reminiscent of a 'Jocks for Jesus' approach reflective of the competitive culture of an American and Western ethos. A so-called muscular form of Christianity can mutate into macho, self-styled hardman images and stereotypes. Such a mentality and manner of relating is rightly called into question, in light of both gender analysis and the gospel which calls for conversion and compassion to counteract hardness of heart and competitiveness. Hastings seems to stretch Christian spirituality to suit sports rather than to call for any change of heart on the part of sports men and women. To attribute the traditional terminology of Christian ministry to sports coaches is to carry the analogy between the realms of spirituality and sport too far and runs the risk of reducing it to the role of cheerleader. In this context the comment of Hoffman calls for consideration: 'The western church's relentless accommodation of popular sports over the past century hasn't been accompanied by a great deal of thought about the axiological implications of such an admixture.'[33]

At a GAA seminar in January 2005 the former Clare hurling player and manager turned television pundit, Ger Loughnane, contributed to the discussion of the connection between spirituality and sport.[34] Eschewing the traditional tie between religion and sport, he refers to the void created by the lack of a spiritual capacity in contemporary society. In a vortex created by concentration on economic forces, disvalues of anxiety, greed, insecurity,

---

32. Ibid., 166
33. *Sport and Spirituality – an introduction*, xii
34. *Exploring the Link between Spirituality and Sport*, DVD produced and distributed by St Patrick's College, Thurles. Other contributors included Therese O' Callaghan and Fr Harry Bohan

bad temper and loneliness have come to dominate. Drawing from his own experience in the world of sport and referring to the value(s) and need(s) of contribution, appreciation and fulfil-ment, he speaks of 'spirit' as giving the best of oneself for the greater good, that of the team. Underlining the importance of 'attitude' in all areas of life, he recognises its presence in the body language of individuals and power in attaining victory. In his contribution, Mickey Harte, the Tyrone football manager, underlines the connections between church/community and county/club, claiming that sport provided a template which permeates the whole of a person's life, promoting both personal fulfilment and selfless dedication, balance and bonding. He speaks of the need to 'win with humility and lose with dignity'. In her study of the precursors of modern Gaelic games another American academic, Dr Angela Gleason, asserts that the analy-sis of sport has been seriously neglected in academic circles.[35] In her view sport holds a mirror up to society, showing the domi-nant value system at play in the wider culture. However, she holds that sport is essentially a spiritual affair and that, in its re-quirement for individuals to sacrifice themselves in submission to the good of the group, it generates attitudes of selflessness and solidarity. Notwithstanding the danger of reducing spiritu-ality to a moral standard, this scenario seems to hold only for team games and contests where the will to win may be hyped up by group dynamics and paradoxically be promoted to an even greater extent.

'God has one hell of a team'
Notwithstanding the irony contained in this interpretation by *The Daily Telegraph* sportswriter Henry Winter, the association of sport and spirituality in explicit confession and celebration of re-ligious faith is an area that is increasingly being explored in the media. *The Observer Sport Monthly* advertised its March 2005 issue with a photograph of English international rugby union player Jason Robinson a foot off the ground clutching a Bible with the caption of 'God's Gift'. The subsequent article is entit-led 'Playing It by the Book'. A 'convert' from rugby league he

---

35. 'What's the name of the game?' *Reality*, 70 (July/August 2005), 8-9

scored his country's only try in the victorious World Cup Final in 2003. A born-again Christian, Robinson attributes his religious conversion to the influence of Samoan-born All Black Inga is Va'aiga (who changed from rugby union to league in 1993). Against the background of his own difficult childhood he confesses to disappointment if one of his own four children would later defect from the Christian faith he and his wife Amanda are trying to form them in. The same theme is played out in the case of All Black Brad Thorn whose 'renewed commitment to Christianity coincided with his crossover from rugby league to union'.[36] (Ben Cohen, a team-mate of Robinson's in the 2003 World Cup victory, is celebrated with the headline 'Born-again Cohen is back', though the piece referred to the rejuvenation of his rugby career rather than to any religious conversion.[37]) A column in the piece on Robinson entitled 'Sporting Converts' refers to English soccer star David Beckham, his former manager Glenn Hoddle and former boxing champion George Foreman. After a near-death experience following defeat in the ring in 1977, Foreman gave up boxing for the Bible. Described as the puncher become preacher, Foreman now devotes his life to spreading the gospel in America and to promoting his world famous (mini) grill. Hoddle experienced a 'spiritual awakening' after a visit to Bethlehem with his club Tottenham Hotspur. However, subsequently as England manager, he encountered ridicule for his reliance on spiritualist/faith healer Eileen Drawer. He was sacked from that post after his statement (in 1999) that people with disabilities were paying for the sins committed in the course of an earlier life. Since then Hoddle has had time, if not indeed reason, to reflect on his own experience of hell on earth.

'Rugby's God squad'[38] displays a new recruit in the figure of

36. 'Convert who convinced on his second coming', *The Irish Times*, 13 November, 2008. See also 'Reluctant Kiwi convert bids to add another jewel to crown of Thorn', *Irish Independent*, 13 November, 2008.
37. *The Daily Telegraph*, 4 November, 2005.
38. Heading in piece profiling Andrew Trimble 'Spreading the Word', *The Sunday Times*, 16 October 2005. (Reference was also made to the fact that as a young rugby league player Jason Robinson fathered children with two different women and had a reputation as a hard drinker. The

Ulster and Ireland player Andrew Trimble. He interprets his ability to play as an opportunity to be a missionary in the midst of the testing world of rugby. Through a local organisation entitled Exodus he travelled to KwaZulu in Natal, South Africa to coach in the townships where a group called 'Rugby balls for Christ' provided 'each kid with his own ball coloured black, red, white, green and black – black representing us in our sin, red for Jesus' blood which cleanses us, white and green representing growth as a Christian'.[39] However, the racial implications of this colour schema – particularly in the context of post-apartheid South Africa – seem to have made no impression on either Trimble or the author of 'Spreading the Word', which features religious faith as the foundation of the rugby vocation of the twenty-year old theology student and proselytiser turned international player. However, his enjoyment of rugby is relativised by his reading of the Bible and the hope of entering the presence of God in heaven: 'Before I play a really big match I often read my favourite passage from the Bible – Psalm 84 … It makes me think that playing for Ireland is absolutely brilliant, a dream come true, and I'm going to love every minute of it. But being in the presence of the Lord is going to be a thousand times more amazing.'[40]

The theme of playing for God connects with other codes and creeds. 'The statement that follows will probably require a second reading, but stick with it because it presages an extraordinary story: Rangers won the Bank of Scotland Premier-league title last season because God was on their side.'[41] This sentence opens a piece profiling the Glasgow Rangers centre half Marvin Andrews who believes that it was God who won the championship for his club against the odds when they pipped their archrivals Celtic at the post. While his team mates celebrated their own victory on the last day of the season over Hibernian at

---

former All Black star Michael Jones honoured a promise to his dying father not to play on Sundays, a pledge he kept throughout his career for both club and country, earning 55 caps in 12 years, eschewing the possibility of earning more.)

39. Idem.

40. 'For God's Sake', *The Word*, January 2008.

41. 'Why Marvin Andrews believes he is walking proof that miracles happen', *The Times*, 28 September, 2005.

a ground ironically named Easter Road, Andrews knelt in the middle of the pitch and prayed, displaying the T-shirt beneath his jersey which carried a quote from the gospel of Luke – 'The things that are impossible with men are possible with God.' Andrews believes that divine intervention miraculously cured his left knee when he rejected the advice of the club's medical staff to undergo surgery. A profile of the *Na Piarsaigh* hurling club in Cork City attributed its origin to a meeting of three teenagers on Redemption Road in 1943 and stated that the formal inaugural meeting took place in the presbytery of the North Cathedral or Chapel as it is known to locals: 'It is refreshing in these post-Catholic times to discover that they retain the club tradition of reciting the Hail Mary in Irish before games.'[42] The club's choice for captain of the county side in 2005 (which won the All-Ireland championship) dramatically declared in a television interview after the thrilling semi-final victory by a single point over Clare: 'I was looking to the Lord to put on a red jersey today. Maybe he did it in the end.' A strong skein and statement of faith served as foundation for both team and supporters of the 2005 All-Ireland football champions Tyrone. (Not surprisingly a banner in the county proclaimed 'God bless the Sacred Harte', a reference to manager Mickey Harte.) Harte and team captain Stephen O' Neill secretly carried the Sam Maguire Cup – while the rest of the party proceeded to the official reception in the county – to the grave of Cormac McAnallen, who played in the first All-Ireland victory in 2003 and died in March 2004 at the age of 24. Reviewing a television programme (shown on the TG4 channel on Christmas Day 2005) which profiled the player, Liam Fay commented that 'McAnallen has been recast by friends, team-mates and the sporting media as a secular saint, an angel in football boots. The fiercely intense fervour of Tyrone supporters has encouraged the growth of a devotional attitude to his memory'.[43] (The trophy for the intercontinental Compromise

---

42. 'Thinking like champions', *Sunday Tribune*, 11 September, 2005
43. *Culture – The Sunday Times*, 1 January, 2006. The thoughts of Tyrone manager Mickey Harte on the deaths of county minor footballer Paul McGirr in 1997 and Cormac McAnallen in 2004 are presented in his 'Spirituality & Sport – Fulfilment – Tragedy' in *Exploring the Link between Spirituality and Sport*.

Rules competition between Australia and Ireland is named after McAnallen.)

Playing for Keeps
In the autumn of 2005 the prominent Irish bookmaking syndicate Paddy Power provoked much discussion and dissension with the publication of its hoarding advertisement featuring the Last Supper scene as a poker classic with the heading 'There's A Place For Fun and Games'. Playing on the original eucharistic event the poster depicts Jesus with a stack of gambling chips before him on the table. With cards strewn around, the scene also shows both roulette and board games in progress. The gospel narrative of Jesus' sacrificial and sacramental self-giving is transformed into a scene of gambling and gaming, more reminiscent of the temple he scourged than the table he served. The advert appeared on ninety two billboards in the greater Dublin area. The inspiration – if that is the correct term – for this venture may have come from the shepherd who became billionaire property mogul George Becali, owner of Rumanian club Steaua Bucharest, who played Dublin team Shelbourne in the Uefa Champions League qualifying round in the summer of 2005: 'Becali, who is in Dublin for the game, is described as "religious" by some of the visiting party, but some church regulars back at home have been upset by his recent decision to commission a copy of Leonardo Da Vinci's Last Supper in which he is portrayed as Christ and the apostles are replaced by the coach and 11 of his players.'[44]

Reaction to the billboard came from different sources. Chairman of the Communications Commission of the Irish Episcopal Conference, Bishop Joseph Duffy, called it insulting and offensive to the spiritual and sacramental sensibility of Catholics, charging that it violated the Code of Standards of the Advertising Authority of Ireland.[45] Adding that while humour was as essential element of Irish natural character, Bishop Duffy asserts that it should not be hurtful to the value and belief systems of others. The editor of *The Irish Catholic*, Garry O' Sullivan,

44. 'It's all Greek to the enemy of the Irish', *The Irish Times*, 27 July, 2005
45. 'Last Supper billboard', letter to *The Irish Times*, 6 October, 2005

responded to this criticism, arguing that the advert offered an opportunity to turn a negative moment into a positive means, that preachers could draw on the gambling and risk-taking instincts of Jesus and the Jewish Passover roots of the Christian Eucharist.[46] Echoing a previous evangelical billboard campaign O' Sullivan states that priests and preachers could be educated to evangelise around the event, with the expression 'Paddy Power Can Change'. In a column ironically entitled 'The Pitch' in *The Sunday Times Culture* magazine Mel Clarke sees the betting poster as a form of shock tactics which 'blasphemously parodied the Last Supper' in a mismatch of the sacred and secular, stating that it sought short term gains in something 'merely cheap and nasty'.[47] This strong journalistic rejoinder, even rejection, adds weight to the religious objections offered from within church circles. A spokesperson for the betting syndicate, Ken Robertson, responded that the iconic status of the Last Supper image was influential in its selection for the ongoing advertising strategy.[48] However, he states that if the scene was significant in Islamic tradition and theology it would not have been employed in such a strategy, adding that the company did not operate in Moslem countries. (A representation of the Virgin Mary and the infant Jesus entitled Icon-caviar, created from black caviar and carrying the words 'Have You Eaten Caviar Lately?', was withdrawn from Moscow's Tretyakov Gallery after objections from the Russian Orthodox church that it incited religious hatred.[49])

Referring to the protest to an Italian car company about their promotional use of the Haka performed by the All Blacks prior to their games, David Quinn draws an analogy with the Irish advert: 'The New Zealand embassy in Italy has objected saying that Maoris revere the Haka and therefore find the ad offensive. Many people will probably support the Maoris in this. A sacred

---

46. 'Last Supper billboard', letter to *The Irish Times*, 8 October, 2005
47. 9 October, 2005
48. Quoted in 'Parody of Last Supper insulting to Catholic faith', *The Voice Today*, 7 October, 2005
49. 'Caviar icon is not to everyone's taste', *The Independent*, 8 October, 2005. A previous piece by the artist Alexander Kosolapov featured the face of Jesus Christ on an advertisement for Coca-Cola with the caption 'This is my blood'.

or semi-sacred act, object or symbol exists for a sacred purpose and should not be used for any other end. To do so is an abuse which, depending on its severity, ranges from merely disrespectful all the way to barbaric. As we know, Christian symbols are frequently misuse by advertisers, among others, as in the ad for Paddy Power bookmakers using the imagery of Leonardo Da Vinci's Last Supper. Hopefully those same people who understood why the Maoris feel aggrieved at the misuse of the Haka will understand why Christian symbols etc should not be misused.'[50] While Quinn is correct in calling for the need for cross-cultural sensitivity and respect for religious traditions, his complaint raises two other issues. Firstly, if the Haka is 'a sacred or semi-sacred act' is athletic contest, particularly the aggressive contact contained in rugby, an appropriate arena for its performance? Secondly, the fact that a few years previously an advertisement campaign for candidates for the Catholic priesthood depended on an analogy with the All Blacks – 'Men in Black' – who were coming to Ireland for an international match raises questions about the relationship of faith and sport and the image of Catholic priests in society.

Paddy Power's presentation features a Mary Magdalene type figure showing her cards to some of the other players in a scene reminiscent of Dan Brown's best seller *The Da Vinci Code*. The parody of this photograph style poster, portraying a camera mounted in the corner that captures the scene presumably for security purposes, is evident on both evangelical and ethical grounds. The hijacking of Christian doctrine and devotion for a billboard 'hoarding' bespeaks the crass commercial considerations at play. The stack of coloured chips, connoting various monetary denominations, set before Jesus in an advert for a casino where betting and gambling is conducted, betrays his concerns and commandments concerning possessions and poverty. Ultimately it reveals a violation of a boundary between the limits of 'fair play' and 'fair game' where, it seems, the measure of anything is assessed in purely mercantile terms, and standards, both theological and aesthetic, can be sacrificed for the sake of gain. The Christian gospel, with its earthly and eschatological

---

50. 'The Haka abused', *The Irish Catholic*, 13 July, 2006

evaluation of the meaning of life and death, is not a game of chance to be considered in the currency of the casino but a gift to be celebrated and cherished. The stakes involved are literally too high to be whimsically caricatured or cashed in.

While spirituality is often seen as a symbol of the search for generativity, growth and a goal in life and the process in pursuit of these, there is a danger – if it has not already happened – of it descending to the level of a slogan. Indeed at another level spirituality could be seen as a critical questioning of such slogans. A plurality of spiritualities in the current of postmodern culture portrays the fluidity of forms of human experience and expression, celebrates diversity and commends the possibility of dialogue. However, there is a danger of developing a lowest common denominator approach, where spirituality in the sense of an avenue towards self-transcendence is sacrificed. Moreover, the separation of spirituality from religion in such a construction (or deconstruction) of reality is a step too far, not only through a rejection of traditional ways of thinking and acting but also by replacement with reductionist modes and models of understanding and praxis of what it means to be human. Ursula King offers a wise reminder in her remark that 'spirituality is a perennial human concern which entails self-transcendence'.[51] Scanning the spectrum of human longing and the depths of human desire, spirituality seeks a horizon of ultimate concern where the dialectic of fulfilment and forsakenness are forged into the freedom of self-forgetfulness and forgiveness. It is here that the drive of innate desire and the draw of the Infinite have the hope of dovetailing. Imagining the immanence of this dialogue remains a problem for the media which give such prominence to the ideas of spirituality and images of sacramentality in its coverage of and commentary on the fleeting and fickle moments of sport.

---

51. 'Spirituality in a postmodern age', in Ursula King ed, *Faith and Praxis in a Postmodern Age*, London: Cassell, 1998, 97

CHAPTER FIVE

Playing God

'Joy is play's intention. When this intention is actually realised, in joyful play, the time structure of the playful universe takes on a very specific quality – namely, it becomes eternity.'[1]

'GOD is a four-letter word ... Pelé – Read the life-story of the greatest footballer of all time.'[2]

In January 2006 Robbie Fowler rejoined Liverpool from Manchester City on an initial six-month loan. Once regarded as one of the greatest strikers and goal scorers greats to have 'graced' Anfield over the decades, his joyful return was described by William Johnson in the following terms: 'The coming of the messiah or the return of the prodigal son? Take your pick of those biblical references to mark what promises to be a highly charged occasion at Anfield on Wednesday'.[3] Not surprisingly his former team mate and friend Steve McManaman opted for a more praiseworthy than penitential title, describing him in divine rather than delinquent terms: 'Waiting for second coming of "God".'[4] On the aforementioned night, Fowler's return and warm-up routine with his team mates before the game against Manchester City took place to the strains of Handel's *Messiah*.

---

1. Peter L. Berger, *A Rumour of Angels*, Middlesex: Penguin Books, 1973, 76-77
2. Poster advertising the autobiography *Pele*, London: Simon & Schuster, 2006
3. *The Daily Telegraph*, 30 January, 2006
4. *The Daily Telegraph*, 1 February, 2006. Writing on the same day Simon Hattenstone, a self-confessed Manchester City fan, took a somewhat different view: 'The headlines, of course. Trumpet, THE RETURN OF THE PRODIGAL SON. Why? Fowler is a blobby has-been, a coke-alluding scally (remember the line-sniffing celebration for which he was fined), a glorified rent-collector and a gay-taunter extraordinaire (the buttocks-spreading gesture he made to Graeme le Saux, then falsely rumoured to be homosexual, earned him another fine'. *The Guardian*, 1 February, 2006

After coming on as a substitute in the second half, he scored in the final minutes with an overhead kick but this potentially winning goal was disallowed for offside. Later that night the presenter of *Sky News Sportsline* stated that 'Robbie is back for the reds but there is no divine inspiration for the man they call God at Anfield.'

In the same week that some newspapers in England were feting Fowler with biblical and theological titles traditionally reserved to describe the divinity of Jesus Christ, the Islamic world erupted in anger at a series of cartoons, initially in a Danish newspaper and later reprinted in other Western media, which satirised the prophet Mohammed. This resulted directly in the destruction of several European embassies and exhortation of renewed suicide-bomber style attacks, such as those which struck London in July 2005. While the German newspaper *Die Welt* supported their publication on the supposed ground that the Western world did not defend a right to shield from satire, the retired Vatican diplomat Cardinal Achille Silvestrini condemned the series as an abuse which amounted to 'nothing less than the feelings of entire peoples who have seen their supreme symbols affected'.[5] Insulting Islam in the figure of its prophetic founder and teacher was widely interpreted as an incitement to inter-religious and inter-cultural tension at a time when issues of Iran's nuclear energy programme were metaphorically raising the temperature of international relations. The alienation of the divine status of the founder of Christianity and attribution of his identity to an individual soccer player seemed to pass unnoticed and unheeded. This chapter probes profiles of sporting personalities, portrayed as 'playing God', particularly through the time-honoured spiritual and theological medium of iconography.

Image of God

'And God saw that it was good'. Like a psalmist's response, this phrase occurs six times in the priestly account of creation in chapter one of the Book of Genesis, culminating in a seventh statement that serves as a symphonic summary: 'God saw

5. Quoted in *The Daily Telegraph*, 4 February, 2006

everything that he had made and indeed it was very good' (1:31).[6] This superlative version comes in the wake of the creation of men and women, considered in their complementarity: 'God created man in the image of himself, in the image of God he created him, male and female he created them.' As Edward Hamel states, 'created last of all, humanity is God's masterpiece, the summit and crown of creation. Whereas for the creation of the other things, the divine command is entrusted to a fulfilling word, in the case of humanity God says, "Let us make man in our image", as if he were in some way giving himself an order. Only people are said to be created in the image of their Maker. Human life is thus seen as a mysterious contact between people and God.'[7] The concept 'image of God' owes its origin to a Middle Eastern worldview in antiquity which invested the image of divinity in the person of the monarch. This development, described in the proverb 'the prince is the shadow of the deity, while the people are the shadow of the prince', entailed a double danger: deification on the one hand and despotism on the other. As Hamel notes, the priestly and Yahwist portrayals of the human family is an ideal, involving a democratisation of the idea 'applied to all persons, as the icon of God, and placed on the earth as God's viceroy and the lord of all creation'.[8] This theological foundation of both human dignity and equality underpins the moral understanding of universal human rights.

In recent decades Catholic theology has explored the connection between theology and anthropology, particularly in light of the work of the German Jesuit Karl Rahner and those who follow his transcendental methodology.[9] The christological cornerstone of this 'connection' is classically and magisterially cap-

6 *The Holy Bible*, New Revised Standard Version, Oxford: Oxford University Press, 1989
7. 'The Foundations of Human Rights in Biblical Theology in Developments following on the Constitution *Gaudium et spes*' in R. Latourelle, ed, *Vatican II – Assessment and Perspectives, Twenty-Five Years After*, Volume Two, New York: Paulist Press, 1989, 462
8. 'The Foundations of Human Rights', 463
9. See Roman A. Siebenrock, 'Christology', Chapter 7 in Declan Marmion & Mary E. Hines, eds, *The Cambridge Companion to Karl Rahner*, Cambridge: University Press, 2005, 112-127

tured in the paragraph headed 'Christ The New Man' in the final document of Vatican II's *Church in the Modern World*: 'In reality it is only in the mystery of the Word made flesh that the mystery of man truly becomes clear ... Christ the Lord, the new Adam, in the very revelation of the mystery of the Father and of his love, fully reveals man to himself and brings to light his most calling.'[10] The triple reference to mystery – God the Father, the Incarnate Word, humanity – reveals Christ as the 'cardinal point' of this connection of divinity and humanity, time and eternity, earth and heaven. In his commentary on the document, 'The Dignity Of The Human Person', Joseph Ratzinger states that it 'culminates in Christ the true image of God which transforms man once more into likeness to God ... Christ's taking to himself the one human nature in every human being is an event which affects every human being; consequently human nature in every human being is henceforward christologically characterised.'[11] Later, as Pope Benedict XVI, he refers to this paragraph in relation to the role that the Incarnation plays in illuminating sport: 'Among the various human activities is sport, itself awaiting to be illumined by God through Christ so that the values it expresses are purified and elevated both at the individual and collective level.'[12]

Paul opens his hymn to the Colossians with a reference to Jesus Christ as *eikon tou Theou*: 'He is the image of the invisible God' (1:15-20). The parallelism in this piece between Christ as 'image/beginning' and 'firstborn of all creation/firstborn from the dead' points to the divinity and humanity of the One in whom 'all the fullness of God was pleased to dwell' (v 19) and in whom universal reconciliation and salvation are revealed and realised. Reflection on and representation of the Christ-event –

---

10. Austin Flannery, ed, *Vatican Council II – The Conciliar and Postconciliar Documents*, Dublin: Dominican Publications, 1987, par 22, 922

11. Herbert Vorgrimler, ed, *Commentary on the Documents of Vatican II – Volume Five*, London: Burns & Oates, 1969, 159-160. (A similar theological trajectory is found in the first encyclical of Pope John Paul II, *Redemptor Hominis*.)

12. '"A light for sports": training for a spiritual medal', Message for the Winter Olympic Games, *L'Osservatore Romano*, weekly English edition, n 1930, 8 February, 2006

incarnation, cross and resurrection – proceed from this proclamation. If Jesus of Nazareth represents, in the words of American Lutheran theologian Joseph Sittler, 'God's absolute involvement with humanity'[13] and is in Karl Rahner's phrase 'an absolute messenger of salvation', the task of Christian reflection and representation is that of (attempting) to articulate and indicate this 'absoluteness' in human, historical terms and typology. (This requires that such attempts are always subject to a 'hermeneutics of reserve', through a humility of understanding and a hesitation of expression.) Nevertheless, 'image of God' in Christ indicates both divine and human dimensions and their dovetailing. Reflection on and representation of Christ remain an ongoing task for the community of faith in continuity with its biblical record and roots, tradition and teaching throughout twenty-one centuries, prayerful devotion of its people, particularly in its saints, and the deliberation of its theologians. While recognising the limits of human articulation and art in regard to the mystery of God (and humanity) in Christ, the church must guard against attempts to reduce it to either ridicule or removal.

Image of Christ
Iconography literally means 'writing images'. The tradition of Christian iconography begins in and with the texts of the gospels. Thought to have perhaps been a painter, this art of writing the image of Christ is particularly associated with the evangelist Luke. From the annunciation to Mary in chapter one to the appearance of the Risen Lord on the road to Emmaus in chapter twenty-four, Luke's gospel is replete with pen-pictures of Jesus and his encounters with and expositions to others, many of which have become the source of spectacular works of art, such as Fra Angelico's depiction of the angel Gabriel's announcement to Mary, Rembrandt's portrayal of the prodigal son and his pitying father, Caravaggio's canvas of Jesus' eucharistic revelation at Emmaus. The words of Anselm Grun capture the genius of Luke in writing the image of Christ: 'Luke was trained in Greek rhetoric. The aim of this rhetoric was to paint pictures before people's eyes. The Roman poet Horace talks of "painting with

---

13. *The Structure of Christian Ethics*, Baton Rouge, 1958, p 25

words". Luke is a master of the art of painting a literary portrait of Jesus for us with words. He makes the figure of Jesus visible by describing his gestures and glances ... He understands the art of telling the story of Jesus in such a way that the whole theology of the incarnation lights up ... Luke doesn't talk about the incarnation of the love of God but tells a story in which the love of God becomes flesh – the story of the Good Samaritan.'[14] For Luke (and the other evangelists) the genre of gospel generated a narrative in which the nexus of encounter with Christ and conversion take place not only historically in the story of his earthly ministry but also hopefully in the economy of the Holy Spirit for those who listen to and hear the word of God in the community of faith. 'When Christ is spoken of as the 'image/ *eikon*' of God, the idea is that he is the visible representation of God.'[15] The incarnation is God's self-communication which calls in faith for the media of language, art and music to indicate intellectually and imaginatively the possibility of encounter with the person of Christ.

Gregory Collins interprets the icon-ic tradition as preserving 'the central mysteries of the faith constantly before us, reminding us of what is most essential in the Christian revelation'.[16] Transposing the image of John Keats, they act as 'mysterious casements', opening windows onto the major moments of the Christ-event, from the incarnation and birth of Jesus through life and crucifixion to resurrection and ascension, as well as the Pentecostal outpouring of the Holy Spirit. (The tradition also indicates and illuminates lives of the saints, especially Mary, the mother of the Incarnate Son of God.) They operate in the *oikonomia* or economy of grace as spiritual epiphanies, enabling encounter with the divine self-expression. In the terminology of Orthodox theology, icons are written, not painted. As sacred text, they serve as 'a visual manifestation of the word of God, a symbolic actualisation of the gospel'.[17] In this perspective, icons are interpreted in a sacramental idiom. 'Reading' icons opens

14. *Jesus: The Image of Humanity*, New York: Continuum, 2003, 13-14
15. Gerald F. Hawthorne, Ralph P. Martin and Daniel G. Reid, eds, *Dictionary of Paul and his Letters*, Leicester: Inter Varsity Press, 1993, 427
16. *The Glenstal Book of Icons* , Dublin: Columba Press, 2002, 5
17. *The Glenstal Book of Icons*, 9

the whole person, body, mind and heart, to the Triune God who is both revealed and related to through the triple media of wood, paint and colour. Icons integrate and instantiate the descending and ascending moments of God's self-revelation and human (self) transcendence, movements from 'above' and 'below'.

An important 'moment' in the tradition and theology of icons is the so-called iconoclastic controversy. This occurred in the Eastern Church during the eighth and ninth centuries, though as Jaroslav Pelikan notes it was 'the eruption into open conflict of deep-seated differences that went back to the earliest stages of patristic theology, perhaps back to the Jewish origins of Christianity'.[18] Focusing on the relation between faith and art, the controversy centred on the use and extent of images in Christian liturgy and prayer. Church councils in these centuries vindicated the venerators of icons, the so-called iconophiles, who interpreted the issue in terms of orthodox belief in both the person and work of Christ. Ultimately, the theo-logic of Christian iconography is a denial of docetism, the heresy that the incarnation is an illusion: 'As John of Damascus might have put it, if all that is material has been made holy by the mystery of the incarnation – has become an 'image of the Trinity' – then the icon is the liturgical paradigm of sanctified matter ... an art of veneration and not of aesthetics or investment.'[19] As the Good Friday liturgy literally proclaims: 'This is the wood of the cross, on which hung the Saviour of the world', the icon presents the mystery of God's 'absolute involvement with humanity' in Christ pictorially and prayerfully. It functions, through faith, as doorway to the divine.[20]

---

18. *The Christian Tradition – Volume 2, The Spirit of Eastern Christendom*, Chicago: University of Chicago Press, 1974, 93

19. *The Month*, June 1987, 227

20. 'The icon itself is matter – wood and gesso and pigment. Its sanctity, its function as a channel of intercession with the Holy, is proof of the cardinal fact of the incarnation. The Word had become flesh, the Divine had become matter; after the Incarnation, matter could lead back to the divine', 229

For an assessment of icons in Western religious art and adoration see Andrew Louth, 'An Invasion of Icons?' *ACE Bulletin*, January 2003, 2-3

Immensity of 'Icons'

The icon has become a cultural construct, interpreted in post-modern times and terms as an artefact to be admired, an object to be observed, a consumer choice in the 'cathedrals' that shopping-centres have come to resemble. Often interpreted and indicated, through advertising, in hyper-inflated terms, icons range from the registers of fashion and design through sport to transport and even to victims of violence: 'Some of the most popular and lasting design icons. This week – Arthur Price cutlery set';[21] 'Routemaster bus – The London icon reaches its last stop;[22] 'The Sun stole my voice – by the 7/7 victim [John Tulloch] whose iconic image was hijacked by politics.'[23] Perpetrators of violence are not excluded as in the presentation of Michael Stone who 'became an icon of loyalist paramilitary violence in 1988 when he launched a one-man assault on an IRA funeral attended by Gerry Adams and Martin McGuinness'.[24] Icons are also interpreted in overtly political terms as in references to Soviet and Chinese ideologies: 'An iconic symbol, a statue beloved of Joseph Stalin called Worker and Collective Farm Girl';[25] 'two of China's major icons, The Long March of 1934 and the Great Wall'.[26] The Archbishop of Westminster, Cardinal Murphy-O'Connor called Bethlehem 'the icon of all pilgrim sites',[27] while Culture Online, a branch of the Department for Culture, Media and Sport established a competition called 'Icons' to determine the essence of Englishness. The first twelve items chosen as 'Icons of England' include *Alice in Wonderland*, the Angel of the North, the FA Cup, Holbein's portrait of Henry VIII, the King James Bible, the Routemaster double-decker bus and the Spitfire. Not to be outdone, in an impromptu survey of journalistic colleagues, Frank Fitzgibbon listed the icons of Irishness as including the Angelus, brown envelope, Daniel O' Donnell,

21. *The Sunday Telegraph*, 11 December, 2005
22. *The Independent on Sunday – The Sunday Review*, 1 January, 2006
23. *The Guardian – G2*, 10 November, 2005
24. *The Independent*, 15 November, 2008
25. 'Soviet icon gets new home', *The Independent*, 1 February, 2006
26. 'A long march to the truth – As China rapidly becomes a global superpower, two books shed light on its most enduring icons', *The Observer*, 5 March, 2005
27. *The Times*, 26 December, 2005

potatoes, the Rose of Tralee. Indicating the role that sport plays in the country at large, he asserted that it was 'impossible to ignore the claims of the GAA to take pride of place on our icons list but now that Croke Park has sold out to the corporate sector and foreign codes, Semple Stadium in Thurles, traditional home of the Munster hurling final, is confirmed as the crucible of Ireland's greatest sport'.[28]

The association of sport and advertising led the well-known writer (author of the classic account of an Arsenal fan's season *Fever Pitch*) Nick Hornby to assert that 'It's just incredible how those guys [Arsenal stars such as Thierry Henry and Patrick Vieira] have become cultural icons that transcend sport.'[29]

In a special issue *Time* published the 'A-list of the world's most influential people'.[30] The 'Heroes & Icons' register included prominent sports personalities such as the American cyclist Lance Armstrong and golfer Tiger Woods, the English athlete Paula Radcliffe and soccer player David Beckham. The categorisation of such sporting successes alongside Nobel Peace Prize winners and leaders of their respective peoples Aung San Suu Kyi, the Dalai Lama and Nelson Mandela raises interesting parallels and intriguing standards of comparison, particularly in the perception and presentation of heroic and iconic status. Allied to his winning of six consecutive cycle racing *Tour de France* titles, Armstrong's recovery from cancer makes his story verge somewhat on the miraculous, though he has had to reject claims that doping drove him to victory. Notwithstanding reservations about equating moral stature (to say nothing of suffering) with physical prowess and sporting success, the reductionism of referring to such individuals as icons is further reinforced by the representation of sports such as fox hunting and the FA Cup in identical terms. The 'Icons' website announced that the public response overwhelmingly declared hunting foxes with hounds as the nation's favourite self-image, despite the fact that parliament outlawed the blood sport in February 2005. (However, political lobbying and pressure-groups may have augmented the so-called and self-styled horse and hound set.) Declaring the

28. *The Sunday Times*, 12 January, 2006
29. *The Daily Telegraph*, 19 May, 2005
30. 26 April, 2004

FA Cup was a worthy icon, Sue Mott asserts that the government's spinmasters had, with its index of cultural icons which included the FA Cup, advanced a notion that was 'absolutely unarguable', and argues that the slate of sporting icons should include items such as the Road Hole (17th) at St Andrews golf course, the cricket Bible Wisden, the Aintree Grand National and Wimbledon. Reviewing the previous weekend's activity in the fourth round of the FA Cup she deems it to have been one of 'fantastic – iconic even – comedy, drama, shame, humility, graft and the glorious pricking of ill-deserved self-importance'.[31] Added to this encomium is the economic dimension, displayed in the launch in 2005 of the magazine *ICON* by former footballer turned television pundit Jamie Redknapp. Intended for fellow professional players and not available to the general public, it holds out what one journalist entitled 'everything a football icon ever wanted' with an article on shopping by helicopter and advertisements that ranged from £21,000 wrist watches through luxury golf resorts to top-of-the-range sports cars. Ironically the icon, in its original moral-theological and spiritual significance, was intended to point away from itself, offering 'a corrective to a self-centred or world-centred culture that gives value only to the here and now'.[32]

'I, Keano'

In what appears almost as a play on the word icon, *I, Keano* is the catchy title of a stage musical which captures the action and atmosphere around Roy Keane's acrimonious departure from the Irish team's training camp in Saipan prior to the 2002 World Cup. Set in a Mediterranean island in Roman times, the drama displays the division between General Macartacus (the then Irish manager Mick McCarthy) and his fiercest fighter who challenges his authority. In real life the events in faraway Saipan – fuelled by the media – engendered comment and controversy in Ireland which endures to this day, as arguments for and against Keane still regurgitate, even if the rage has largely died down. Never a stranger to conflict – not least in the manner of his de-

31. *The Daily Telegraph*, 10 January, 2006
32. John Chryssavgis, 'Iconography', in *The New SCM Dictionary of Spirituality*, ed. Philip Sheldrake, London: SCM Press, 2005, 353

parture from Manchester United in the 2005/6 season – Keane is generally considered to have been the most complete, committed and consistent player in the Premiership since its inception in the mid 90s, captain of both his club and country. Tom Humphries, whose interview with Keane in Saipan for *The Irish Times* initially indicated the intensity of his feelings about the inadequacy of the Irish team's conditions in preparation for the World Cup in Japan/South Korea, includes Keane in the classical iconography of Ireland, alongside Éamon De Valera, John F. Kennedy and the Sacred Heart of Jesus, interpreting his autobiography as a 'sacred text'.[33] After Keane's return to the Irish team (under Brian Kerr's management) the same journalist sees him in Norse mythological terms – 'Calling on our own god of war' – as he prepared to play in the 2006 World Cup qualifier against the Faroes Islands in Torshavn, a town which takes its name from the harbour of the Norse god of war, Thor.[34] While Humphries hails Keane's return in moral terms – 'Winner or sinner?' – his colleague Keith Duggan, in the same issue, estimates his reprise of international duty eschatologically, as a 'Second Coming'.[35] Conferring the freedom of the city on Keane and Cobh athlete Sonia O' Sullivan, the Lord Mayor of Cork states that their efforts and achievements have left audiences and admirers in 'stupified satisfaction' as they 'had hammered their God-given natural talent into something special through dedication and hard work and were examples of modern icons'.[36] Prior to his sudden departure – or dismissal – from Manchester United, Paul Wilson employed a similar perspective on estimating the footballer's future: 'Keane must tone it down in next life'.[37] (Keane's namesake, Spurs player Robbie, was chosen as captain for the first game by Ireland under manager Steve Staunton partly because he was considered to be an icon.[38])

Before Ireland's 2005 World Cup qualifier against Israel in

---

33. *The Irish Times*, 28 April, 2003
34. *The Irish Times*, 8 June, 2005
35. *The Irish Times*, 17 April, 2004
36. *Irish Examiner*, 15 June, 2005
37. *The Observer*, 2 October, 2005
38. 'Keane the "icon" leads Staunton's new era', *The Independent*, 1 March, 2006

2005 Ken Early describes Keane as more than a mere footballer, 'at once a national icon, a symbol of something bigger than himself, the most transformative figure in Irish sporting history'.[39] In a profile published under the heading of 'Messiah goes to the Promised Land' Early exclaims that '"they are not made whole that reach the age of Christ" so wrote Thomas Kinsella in 1961. But as he journeys towards the Holy Land at the messianic age of 33, that's not strictly true of Roy Keane.' Referring to the course of the Saipan controversy in Ireland as religious schism, he confesses that 'a grieving people were not to know that one day he would rise again, as the saviour of Irish sport.'[40] (A 2008 account of Keane's first season as manager of Sunderland is entitled *In Keane We Trust*.) Characterisation of Keane in christological terms – Messiah, Saviour – appears as both clever and catchy in the context of a competitive match in Israel, converting the language of iconography to the level of incarnation. Given that the Christian doctrine of the incarnation is the cornerstone of both the form and content of icons, this conflation creates a cognitive and confessional dissonance when doctrinal titles and theological terminology are converted to describe sporting contestants.

God's Tiger

In his book *Christianity Rediscovered*, Maryknoll priest Vincent Donovan recalls and reflects on the seventeen years of missionary work among the Masai people in East Africa. Referring to the Masai proverb, 'In the end the lion is God', he repeats belief in the power and transcendence of God found in traditional religion(s).[41] Analysis of the mental strength and physical skills of golfer Tiger Woods enjoy similar attributes. James Lawton likens the influence from childhood of his father Earl to lines usually reserved for divine revelation: '*Honour thy father* is a command of Biblical authority and how better could Woods do this than with another confirmation that when the old jungle fighter declared that his son was a "chosen one".'[42] A year before

---

39. *Village*, 19-25 March, 2005
40. Idem
41. London: SCM Press Ltd, 1982
42. *The Independent*, 4 April, 2006

Tiger's first victory in the Masters (1996), his father already talked of him transcending the game and taking it to new levels, including that of humanitarianism, by virtue of his ethnicity, which especially empowered him to perform miracles.[43] Lawton proclaims that 'as prophecy went, this was probably unprecedented since John the Baptist announced the arrival of the Messiah'.[44] While Woods' level of preparation is legendary he is also a lucky player and this has played no small part in his progression to the so-called pantheon of golfing gods, a factor which writers and commentators seem to ignore, perhaps out of fear of falling out of favour. While some may consider calling Woods lucky a heresy, others may see it as at least a sign of divine favour or a proof that the 'gods' generate their own share of luck.

James Lawton attributes Woods' success as much to the influence of divine inspiration as to his individual resolve, stating that he 'so often appears to work directly with God' and that 'We always know that somewhere along the line with Tiger there is the certainty of redemption.'[45]

Writing about Woods on his first round in the 2005 British Open – in a piece entitled 'Masses flock to worship at Tiger's feet' – Matthew Pinsent casts him in explicitly cultic categories: 'If golf is a religion, and many millions spend far longer on a course than in any place of worship, then Tiger Woods is the highest of all priests.'[46] Mixing his metaphors, Pinsent portrays him as a 'biblical character' entering 'his cathedral', while the people who followed his round are at once characterised as both a congregation and pilgrims, 'crowding his every move, as if touching his hem was going to cure them'. When Woods threw

---

43. In a profile of the player prior to the 2006 Masters Lewine Mair comments on the different backgrounds of his parents: 'The most obvious sign of where the American meets the Thai surfaces on a tournament Sunday [when] the world number one always plays in a red shirt because red, in Thai culture, symbolises power … Like so much else from his upbringing, this little ritual contributes to his seemingly bottomless well of belief.' *The Daily Telegraph*, 6 April, 2006
44. *The Independent*, 4 April, 2006
45. 'Wonder of Woods rooted in resolve as much as flashes of divine inspiration', *The Independent*, 17 June, 2006
46. *The Times*, 15 July, 2005

away a broken tee on the fourth hole, the marshals have to 'decide who got the precious relic'. His two playing partners, Australian Robert Allenby and Spaniard Jose Maria Olazabal, are presented as 'altar boys', while the piece finishes with a 'Note to the faithful – the service [second round] today starts at 1.31 pm.' However, the hyperbole – and even hysteria – of this passage are only heightened by the Achilles' heel like reference to the day's events as a 'circus', which leaves readers wondering whether, in such an arena, Woods should be cast as a tiger or tamer. Further evidence of evangelical flavour and fervour are found in reference to Woods' preaching 'the gospel of accurate driving being a holy necessity around Baltrusol' [USPGA 2005] though he is reported to have made 'the devil's mess of his front nine'[47] on the first day and the example of (sporting) compassion shown to fellow competitor John Daly when he 'three-putted away what would have been one of the most spectacular redemptions seen this side of the Sea of Galilee.'[48]

Included in *Time*'s hall of 'Heroes and Icons' in 2004, Woods earned the superlative estimation of fellow golfer and Major winner Sandy Lyle: 'He's taken things to a different level and is already an icon, so what's the stage beyond icon? Is there a word for that?'[49] This remark raises the issue of the intensification of iconography in the context of sports individuals and institutions. An article on English soccer legend and 'icon' Bobby Moore quoted words used about another American sporting legend: 'In the United States, [Joe] Di Maggio became the icon of icons because, as the baseball writer David Halberstram put it, he "transcended the barriers of sports in terms of the breadth of his fame".'[50] Referring to speculation about the possibility of Italian seven times World Championship motorcyclist Valentino Rossi switching to Formula One motorcar racing in a Ferrari, Paddy Agnew asserted that 'it would be the case of an icon driving an icon', though he quotes his disclaimer 'I am Valentino Rossi, not an icon.'[51] Writing about the reconstructed Wembley

47. *The Independent*, 12 August, 2005
48. 'The unforgettable compassion of a true master', *The Independent*, 11 October 2005
49. *The Daily Telegraph*, 11 August, 2005
50. *The Observer Sports Monthly*, August 2005, 18
51. *The Irish Times*, 5 May, 2007

stadium, sportswriter Hunter Davies proclaimed that 'the new Wembley, with its arch, is already an icon', adding 'Funny how icons are immediately made these days. Used to take for ever for such recognition'.[52] The juxtaposition of 'immediately' and 'for ever' highlights the confusion and crisis in characterising such players and places as icons.

'God's little foot'

The headline for an exclusive interview with David Beckham – 'This will be my life after football'[53] – could be interpreted in immortal, rather than merely mundane, terms if the thoughts and feelings of his fans were to be taken into account. Less than two months later *The Times* talked of the 'wow factor' that could 'turn Beckham into an American idol' if he were to take up his boots and play in the Major Soccer League there. However, George Best, considered by many pundits to have been the greatest player in the history of English and perhaps even European soccer, gave Beckham the equivalent of a B minus for his skill levels. Notwithstanding the hype, even hysteria at times that has surrounded his Manchester United, Real Madrid and English careers to date, the player has never been charged with showcasing either professional or personal hubris. He is generally considered to be a nice person who has opened a sports academy for children in Greenwich, London to develop their lives. Nevertheless, the suspicion remains among some soccer pundits that Manchester United pulled off an economic coup, whatever the emotional costs, in transferring a beyond his sell-by-date Beckham to arch-European rivals Real Madrid. The ability of 'Brand Beckham' to advertise the Spanish club's jerseys and other products may have been a factor in his acquisition, especially for the burgeoning and fiercely competitive Asian fan market. One estimate of his economic worth to Real Madrid equalled twenty times his transfer cost of twenty million sterling, an amount assayed as 'peanuts' by Jose Angel Sanchez, the club's marketing director.[54]

---

52. *The Sunday Times*, 20 May, 2007
53. 24 February, 2006
54. See John Carlin, 'Why Beckham and branding are key to Real's world domination', *The Independent*, 17 February, 2006

Referring to the 'Beckham caravan' rolling on, James Lawton reckoned that he 'is an immovable, untouchable factor in the nation's football … the extraordinary reality of his life and times'.[55] His commercial contribution has increasingly out-weighed his competitive importance for both club and country. Moreover, he has incurred the cost of both celebrity and star-dom with the intrusion and even the risk of invasion into his personal life which involved the attempted kidnap of his wife, former Spice Girls member Victoria and lurid accounts of extra-marital activity. He has had to learn that being in the spotlight does not cease when the game concludes, that the media circus never leaves town without its proverbial pound or two of flesh. A sporting 'fall from grace' can be both fickle and furious.

Prior to the 2002 World Cup finals, Beckham broke a metatarsal bone in his foot. To employ the title of a well-known soccer book, anxiety and analysis reached 'fever pitch' levels among English fans and media before Beckham was cleared fit to play. The television celebrity Uri Geller led prayers for his re-covery. (A similar situation developed around Wayne Rooney before the 2006 competition.) Sent off against Argentina in their 1998 encounter (a harsh refereeing decision by some estimates) which England lost in a penalty shoot-out, in 2002 Beckham scored from the spot in a 1-0 victory. Tom Humphreys greeted the result with a reference to the continuation of 'football's eternal mysteries', while two posters at the game gave a divine riposte to the infamous 1986 'Hand of God' incident when Argentina won 2-0: 'Jesus took the penalty'; 'The Foot of God'. The latter theomorphism – a human being or part of a person taken as an attribute or addendum of God – captures the fervour and flavour of some of the commentary that had attended Beckham's injury before the competition, with the additional el-ement of divine justice. It seems there are no depths to which divinisation cannot descend.

The 'iconisation' (a term used by Suzanne Harrington in her survey of academic devotion to 'Beckhamology'[56]) investing Beckham with spiritual and salvific status has acquired inter-re-

---

55. *The Independent*, 4 October, 2005
56. 'Academia image gets the boot with Beckhamology', *Irish Examiner*, 5 November, 2002

ligious dimensions. In May 2003 *The Observer* referred, in almost scriptural terms, to people of different races, sexes and ages worshipping at 'at David's feet, the corn-rowed man-god' (a reference to his latest hairdo), while in December 2004 a celebrity waxwork nativity scene at Madame Tussauds in London depicted David and Victoria Beckham as Joseph and Mary, with 'Posh 'n' Becks the Stars of Bethlehem'.[57] In an assessment of England's surprise World Cup qualifier defeat to Northern Ireland in 2005 the veteran soccer writer David Lacey speaks of the 'crosser' (Beckham's soccer trademark) 'proving an awkward cross to bear'.[58] In a piece entitled 'Beckham as the Messiah' Gerard Senan opines that 'There may be some superficial similarities – boy from lowly background achieves an international following, perhaps – but the chances are that when most Christians get down on their knees on a Sunday morning to prepare for the second coming, they are not thinking of David Beckham.'[59] Senan's statement was occasioned by an international academic conference which heard that 'the footballer may be the nearest thing modern society has to a new Messiah ... that Beckham is steeped in pseudo-Christian iconography'.[60] In the build-up to the Commonwealth Games in Manchester in 2002, in a series of Indian-inspired artworks, David and Victoria were depicted as the Hindu god Shiva and goddess Parvati while their son Brooklyn, seated on his father's knee and kitted out in Manchester United colours, was portrayed as the elephant god Ganesh. The authors appealed to the 'trinity' of both Shiva, Parvati and Ganesh and sport, media and pop celebrity to justify their 'light-hearted' artistry.[61]

Contemporaries of Beckham have also received similar divine accolades. These include the Italian striker Roberto Baggio, on whom the title *Il divino* (The Divine One) was bestowed in his native country. A Buddhist, Baggio's trademark hairstyle also earned the epithet 'God's ponytail'. Beckham's fellow English forward, Alan Shearer, has been the subject of fanatical reli-

57. *Irish Independent*, 10 December, 2004
58. *The Guardian*, 10 September, 2005
59. *The Guardian Weekly*, 23-29 September, 2005
60. Idem
61. *The Guardian*, 27 February 2008

gious-like devotion, largely because of his decision to reject the offer of clubs like Manchester United and opt instead to play for his native Newcastle United. The subject-matter of a Masters thesis dissertation entitled 'The King of Newcastle – Alan Shearer is Above Football' he is described by Swedish author Jenny Lindstrom as possessing 'a consistent capacity for action that surpasses the norm of man, just like the ancient heroes'.[62] More a messianic than a mythical figure for Newcastle fans, Paul Hayward hailed his 'decision to play the prodigal son was either the biggest miscalculation by a world-class footballer in modern times or the greatest declaration of spiritual integrity'. [63] Amidst the ongoing managerial crisis at the club Shearer is regularly referred to as the figure who can rescue the fortunes of his beloved Newcastle, not least by his former manager Sir Bobby Robson who 'identified [him] as the saviour of St James' Park ... convinced that, despite the absence of managerial credentials on Shearer's glittering CV, the iconic Geordie has what it takes to revitalise the strife-torn Tyneside club'.[64] Marina Hyde expresses the extent of such 'iconisation': 'If we are to interpret Lee's annunciation correctly, he suspects that [present owner Mike] Ashley will not finalise a sale by January and will therefore find himself in a bit of a spot, with a serious face-saving challenge to pull off – much as the Virgin Mary did all those Christmases ago when she found herself with a child. And so thoughts turn to Shearer as saviour. Or Shearer's thoughts do, evidently ... Still, it is the season of hope and the word "messiah" is bandied about so regularly in relation to Newcastle that there is no earthly reason we should not slap it once again on to the island-tufted head of Alan Shearer and cross or fingers that it will all end happily ... as long as you count inevitable crucifixion followed by iffy resurrection as a happy ending, obviously.'[65]

---

62. *The Independent on Sunday*, 23 April, 2006
63. *The Daily Telegraph*, 2 April, 2005
64. 'Shearer's love for Newcastle can save club from sinking', *The Daily Telegraph*, 20 October 2008
65. 'Out of the mouthpiece into Shear hell', *The Guardian*, 20 November, 2008

Gaelic Gods

In the past decade two players – D. J. Carey (Kilkenny) in hurling, Peter Canavan (Tyrone) in Gaelic football – have been deified by devoted fans and described as 'god' in their respective counties. On All-Ireland final day in September 2003 legendary Kilkenny forward Eddie Keher referred on RTÉ radio to this title for Carey, as his team went on to defeat Cork for the championship. A month later Tom Humphries profiled Carey for *The Observer Sports Monthly*, calling him 'the epitome of Irish character'.[66] In hyperbolic style, Humphries refers to hurling as the 'Alpha and Omega', the force holding sport, culture and community together, 'a game for gods played by men [where] D. J. straddles the gap between gods and men' which attracted devotion in its 'cathedrals', a superstar who 'saved hurling with what he was given'[67] and who enjoys an international reputation and recognition in the company of professional golfers. When a rumour spread that he was about to join their ranks, he received twenty-five thousand letters within a few weeks and returned to hurling. Canavan captained Tyrone to their first All-Ireland success in 2003 and played a pivotal role in their second success two years later. Describing him in 2003 as 'the spiritual fulcrum', 'upon the rock Peter they built their team', two years later Humphries extols him in explicitly divine terms: 'God had a walk-on part in yesterday's thundering Croke Park drama.'[68] In a preview of the 2005 game against Kerry, Humphries' colleague Ian O' Riordan characterises Canavan as a Christ-like figure walking on water, whose 'witnesses to his miracles are true believers'.[69]

In the Anglican Cathedral of St John the Divine in New York a stained-glass window enshrines players of baseball and other field sports. During the 2005 Championship season a variation of this theme appeared throughout Ireland in an advertisement for Lucozade sports drinks. Under the mantra 'Achieving Starts with Believing', two Gaelic footballers are depicted in stained-glass style as they compete aerially for a ball. The bringing to-

---

66. October 2003
67. Idem
68. 'Water to wine for Canavan', *The Irish Times*, 5 September, 2005
69. *The Irish Times*, 17 September, 2005

gether of belief and sporting battle in this medium masks its religiously iconic meaning, making for a substitution of faith and prayer by sport and play. Advertising's appeal to ritual, as in the Paddy Power parody of the Last Supper, appears, if not acts, as an alternative to religious worship. Prior to the county's 2005 All-Ireland victory a banner in Dungannon proclaimed 'Sam [Maguire] is coming back to Tyrone thanks be to the Sacred Harte.' This refers to the county manager Mickey Harte and in a fascinating reference to the deaths of former Tyrone players, Harte states that 'We didn't think it was right to put them to the forefront of our language as it were.'[70] However, advertisers, fans and journalists do not seem to share a similar hesitancy when portraying and proclaiming coaches, players and places in terms of Christian images and language. Recourse to such means represents what Michael Paul Gallagher calls 'a wounded imagination', where 'according to [Cardinal] Newman, 'imagination is the high road of faith' and yet 'can sink into superficiality'.[71] Perhaps superficiality is too soft a term for this process of interpreting Christian iconography in sporting symbols and statements.

'The Hand of God'

In a biography bearing this title, Jimmy Burns states that his main interest is 'to investigate Maradona as a unique social, political and religious phenomenon', describing it as a story about 'a natural-born football talent who grew up to believe he was God and suffered as a result'.[72] In a career that covered his native Argentina, Spain and Italy, his crowning achievement was to captain his country to World Cup victory in 1986. Passage to the final (and victory over West Germany) included the incident for which he has become infamous – the 'hand of God' – goal against England in the quarter-finals when he palmed the ball into the net over the approaching English goalkeeper Peter Shilton. Billed in advance by the British tabloid media as a replay of the Falklands/Malvinas war, with talk of

70. *Irish Independent*, 26 September, 2005
71. *The Tablet*, 259, 10 September 2005, 10
72. *The Hand of God*, London: Bloomsbury, 2002, xi-xii

'exclusion zones' around Maradona, this score soured the result and subsequent championship victory. The irony is that Maradona went on to score a second goal against England, considered by many pundits and fans as the greatest goal in the history of the World Cup. Getting the ball inside his own half, he left a handful of English defenders trailing in his wake as he, on this occasion, waltzed the ball past the hapless Shilton. (One version of his run that resulted in this second goal viewed it as 'magical, mystical'.) However, the fact that Maradona maintained that his first score was the 'hand of God' has forever marked – and marred – that match. In an interview with BBC Match of the Day anchor (and opponent on that fateful day in 1986) Gary Lineker twenty years later, Maradona accepted responsibility for the role his hand played in the score, though reiterating that 'God gives us the hand' and claiming that it was not cheating but rather cunning and craftiness.[73]

Despite subsequent success with Argentina and at club level with Naples in the bearpit of Italy's *Serie A*, Maradona's life became a headlong descent into a drug fuelled existence which eventually extinguished his footballing genius and seriously harmed his health. This descent has been well documented by the media, most tellingly in Burns' book which has been dubbed a 'modern footballing classic'. His dalliance with politics, particularly with the Cuban dictator Fidel Castro, has also provided much material for commentary and speculation. His return to health, public visibility and a television career have become the subject matter of renewed media interest and interpretation. Described as 'speaking in parables', his return to health and prominence have been depicted in theological terms: 'Maradona's road to redemption';[74] 'Diego's resurrection';[75] 'Maradona – the story of his return from the dead'.[76] (His autobiography – *El Diego* – includes chapters entitled 'Passion', 'Resurrection' and 'Glory' which refer to periods of his football career, at Argentinian club Boca Juniors, Napoli and winning the World Cup respectively.) A claim that his life-story is 'a remarkable tale

73. *The Sunday Telegraph*, 30 April, 2006
74. *The Sunday Times*, 9 October, 2005
75. *The Independent*, 11 November, 2005
76. *The Observer Sports Monthly*, January 2006

of personal redemption, almost resurrection'[77] connotes a sense that he may well have reinvented himself in the sense of recovery but collapses the christological meaning of redemption and resurrection. Maradona has passed the torch on to fellow countryman 18-year-old Barcelona player Lionel Messi, who has been portrayed as 'the new Messi-ah'.[78]

A host of headlines greeted his appointment as manager of Argentina in October 2008. Under the banner 'Gambling on God' (with a picture of Maradona as a player in prayer like pose) Ian Hawkey writes that 'Argentina are placing their faith in the divine yet untried hands of Diego Maradona'.[79] Describing 'Maradona's latest crusade', Dion Fanning defines him as 'Argentina's salvation once more'.[80] Much space is devoted to the Maradonian Church in Buenos Aires which depicts time in terms of the year DD, *despues de Diego* or 'after Diego'. Shane McCabe describes the delight of members on hearing news of their hero's elevation: 'In the *Iglesia Maradoniana* they were jumping for joy at the news of their high-priest's appointment as the new pontiff of the country's unofficial religion. There is a replica World Cup at the centre of the spacious club-room, a mural celebrating *la mano di Dios* (the hand of God) and no shortage of disciples. They have a Maradona version of the Our Father, petitioning "Our Father Diego" to "forgive the trespasses of nasty journalists, as forgive the Naples Mafia".'[81] Estimating their numbers in excess of 100,000 Joel Miller defines devotion to the star turned saviour as 'indicative of the divine-like status he is afforded in his home country, and indeed across the globe'.[82] With a caption 'Mascherano applauds appointment of idol Maradona', Andy Hunter writes that the Liverpool player 'has dismissed the scepticism surrounding Argentina's appointment of Diego Maradona as national team coach and said the iconic talent, though a managerial novice, can reproduce the success he

77. Chris Taylor, 'The Observer Profile', *The Observer*, 6 November, 2005
78. 'In Maradona's footsteps, the new Messi-ah', *Irish Examiner*, 7 March, 2006
79. *The Sunday Times*, 2 November, 2008
80. *Sunday Independent*, 2 November, 2008
81. *Sunday Independent*, 2 November, 2008
82. 'Evening worship at the church of Maradona', *Irish Examiner*, 17 November, 2008

orchestrated so brilliantly as a player', quoting his words that 'It's great to have such a legend as manager. To us he is like God. He's the best player we've had in our history, the best player football's ever had.'[83]

The 'hand of God' is a biblical concept connoting primarily the sovereign power of God. In the Old Testament 'the hand of Yahweh' appears often, as a figure of punishment but also offering deliverance and protection. If the Lord's hand is indicated as being with somebody, it is interpreted as a statement of strength and support, as in Psalm 89:21 – 'My hand will always be with him [David], my arm will make him strong.' In the New Testament, the christological content of this care and commission is clarified: 'The Father loves the Son and has entrusted everything to his hands' (John 3:35). Theologically, the most beautiful reference to the image of God's hand(s) occurs in St Irenaeus' indication of Jesus Christ and the Holy Spirit: 'For God did not stand in need of these [beings] in order to accomplish what he had determined with himself beforehand should be done, as if he did not possess his own hands. For with him were always present the Word and Wisdom, the son and the Spirit, by whom and in whom, freely and spontaneously, he made all things to whom he also speaks.'[84] If Maradona's appeal to divine intervention decries moral evaluation, it also demands deconstruction.

Best Mates

George Best died in November 2005. The huge outpouring of grief in Manchester and his native Belfast drew comparisons with the death and subsequent mourning for Princess Diana. Considered a certain candidate for a World XI by most soccer pundits, his skills and scores rate comparison with players like Cruyff, Di Stefano, Pele, Puskas and Maradona. Calling him 'Football's First Icon', *The Observer* editorialises him as 'an angel on the pitch', portraying a pair of boots with angelic wings as a tribute to his memory.[85] He was at least as famous for his es-

83. *The Guardian*, 6 November, 2008
84. *Against Heresies*, Book 4, Chapter XX1, in A. Robert & J. Donaldson, eds, The Ante-Nicene Fathers, Grand Rapids: Eerdmans, 1956, 487-488
85. 27 November, 2005

capades off the field as his exploits on it and the media had, (no pun intended) a proverbial field day in the events leading up to his death and funeral. As addiction to alcohol robbed him of his athletic talent and tragically of his life, Tom Humphries' analysis captures the sense of the circus that he had both been cause and casualty of: 'George Best died as he had lived, with the bright lights and the media mob sucking away his dignity and his privacy. He was George and we took him and made him Georgie [the fifth Beatle] and turned him into a deity and then into a cautionary parable'.[86] An international player for Northern Ireland, his death drew on a sense of sympathy, if not indeed solidarity, that transcended sectarianism.

The Independent featured a photograph of a fan praying at the shrine set up to his memory outside the Manchester United ground Old Trafford, a scene which is described by Henry Winter in the following terms: 'Manchester's rain extinguished the candles lit in the shrine to George Best on Sir Matt Busby Way … but it couldn't wash away the memories of those gathered in the cathedral of Old Trafford.'[87] Eulogies extended from the ecstatic to the evangelical through to the eschatological: 'Blessed with a talent only God bestows', he was seen as both 'myth and saint of soccer', 'a titan who sinned but was redeemed', the returns of the 'earthly remains of a heavenly body' to Belfast heralding 'a common religion'. The categories of 'icon' and 'miracle worker' captured both the tone and theme of the media treatment of Best's career as a footballer which reached its crowning moment in the 1968 European Cup final, in which 'Best had a transcendent game, his sublime contribution confirming his genius',[88] including two goals in Manchester United's 4-1 victory over Benfica. If 121,000 people were reported as genuflecting in front of 2006 German Grand Prix winner Michael Schumacher, the grief expressed at Best's passing rated him, in media calculations, as a candidate for instant sanctification. In his case the overdrive of media opinion transcends the traditional pantheon of soccer greats, seeing him as an 'unrivalled icon' who made 'prayers with his feet', a man-made

86. *The Irish Times*, 28 November, 2005
87. *The Daily Telegraph*, 1 December, 2005
88. 'Obituary', *The Daily Telegraph*, 26 November, 2005

deity who suffered the fate of crucifixion by the media and merited at least passing comparison with the Dalai Lama.[89]

The association of football and faith around the death and funeral of George Best brings to the fore the sense that sport, especially soccer, functions as a surrogate spirituality, a replacement for traditional religious forms in a largely secularised Western world. The prominent soccer writer Jimmy Burns synthesises this viewpoint in a piece on Best in the English Catholic weekly *The Tablet*: 'The sheer volume of media output and commentary devoted to Best was a reminder of the extent to which football has become almost a substitute religion, generating lifelong loyalties, and a passionate transference of beliefs and inner failings from fans to celebrity stars. Football is regarded by billions as of crucial importance, its main protagonists elevated to iconic status, more important than presidents or bishops'.[90] The reference to transference may suggest the need for a sociopsychological analysis of this phenomenon. At the same time identification of sports stars as 'icons' suggests intimations of transcendence and raises issues which require both philosophical reflection and theological response. Best's death and funeral bring together issues of both morality and mortality, questions about the meaning of life and death. The media spectacle and mass grief that surrounded both his final days and funeral invite comparison with another occasion earlier in the year, the death and burial of Pope John Paul II. Beyond factors of the force of personality and the formation of cultic following, themes of transience – the artistry of football, the achievement of fame, the adulation of fans, the ageing and abandonment of once flourishing skills and strength – tell a tale of tragedy or take it to the threshold of transcendence. Reminders both of human frailty and its historical finality, John Paul II and George Best serve as representatives of the faithful and fallen, who focus the mind (and hopefully the media) beyond the vicissitudes of life, the vagaries of victory and valediction to questions of ultimate concern and consideration. Sport may serve a religious function in raising questions that transcend the immediacy of involvement

89. Billy Keane, 'It's about as near as any of us can get to reaching sainthood', *Irish Independent*, 3 December, 2005
90. 259 (3 December 2005), 11

on the playing fields, interest on the terraces and interpretation in the media. The death and funeral of both Pope and playboy, once proud performers on the stage and soccer pitch respectively, hold up what Burns terms 'a mirror to the vulnerability of the human condition, its possibilities and limitations'.[91] Among the tasks of theology is to see what this mirror reflects in the light of revelation.

A few weeks before George Best's death the equine racing world experienced shock and sadness with the sudden death of triple consecutive Cheltenham Gold Cup and King George VI Chase winner Best Mate during a routine race at Exeter, after suffering acute heart failure on the track. Attendance at the meeting had doubled in anticipation of the horse's return after injury earlier in the year had prevented him from defending his Gold Cup crown, considered the Blue Riband of National Hunt racing. Reactions to the event ranged from disbelief through a sense of poignancy to tragedy. The tenor of tragedy was added to by the fact that the horse had won the prize for the best-turned out before the race. The wishes of owner Jim Lewis to bury the remains of the beloved Best Mate resulted in questions in the House of Commons about regulations concerning the disposal of animals by cremation considered 'commercial', in the wake of the BSE and foot and mouth crises. Called the 'people's horse', his death featured on the front pages of many papers the day after. A feature of his popularity was the fact that he had helped raise thousands of pounds for charity purposes.

A DVD of the horse's career, called *Best Mate –The Icon*, was produced and featured as 'DVD of the Week' in *The Independent on Sunday*.[92] In an article entitled 'He Was Our Icon', trainer Henrietta Knight speaks of him lovingly as 'Matey, the horse of our dreams and a racing icon', referring to the steady flow of visitors to see him and personal fan mail sent to him over the years.[93] After his death he was immediately installed in horseracing's Hall of Fame alongside the Irish icon Arkle. (Simply called 'Himself', Arkle has been hailed as both a shrine

---

91. Idem
92. 5 March, 2006
93. 'Best Mate Tribute', *The Daily Telegraph*, 4 November, 2005

and a saint, 'the first horse who truly became a public figure, an equine god who took his place alongside the Beatles, Jackie Kennedy and El Cordobes in popularity polls'.[94] Best Mate's owner expressed the hope that he would be taking on Arkle in an equine eternal venue. As an institution in the world of horseracing, Best Mate was considered a legend, listed as a thoroughbred that 'transcends the insular world occupied by horsemen and betting shop punters to prick the consciousness of the nation'.[95] Prominent racing presenter and columnist Clare Balding hails him as one of 'a handful of racehorses who have transcended the confines of the racing pages ... more than a headline act, a show-stopper, a beautiful physical specimen who age shall not weary'.[96] At the same time Animal Aid director Andrew Tyler criticises the suffering experienced in the equine pursuit of prestige and prize money, glamour and glory, stating that their selective breeding for speed at the expense of bone density and general health considerations contributed to their vulnerability and fragility.[97]

The anthropomorphism and associated iconography articulated in the aftermath of Best Mate's death ask fundamental questions about the meaning of sport that involves the association of animals and humans. Similar outpourings of grief and obsequies of glory attended the departure ceremonies for Desert Orchid,[98] an animal Lise Hand describes as 'an iconic local-boy-done-good'.[99] Henrietta Knight's quote from the poet Byron –

94. Sean Magee, 'The day when Arkle became the greatest', *The Guardian*, 5 November, 2005

95. Richard Evans, *The Daily Telegraph*, 2 November, 2005

96. *The Observer*, 7 November, 2005

97. 'Don't be blinkered to the cruelty of racing', *The Guardian*, 10 November, 2005

98. 'With Desert Orchid, non-horsey people suddenly saw the point. They saw a beautiful, courageous, generous, powerful, athletic, brilliant, character-filled individual ... Oh, brave old world that has such creatures in it! To share a planet, to share a life with such marvels ... He will be lavishly anthropomorphised and sentimentalised and wept over. But why not? He was the horse for all sorts and conditions of humankind, he was the horse for everyone, and above all, he was wonderfully and perfectly suitable for playing the part of Everyhorse.' Simon Barnes in *The Times*, 14 November, 2006

99. 'Our darling little Dessie', *Irish Independent*, 18 November 2006

'those whom the gods love die young' – and her farewell, in the form of the traditional Requiescat – 'He was unique and the memories will last for ever. May he rest in peace'[100] – raise intriguing parallels between human and equine existence, not only in earthly terms but even extending into eternity.[101] Are such interpretations simply inferences of intimacy around the proverbial bond between 'man and beast' or do they involve a shading of animal life into human existence? Or do the attribution of human and even divine qualities and powers to animals such as Best Mate attest to an increasing sense of social isolation and loss of traditional religious belief? While Kauto Star's victory in the 2007 Cheltenham Gold Cup occasioned the headline 'Bloodied and bruised punters follow Star to salvation',[102] his easy eclipse by stable companion Denman a year later showed how fickle fame and faith in horses can be as their 'battle for immortality'[103] bore witness. Chris McGrath engages in explicit religious description in his evocation of the Epsom Derby: 'Last year, it all boiled down to whether or not you could accept the Authorised [2007 winner] version. But the 229th Derby is open to all manner of interpretations, and nobody at Epsom today can be certain that he is reading gospel, or counterfeit scrolls.'[104] (The field included Tajaaweed, defined in the same piece as 'Set of rules governing the correct way to recite the Koran'.)

From Icons to Idols

In a 'symbol saturated society',[105] the shift from 'icons' to 'idols' seems only a short step to take. Earlier reference was made to the so-called 'wow factor' as a sufficient catalyst to convert David Beckham into an American idol, in pursuit of promoting

100. 'He Was Our Icon', *The Daily Telegraph*, 4 November, 2005
101. 'With Desert Orchid and Best Mate now grazing in that great paddock in the sky, which horse will be the next to hold the mantle of Britain's favourite racer?' Sergeant Cecil in *The Times*, 14 November, 2006
102. *Sunday Independent*, 18 March, 2007
103. *The Independent*, 14 March, 2008
104. *The Independent*, 7 June, 2008
105. Scott Lash and John Urry, *Economies of Sign and Space*, quoted in Timothy A. Radcliffe, *What is the Point of Being a Christian?* London: Burns & Oates, 2005, 18

a sport which struggles to capture the public imagination despite the staging of the 1994 World Cup there. An advertisement during the Lions tour of New Zealand in 2005 sported captain Brian O'Driscoll with the slogan 'In BOD we trust'.[106] Prior to the 2006 European opening Formula One race at Imola, the future of the sport's superstar Michael Schumacher seemed in doubt, leading one columnist to suggest that 'time was running out for Ferrari idol'.[107] Two weeks later his victory in the European Grand Prix on home soil at the Nurbirgring was greeted by '121,000 genuflecting Germans',[108] which seemed to galvanise him and breathe new life into his career (and the championship race.)

As well as the imagery of iconography, the language of idolatry is being interpreted to indicate both the nature of sport and the prominence of sports personalities, both on and off the field of play. This development dovetails with the merchandise and marketing wars associated with brands of sportswear and accessories, which reached fever-pitch proportions in and around the 2006 World Cup in Germany. Branding now appears to be the bearer and vehicle of meaning. The 'brand' as transmitter of meaning in the context of post-modernism and globalisation provides the basis for both anthropological and philosophical studies. The 'trinity' of film, music and sports stars as the wearers of such brands and bearers of meaning is a related area calling for deeper reflection and discernment. The 'battle of the brands' is not an insignificant element in the encounters of sports men and women, whether engaged in competition or recreation. The sporting challenge is clouded to a certain extent by the hype and even hysteria engaged by who wears what and for whom. The cult of celebrity, rather than the context of competition and contest, creates a certain identity crisis for sport.

Recourse to idolatry in conceiving and communicating sport constitutes a fundamental faith challenge for Christian communities, spirituality and theology: 'The idol is a product of human ingenuity, which receives the longing and desire of those who

106. *Irish Independent* deputy sports editor Sean Ryan discusses the social and religious significance of such sports personalities in 'Idolising sports heroes is a danger', *The Voice Today*, 18 November, 2006
107. *The Daily Telegraph*, 22 April, 2006
108. *The Daily Telegraph*, 8 May, 2006

make it. It is a screen reflecting back projections arising from the one who worships it. The idol cannot give authentic access to the infinite, for it is a closed object, sufficient to itself. Idols are essentially opaque.'[109] Idols, by their very nature, are incapable of intimating or inviting to transcendence, denying a doorway out of and beyond an existence that is entirely envisaged in innerwordly terms and categories. Involved in the subject's narcissism or projection they are mirrors of immanence. The worship of idols is antithetical to Judaeo-Christian revelation and the requirement of the First Commandment: 'You shall not make for yourself an idol, whether in the form of anything that is in heaven above, or that is on the earth beneath, or that is in the water under the earth'.[110] John Calvin's claim that human nature is 'a perpetual factory of idols'[111] could count the sport-media complex among its targets. Traditionally the distinction between the 'icon' and the 'idol' involves the difference and, to employ a spatial metaphor, the distance between transcendence and immanence. Poetically, adapting an image of Keats, the icon invites from beyond the 'mysterious casement' while the idol is imprisoned before it. Theologically, the distinction involves issues of truth and falsehood, being and non-being, authenticity and alienation, salvation and perdition, heaven and hell. Recourse to the register of idolatry to represent sport and references such as 'diabolical' to report games and matches[112] further suggest a reduction of religious belief and loss of a sense of transcendence. In his homily at the *Esplanade des Invalides* during his visit to France, Pope Benedict XVI states that idolatry obscures reason as well as faith and intercedes with God 'to help us purify ourselves from all idols, in order to arrive at the truth of our being, in order to arrive at the truth of his infinite being.'[113]

---

109. Gregory Collins, 'Christ, Idols and Icons', *Doctrine & Life*, 52 (July/August 2002), 337
110. Exodus 20:4.
111. Quoted in 'Editorial – No Other Gods', *Interpretation*, 60 (April 2006), 131
112. 'Flintoff's folly and diabolical fielding lets Sri Lanka off hook', *The Independent*, 16 May, 2006
113. 'Shun worship of idols, raise the cup of salvation. God alone gives true happiness, teaches true values', *L'Osservatore Romano*, weekly English edition, no 38, 17 September, 2008

Sporting Identity

A *Demos* pamphlet by John Holden[114] interrogates three mode(l)s for measuring the values of the arts in society: instrumental, institutional and intrinsic. Applied analogously to sport these afford three very different analyses of its worth and meaning. The instrumental analysis argues that sport is worth subsidising – by the state or private sector– for its social consequences. These consequences span a spectrum from individual health and leisure activity through bonding and providing role models to creating a communal and national sense of identity. In this perspective, sport could be employed as a means to advertise, even exorcise, issues such as racism and substance abuse. Moreover, spending on sport is a considerable source of tax revenue for government. The provenance of sport for the production of effects beyond immediate enjoyment extends to the expansion of the public realm, in the institutional analysis. Both public provision and social participation are promoted in this perspective which bears some connection with the bread and circuses approach of 'classical' antiquity. In an age increasingly characterised by privatisation and attendant dangers of isolation, fragmentation and alienation, sport is seen as increasingly important for social connection, contribution and coherence. The intrinsic model interprets the investment of individuals, teams, clubs and supporters in terms of leisure, pleasure, effort and achievement. This often acquires an aesthetic aura, as in, for example, repeated references to soccer as the 'beautiful game'. In this scenario 'sport for sport's sake' moves beyond the level of slogan to mantra status. Elements of exercise, exhibition of stamina and skills, enjoyment, even ecstasy combine to create the celebration of athletic attempts and achievement in sports ranging from archery through football in its many forms to World Cups in a myriad of codes and disciplines, to fields spanning the globe from Croke Park to Melbourne's MCC and Wembley. Arguments for the intrinsic value of sport attempt to integrate amateur and professional practices in a seamless garment, though this interpretation is stretched, if not shattered by the scale of salaries and prize monies for professional participants, to say nothing of issues of corruption.

---

114. See *The Guardian*, 20 May, 2006

The Daily Telegraph correspondent Sue Mott speaks about 'the iconic nature of sport'. The Brazilian footballer Pele has been called 'the most famous sporting icon on the planet'.[115] Describing him as a 'global icon' Alex Bellos declares: 'Pele always says that "Pele has no colour or religion". Aside from the perceived self-importance of referring to himself in the third person, what he means is that as an icon he crosses boundaries of creed and faith – he has travelled the world and is idolised everywhere.'[116] The terms of such sporting iconography state a standard of socio-cultural transcendence which is convertible into global, universal status. (However, while he has been compared by some commentators to other world figures such as Muhammad Ali and Nelson Mandela, Pele has also been criticised for a lack of commitment to the cause of black economic and political rights.) Reference to crossing 'boundaries of creed and faith' raises the spiritual and theological tradition of 'seeing' icons as not only intimations of but also invitations to divine grace. This interpretation of iconography 'from above', that is, from the intentionality and involvement of God's absolute in human history in the incarnation, clashes with and contradicts a conception of icons (and idols) coming completely from humanity and contained in every corner of human life, ranging from fashion through politics to sport. In an age characterised as the 'most illusioned' by the American writer Daniel Boorstin the presence and power of imagery is immense. At the same time illusion can easily turn into disillusionment if issues of authenticity, integrity and truth are ignored or if the 'censorship of indifference' (to use a phrase of the critic and poet John F. Deane) comes to dominate cultural standards of interpretation and representation. If, to transpose the claim of Shakespeare that 'the purpose of playing, whose end ... is to hold, as 'twere, the mirror up to nature',[117] then the image of sport's relation to and representation of contemporary society should best be conceived as a mirror rather than an icon.[118]

---

115. *The Guardian*, 20 May, 2006
116. *The Sunday Times*, 21 May, 2006
117. *Hamlet*, London: Penguin Books, 2005, III.2, 71
118. This idea is suggested by the title of Denis Muller's articles *'Le football comme miroir'*, *Etudes*, no 4045 (Mai 2006)

The argument that language is 'out there' in a free, floating fashion and can be both accessed and availed of at will is adduced in support of sport and sports journalism having the right of recourse to refer to religious and theological terms, including iconography and idolatry. This approach is evidence of both a (free) market and consumer conception of communication. In this scenario both the eye of the beholder and the expression of the bearer are commodities that can be bought and sold, often by the highest bidder. A restriction of sports coverage and commentary to its own 'language game' could serve to preserve its proper autonomy and aesthetic appeal from the alienation of advertising and avoid the criticism of All Black coach Graham Henry about 'cliché-ridden sports hacks' copy'.[119]

---

119. 'Henry: the man they love to hate', *The Sunday Telegraph*, 23 November, 2008

CHAPTER SIX

Sport and Morality

'[Albert] Camus probably has to be the chief witness for football's defence. He did, after all, once declare: "All I know most surely about morality and obligation I owe to football".'[1]

'My favourite quote of the World Cup so far came last Sunday from Portugal's coach, Luiz Felipe Scolari, after the match that evening between his team and Holland, which gained instant notoriety for producing 16 bookings, including four red cards. Asked about captain Lius Figo receiving a yellow card for headbutting an opponent, he replied by citing the provocation his skipper had been subjected to and said: "Jesus Christ said we should turn the other cheek, but Figo's not Jesus Christ".'[2]

Events both on and off the fields of play in two sporting codes in England and Ireland in autumn 2006 created news headlines and heralded the necessity for situating sport in the context of morality. An angry sideline exchange between Arsenal's Arsene Wenger and West Ham United's Alan Pardew, which resulted in the two managers having to be separated after West Ham's last-minute 1-0 victory, raises questions that reached beyond etiquette to ethics. Pardew's post-match apology did nothing to appease Wenger who, having left the pitch without the traditional handshake to his opponent, exited the stadium without speaking to the media. In the wake of that incident (and the previous week's match between Chelsea and Barcelona in the Champions League) James Lawton refers to a 'voiding of conscience' in a code where 'a large section of the audience seem to have the moral grounding of a dinghy caught on a rough day in the Bay of Biscay', claiming that Wenger was 'congenitally

1. James Lawton, 'The thud and blunder of the football field still a far cry from the world's killing fields', *The Independent*, 2 January, 2007
2. Denis Campbell, 'For the Love of football', *The Tablet*, 1 July 2006, 12

incapable of dealing rationally with defeat'.[3] In Dublin the hybrid International Rules second test between Australia and Ireland (involving professional Australian Football League and amateur Gaelic footballers) provided and proved a bruising encounter resulting in one Irish player being carried unconscious from the field. Media captions characterise the contest in a spectrum ranging from 'Rules out as hybrid code sinks' through 'Game looks beyond Rules' to 'No Rules'. Tom Humphries pulls no punches in his sober verdict on the spectacle: 'In the corrupted idiom of modern sports, surely the most pernicious word is a recent and annoying sexist coinage. Handbags. Sometime some clown who never threw nor received a punch in his life will blowhard and dismiss yesterday's first-quarter violence in Croke Park as handbags … Until handbags becomes a legal defence in assault cases, let's hear no more of them.'[4] Scenes of provocation, aggression and retaliation spoiled the game played before more than 80,000 spectators, of whom a quarter were children. However, freelance journalist Paul Daffey asserts that an Australian need for atonement after their poor performance in the First Test the previous week and direct 'in your face' style of play, which contrasted with Irish cunning, were the real reasons for the robust scenes in the Second Test.[5] The future of the so-called compromise rules series was immediately called into question only a day after by *The Irish Times* GAA correspondent. Seán Moran headlined his column with the hope that 'Third Test may be resurrected'. Playing on the title of the Australian national anthem – '*Australia fair* has whole other meaning' – Moran's colleague Keith Duggan asked, 'Could the GAA people responsible for the future of this series live with the moral repercussions if something unthinkable did come to pass?'[6] The 2008

---

3. *The Independent*, 7 November, 2006. Two weeks later the clash between Wolverhampton Wanderers and Sunderland brought their managers – Mick McCarthy and Roy Keane – together for the first time in four years after their showdown which resulted in Keane's being sent ignominiously home from Saipan. Media interest in their 'reconciliation' raised the profile of the game.

4. 'This should be the end of it', *The Irish Times*, 6 November, 2006

5. 'Enmity the upshot of culture clash', *The Irish Times*, 10 November, 2006

6. *The Irish Times*, 11 November, 2006

return series in Australia passed without serious incident which seems to guarantee the future of the competition for the foreseeable future. On the question of violence in sport, Professor Conal Hooper of University College Dublin's Centre for Sports Studies believes that 'a lot is down to the size and fitness of the players now involved, the hype surrounding competitions and the "win at all costs" mentality' and that this 'will surely affect participation rates [which] is the last thing we need right now with so much concern over health and obesity levels.'[7]

'Serious sport is war minus the shooting'[8]
The morality of warfare has traditionally been treated by ethicists and moral theologians in terms of the so-called 'just war' paradigm, which attempts to regulate the conditions for both going to war (*ius ad bellum*) and governing conduct in the course of conflict, including its cessation (*ius in bello*). Orwell's statement may seem somewhat tongue in cheek yet the description (at times) of phases of play in rugby as trench warfare and other martial metaphors for matches and games mean that sport is often presented as a form of conflict conducted on the fields of play rather than on battlefields. In *The Soccer War* the Polish foreign correspondent Ryszard Kapuscinski describes the 1969 conflict which broke out between Honduras and El Salvador.[9] The catalyst for the so-called '100 Hour War' was a concatenation of events before and after the respective home fixtures, including the suicide of a distraught Salvadorean fan who was favoured with a state funeral. (El Salvador progressed to the following year's World Cup competition in Mexico.) Casualties in the conflict (which ceased after the intervention of other Latin American States) included 6,000 dead and over 12,000 injured with large scale destruction of property and displacement of people. The Six Nations Rugby international game between England and Ireland in Dublin and the playing of the respective

7. Quoted by Cliona Foley in 'Violence in sport now a growing problem for all codes', *Irish Independent*, 16 April, 2007
8. George Orwell, in ed, David Pickering, *Cassell's Sports Quotations*, London: Cassell, 2002, 33
9. In *The Granta Book of Reportage*, London: Granta Publications, 3rd Edition, 2006, 3-25

national anthems at Croke Park in February 2007 recalled memories of the 'Bloody Sunday' shooting dead there of players and spectators by Crown forces, the so-called Black and Tans, during the Dublin versus Tipperary Gaelic football match in November 1920. England's first international soccer encounter with Argentina after the Falklands/Malvinas war occurred in the 1986 World Cup which occasioned comments like the need to create an exclusion zone around the English penalty area to keep Diego Maradona and company at bay. However, Maradona's second goal resulted in a run from deep within his own half which left more than half the opposition floundering and even falling to the floor.

In his review of *On the Corinthian Spirit: the Decline of Amateurism in Sport*, Jim White comments: 'We might think football's ethics are in steep decline, but there is nothing new in its loss of moral core. George Orwell spotted it long before [Wayne] Rooney's father – "You play to win, and the game has little meaning unless you do your utmost to win".'[10] Reference to the disappearance of a moral centre in the game of soccer raises the question of morality in relation to sport in general. Does sport support a code of morality that governs players and participants or is sport a sort of survival and success of the fittest, fastest and fiercest competitors? Do extreme efforts to win entail considerations of means that are employed and ends that are envisaged? Is the slogan 'achieve victory and avoid defeat' to be seen as the supreme principle of sporting activity which justifies the prize of winning at any cost? What is the relationship between the means of contest and the manner of conquest in sport? Does a system of morality hold a mirror up to sport or does sport reflect the standards that are acceptable as normal and normative in society at large? Are the words of former Ireland and Lion rugby great Willie John McBride that 'it matters a great deal who is going to win, but not at all who won' a treasure of moral wisdom? The value(s) of sport call for an estimation which extend beyond the range of economic and financial results, that is, an evaluation that is properly ethical.

---

10. *The Daily Telegraph*, 20 May, 2006

Morality and Ethics
Too often interpreted individualistically, morality involves interpersonal, communal, social and international relations, rights
and responsibilities. Rooted in the generally – if not universally
– recognised distinction between good/evil and the concomitant call/sense of obligation to realise what is right while avoiding or at least minimising wrongdoing, morality both mediates
and measures the character and conscience of persons. The
moral life is concerned with how, in the words of Gernot Bohme,
'one must form oneself as a person in order to be[come] a human
being, not just somehow, but well.'[11] Ethics extends beyond expression and description of customs in culture and society to
questions of their prescription and justification. As a normative
science, ethics deals with the determination of principles that are
defensible in terms of rights and duties as these affect the well-
being of individuals and society. However, as Julia Driver
states, a 'central problem in ethics has to do with accounting for
the source of normativity.'[12] Noting that normativity is concerned with claims that are evaluative by nature, Driver declares
that 'in ethics the kind of evaluations that occur are those that
have to do with moral value and disvalue, moral rightness and
wrongness' and furthermore that 'these claims are thought to
have a peculiar authority over us'.[13] Notwithstanding the pecul-
iarity of the adjective that qualifies authority, ethics proceeds to
probe and pronounce on the areas of attitude and action, dispos-
ition and deeds, character and conduct which characterise
human culture and its cognate morality.

As relational and responsible beings, persons experience
each other in a drive-draw dynamic which demands that 'being-
human-well' (Bohme) is about the realisation of certain states of
affairs contributing to and creating a common good. The oft-
quoted assertion of a former British Prime Minister that 'there is
no such thing as society' belies the belief that human beings do
not flourish in isolation from one another. Moral solipsism is
both logically and ethically a contradiction in terms. Moral

11. See his *Ethics in Context – The Art of Dealing with Serious Questions*,
Oxford:Polity Press, 2001
12. *Ethics – The Fundamentals*, Oxford:Blackwell, 2007, 5
13. Idem

philosophers and theologians discern a gift-call, invitation-response structure in the social interaction and situation of human existence. The dialogue and dovetailing of self-giving and receiving love looks to the protection of individual dignity and rights while promoting the demands of justice and equality for all. This moral vision is described by Pope John Paul II in terms of solidarity which is 'not a feeling of vague compassion or shallow distress at the misfortunes of so many people, both near and far. On the contrary, it is a firm and persevering determination to commit oneself to the common good; that is to say, to the good of all and each individual, because we are all really responsible for all.'[14]

Historically, philosophical ethics has articulated various theories which have attempted to systematise morality founded on foundational or final values such as happiness, duty, pleasure. These theories have often been translated through stories and narratives and as such described in literature and depicted in film. Moral theology and theological ethics probe the meaning of morality, its origin and outcome(s), in the light of the Revelation that is God's self-communication in the Christ-event and the continuing mission of the Holy Spirit in the life of the church. The gospel narratives of the life, death and resurrection of Jesus of Nazareth, remembered and reflected on through the light of faith, represent a unique Christian source for mediating the moral point of view of believers, making an original vision of life and death available and marking an authentic account of value and virtue.[15]

Sporting Ethics
The language and logic of ethics, whether philosophical or theological, may seem light years away from the arena of sports and its associated activities, especially when one considers the words of Orwell and the wit of American baseball coach Leo Durocher that 'nice guys finish last' and 'show me a good loser

---

14. *Sollicitudo Rei Socialis*, Rome: Vatican Press, 1987, par 38
15. On the role of the Resurrection narratives in particular see Brian V. Johnstone, 'Transformation Ethics' in Stephen Davis, Daniel Kendall and Gerald O' Collins, eds, *The Resurrection*, Oxford: University Press, 1997, 339-360

and I'll show you an idiot'.[16] In a worldview formed by attitudes such as those articulated by English racing driver Damon Hill that 'winning is everything'[17] and former American football coach Vince Lombardi that 'if it doesn't matter who wins or loses, then why do they keep score', sport seems to be at odds with any concept of the common good. 'To the victor the spoils' means that for the loser(s) there is nothing left to be shared out, except perhaps sympathy. Struggle and success might seem the logical outcome of natural selection in the sporting arena. If, as Orwell suggests, sport is war conducted without shooting, the options preclude any form of truce or draw, leaving triumph and defeat as the only possible outcomes. Here the evaluation of means and ends may take on a mercenary, mercantile character, measuring success solely in terms of domination for one party and defeat for the other, negating any sense of solidarity and separating the victor(s) from the vanquished. In this context political considerations can contribute ideological elements to sporting competition, adding elements of division and even exclusion. Here sporting prowess and success can be perceived and portrayed as racial superiority or cultural inferiority. Thus sport can be politics or even economics by another means.

The extension of ethics to the world of sports has individual, interpersonal, institutional and international applications. On the individual level the question of integrity involves issues of abiding by the rules and not seeking to gain an unfair advantage. A good example of such integrity was the action of golfer Darren Clarke at the Irish Open in 2006. Resuming play in the postponed fourth round, he held a two-stroke lead but discovered that his ball had been moved from the heavy rough, a lie that would have prevented him from attempting to reach the green. He opted to play out sideways, forsaking the advantage achieved 'as if the leprechauns had been at work flattening the grass and improving his lie'.[18] The European Tour subsequently

16. *Cassell's Sports Quotations*, 281 and 129
17. *Cassell's Sports Quotations*, 366. The full quote includes 'The only ones who remember you when you come second are your wife and your dog.'
18. 'Sporting Clarke loses title but wins respect', *The Daily Telegraph*, 23 May 2006

awarded 'shot of the month' to Clarke for what he stated was 'doing something that was just my way, the right thing to do'.[19] ('Being a good sport' involves a spirit and standard of self-regulation in games such as golf where a referee does not get involved in every phase of play.) One commentator contrasts his action with the 2005 'Jakartagate' scandal, where Colin Montgomerie gained obvious advantage in replacing his ball after a weather delay and complimented Clarke's selfless action as making a point or two.[20] In a piece cleverly entitled 'Golf: The final bastion of sport's fair ways', James Lawton plays on the conjunction 'fair way' and comments that the game's administrators are 'engaged in a sport that still, however clumsily, recognises there is some considerable difference between right and wrong'.[21]

The interpersonal dimension of sport demands not only that contestants abide by the rules but also display an attitude of respect for one another. Targeting individuals for hard and possibly hurtful treatment is often a feature of team play on the field, where intimidation, insult and even injury are tactics taken to 'soften up' opponents and show them which side is in charge and intends to win, by fair means or foul. A policy of pre-emptive strike or 'getting one's retaliation in first' vitiates the spirit in which sport is supposed to be conducted. Unfortunately the desire to win at all costs is often inculcated in sports players from an early age, forming attitudes of aggression and antipathy towards opponents. While some sports involve greater proximity to and contact with the opposition, with higher degrees of physical effort and expression, players can be prepared psychologically to operate within the limits laws lay down for such close encounters. Beating opponents with sporting tools, biting and gouging them in various parts, striking and spitting at them, are not only unseemly but unacceptable, not least for the horrendous injuries that sometimes result from such incidents. While nobody supports that sport should become part of the 'Nannystate' and all accept that competitive games are not gov-

---

19. Quoted in *The Sunday Times*, 3 December, 2006
20. James Corrigan, 'Clarke takes high ground', *The Independent*, 23 May, 2006
21. *Irish Independent*, 4 June, 2005

erned by the niceties and nuances of diplomatic encounters, interpersonal exchange on (and off) the field requires restraint and a requisite level of respect. For example, controversy over the 'spearing' of Lions captain Brian O' Driscoll in the opening minutes of the first test against New Zealand in 2005 is unlikely to ever fade away completely.

The institution of sporting ethics involves more than individual and interpersonal dimensions. Administrators, agents, coaches and managers constitute important 'players' in the sporting process that extends far beyond the confines of course, court and pitch. A code of conduct for sports men and women, both amateur and professional, is an important phase in the elaboration of such an ethic but responsibility also reaches into areas of preparation, tactics and post-match analysis. While sporting culture may be difficult to condense into a code, clarification of a set of commonly accepted principles governing competition and guiding conduct in the course thereof should not prove insurmountable. The association of sport with business and media in the context of ownership, sponsorship and advertising raises the stakes above the actual events themselves and thus adds pressure to those participating in games and matches. The situation has not yet – thankfully – been reached where sports men and women are the 'playthings' of wealthy and powerful individuals and groups but there are worrying signs in that direction, as evidenced with the takeover of some prominent soccer clubs. Corporate raids and sell-offs of clubs and their players reveal that sport is seen as a legitimate arena for market speculation. The branding of clubs and individuals is a constitutive dimension of market dealing and development. Allied with media, the manipulation of sporting markets, for example in America and Asia, makes competition off the pitch as important as on it. Sport has mutated into a market of selling and buying of people and products, individuals and image rights where business can sometimes relegate what happens on the ball, in the basket and ring to secondary importance. Sport is seen as 'fair game' for mercantile interests and investment by both individuals and financial institutions where sentiments of identity and community can be subject to fluctuating forces and given short shift. For this reason the ethics of sport enters into and engages business ethics. Sport needs to be studied as an element, extension and expression of business ethics. Issues of corporate social responsibility need to inform both the institution and investigation of sport. At the same time it is only fair to acknowledge the sponsorship of certain community based and international events by the business world. In this regard the recent Special Olympics in Ireland is a fine example of sponsorship and support by the business community.

The international dimension of sport necessarily involves political considerations. Boycotts of tours and tournaments, for example as happened in the case of apartheid South Africa and the 1980 Moscow Olympic Games after the Soviet invasion of Afghanistan, bring both moral and political considerations into play. As an integral part of social and cultural life sport is not exempt from ideological interpretation and manipulation. The question of racism and attempts to eliminate it find a particular focus and force in the field of international sport where people of different ethnic, racial and religious identities regularly encounter each other and engage in a contest of equals. Notwithstanding the necessity of competition and consequent defeat for one party or side, sport offers the opportunity for the celebration of diversity and plurality. The spectacle of a multiracial Springbok (South Africa) rugby team facing the All Blacks doing their pre-match Haka, the magic of a Brazilian soccer team, the sight of Seán óg Ó hAilpín leading Cork to the All-Ireland hurling championship are a few examples of the power of sport to transcend and break down barriers that may have been constructed once on the basis of colour, creed or culture. Alan Hubbard engages in scriptural, if not sporting, licence, in profiling the vision of Jordan's Prince Feisal to promote reconciliation between warring nations through sport: 'Just down the dusty road from the Jordanian shores of the Dead Sea lie what used to be the seedy Biblical cities of Sodom and Gomorrah. With all that is happening off the playing field these days it seems a rather appropriate base camp for a new sporting enterprise. Yet if it succeeds, it could turn out to be a veritable Garden of Eden … The World Cup and Olympics may be a princely pipe dream for the moment, but as you stand atop Mount Nebo, where Moses is said to have looked across at the real thing, you can believe that sport's Promised Land in Jordan may not be that far distant.'[22]

The interpretation of sport in individual and interpersonal, institutional and international dimensions of life promote human development which provide us, in the words of the German moral theologian Dietmar Mieth, 'with a unique set of qualities or values which are attractive because they cannot be achieved (or so it appears) as efficiently by other means: health and fitness, energy, the experience of competition, a feeling of achievement and success, discipline, social contact, educational and cultural opportunities, a model of fair play, solidarity, social advancement and integration'.[23]

Fair Play

In a piece entitled 'Why I now loathe this sporting life', Geoffrey Wheatcroft states that 'sports of every kind are now tainted almost beyond redemption'.[24] His lament for sport leads him to summarise it as a life too often characterised by 'cheating, bribery, corruption, and young men conditioned to think that losing is literally worse than death'.[25] His recourse to a theological and doctrinal term to describe the desperate situation of sport is interesting, raising the possibility that a trans-ethical interpretation of the significance and state of sport is not only desirable but demanded.

Cheating is a chameleon that assumes different forms of concealment and corruption in different codes of sport. Forms of cheating range from the feigning of injuries which may result in free kicks being awarded and further sanctions for opponents, both on and off the field. The phenomenon of 'diving', particularly in the penalty area in soccer, has increasingly incensed opponents, fans and commentators in recent years. James Lawton captured the issue with the caption, 'Pearce's honesty stands out in an era of diving morals', which commended the recognition

22. 'Prince: how sport can give peace a chance', *The Independent on Sunday*, 16 July 2006.
23. 'Towards an ethic of sport in contemporary culture' in *The World Of Sport Today – A Field of Christian Mission*, 23-43 at 24
24. *The Observer*, 30 July, 2006
25. Idem

of the City manager that one of his players in the Manchester derby deserved dismissal 'for a dive outrageous even by the standards that are mostly accepted with shrugs of resignation'.[26] Stuart Pierce's support for the referee stands in marked contrast to the harassment of referees by players – often in raging packs – and the post-match remarks of managers about officials and their (lack of) objectivity. The scourge of many referees in the course of his passionate playing career, now the manager of Ipswich Town, Roy Keane expressed his embarrassment at the cheating antics of players who 'dived' during games. Sent off eleven times, Keane complained that some players in the Premiership (a competition in which he captained Manchester United to seven championships) fake injury and try to force referees to take disciplinary action against opponents: 'Players have to treat referees fairly. When they go down it must be genuine ... Lads I've played with dived and it drove me crazy, going down like they've been shot. If I'd done that and after the game you have to go and see your family, they'd disown me if I was trying to get another player in trouble.'[27] In 2008 the English FA announced their 'Respect' campaign for referees though the message appears to have fallen on deaf ears 'with a number of high-profile Premier League managers failing to honour the code of conduct by making outspoken criticisms of match officials'.[28]

Former Italian international soccer player Gianluca Vialli (who played for Chelsea in the English Premiership) refers to sporting realpolitik in his book *The Italian Job*: 'Italians are taught that many succeed by cheating ... When I was growing up, I was not encouraged to take a dive, yet I picked things up in subtle ways. Many did not view such tricks for what they are, cheating. They were seen as clever or, as we say in Italy, *furbo*.'[29] Gaining unfair advantage over opponents may be clever but not correct, if the rules of the game and the standards of morality are followed. Vialli's view that the 'real world' is reflected on the play-

---

26. *The Independent*, 11 December, 2006
27. Quoted in 'The game is full of cheats. I'm glad I'm not playing any more', *The Daily Telegraph*, 10 November, 2006
28. 'How FA's crusade lost game's respect', *The Daily Telegraph*, 11 November, 2008
29. Quoted in *The Times*, 25 April, 2006

ing field, that sport shows a mirror to life, serves up a Machiavellian scenario where means and ends are inverted in a form of political power play. The most in-famous example of cheating in sport involved the incident where Diego Maradona 'interpreted' his hand-scored goal against England in the 1986 World Cup as 'the Hand of God' and denied allegations of cheating: 'I don't think it's cheating, it's cunning. Is it cheating handling the ball? Oh no, no, no it's not cheating. I don't think it's cheating, I believe it's a craftiness, maybe we have a lot more of it in South America than in Europe but it's not cheating.'[30] Ironically, Maradona's second goal in the same game is generally considered the greatest goal to have been scored in the history of soccer's World Cup finals. Describing Maradona as 'a genuine villain, a genuine genius', Simon Barnes wonders 'Were we right to half-forgive him after that subsequent and brilliant run-and-score through the entire England defence?'[31] However, in his *The Corinthian Spirit – The Decline of Amateurism in Sport*, D. J. Taylor decries the so-called realistic view of sport in favour of a romantic vision, denouncing Maradona's deceit: 'Sport is a rom-antic activity. The sports field is where you project your myths and if something is romantic it is, *ipso facto*, moral. If you are going to invest so much emotional capital in a game then it must have a fundamental moral basis otherwise it means nothing at all and is pointless. I found what Maradona did repulsive.'[32]

Another incident of unfair handling is Leicester flanker Neil Back's illegal prevention of the put-in to the Munster scrum in the 2002 European Rugby Cup final against Munster. Munster player Anthony Foley later stated: 'We've never blamed the re-sult on Neil Back. *Fair play to him.* The Leicester team of that era had a very ruthless and dominant streak that, under no circum-stances, were they going to lose. You've got to credit them for that.' Interpreting the four words highlighted as a 'pefectly ludi-crous use of the Irishism', a euphemism for engaging in deliber-ate foul rather than fair play, Wheatcroft expressed his evalu-ation in trenchant terms: 'Foley summed up the spirit of the age,

30. Interview with Gary Lineker, *The Sunday Telegraph*, 30 April, 2006
31. 'Dastardly Schumacher proves the embodiment of a genius loved and loathed in equal measure', *The Times*, 20 October, 2006
32. Quoted in *The Observer*, 28 May, 2006

in the same way that football writers will say a striker "went to ground" to win a penalty as if it was all part of the game. And anyone who disagrees is treated as a prig or prude; that's the way it is, grow up, get a life. There is answer to that. Cheating is cheating, diving is cheating, handling the ball in a scrum is cheating. If these are acceptable – or at least accepted – parts of their games, then why should it be any less acceptable to bribe a referee to ensure that your team wins a match?'[33]

In response to the chant of Gloucester supporters 'Same old Leicester – always cheating', former player turned television pundit Austin Healy commented that 'It's only cheating if you get caught.'[34] The claim of Munster out-half Ronan O'Gara needs to be considered in similar vein: 'All the best teams cheat', suggesting that if a Munster player had done what Neil Back did in the 2002 final 'he'd be a legend.'[35]

Seven times Grand Prix world champion Michael Schumacher was accused of cheating in the qualifying round for the 2006 Monaco event and was relegated to the back of the starting grid for the race. Holding pole position for the fastest lap time, Schumacher parked his car across the line at the exit from the second last corner, claiming that the steering had seized up and that he had run out of space, which necessitated the marshals to manifest warning flags and slow the approach of other drivers. In *Pulling a Fast One*, Martin Brundle states that 'the whole saga puts another question mark against Schumacher's conduct and attitude [which is] a shame, because he's so good that he simply doesn't need to get involved in this type of alleged tactics'.[36] Sport is not immune to so-called dirty tricks, that is, efforts to gain advantages over opponents achieved by tactics employed off the field of play.[37] In tennis, coaching from outside the court is considered to be against both the spirit and law. However, in the opinion of champion Rafael Nadal, clandestine tactics in the

---

33. *The Observer*, 28 May, 2006
34. Quoted by John Inverdale in *The Daily Telegraph*, 16 May, 2007
35. John O'Donnell, Review of *Ronan O'Gara: My Autobiography* in *The Irish Times*, 11 October, 2008
36. *The Sunday Times*, 28 May, 2006
37. 'Dirty tricks that helped to win Rugby World Cup', *The Sunday Times*, 25 June, 2006

form of bodily gestures and verbal calls are resorted to by ninety per cent of professional coaches.[38]

Cheating is often contrasted with gamesmanship, defined as 'the art of winning games or defeating opponents by clever or cunning practices without actually cheating'.[39] In both cases, however, the spirit of fair play is compromised in favour of an attitude that seeks victory at all or at least greater cost. The 'good' of the game is calculated not in terms of participation, prowess and performance but estimated as the prize of victory. To be fair to sportsmen and women, whether amateur or professional, they do not engage in contests to fail. Indeed if they should seek to lose they are suspect of throwing a game or match for commercial or other corrupt considerations. However, the nature of competition necessitates that at the end there are both victors and vanquished. The comment of the author of schoolboy fiction John Tunis that 'losing is the great American sin' calls for the balance of the 'Galloping Major', the great Hungarian soccer player Ferenc Puskas, in his observation that 'the loser must have no spite'. The spirit of fair play in sport that gives the lie to a list of activities ranging from a mere gaining of advantage through gamesmanship to cheating is admirably articulated in the words of the author who created *Biggles*, Captain W. E. Johns: 'I teach that decent behaviour wins in the end as a natural order of things.'[40]

Reference to 'a natural order of things' raises the question of drug abuse and doping in sport, whereby competitors seek to enhance performance by themselves (or their animals, as in the case of canine and equestrian contests) by taking banned or illegal substances. Such a scenario also extends to the doping of animals in order to acquire advantage, either with the aim of boosting performance or deliberately causing the animal to underperform with a view to its future prospects. The intensity and pressure on individual performers may also lead to their use of so-called recreational drugs and their influence, for good or ill, on subsequent capacity to participate and compete. High profile

---

38. Nick Bolletteri, 'Nod and a wink to covert operations', *The Independent*, 1 June, 2006
39. *The Times English Dictionary*, 1st ed,Glasgow: Harper Collins, 2000
40. Quoted by Sean Diffley in *Irish Independent*, 4 November, 2006

cases of participants and winners testing positive for banned substances brings sport as a whole into disrepute and makes a mockery not only of the notion of 'sport for sport's sake' but also of the concept of the so-called level playing pitch. The imitative effect of drug abuse and cheating on young players of various sports is an issue that invites not only evaluation but efforts aimed at elimination. If the Olympic ideal of *altius, citius et fortius* – higher, faster and stronger – and the traditional invocation of 'may the best or better competitor or team win' are to be maintained with any moral meaning, the incidence of drug abuse needs to be eradicated from the arena of sport. Issues of human identity and integrity are involved in the interpretation of competitive sport which 'in its truest form should be a test of speed, strength, reflex, agility, mental fortitude and physical endurance'.[41] There is nothing less than the soul of sport at stake. Otherwise sport not only sacrifices its integrity but also risks selling out its human identity. The influence of sport to promote a healthy, human lifestyle is pointed out by the head of the Vatican's office for Church and Sport, Fr Kevin Lixey: 'We all know kids look to athletes as role models. And while it's easy to see the negative side of sports – be it doping, fan violence, or millionaire athletes who aren't always the best role models – there's also the positive side of sport that isn't being promoted on any grand scale. And we want to change that.'[42] In addition to reasons against doping in sport on the grounds both of protecting the health of participants and preventing them gaining an unfair advantage, Mieth adduces two other moral arguments: firstly, the fact that the player is committed, both personally and publicly, to a contract with organisations associated with the sport in question carries rights as well as responsibilities; secondly, involvement with wider social institutions, such as media and medicine, increase the value of sport, both economically and ethically, which would be compromised in the event of doping being discovered.[43]

The issue of injury incurred in the course of sporting activity

---

41. Brian Viner, *The Independent*, 29 July, 2006
42. Quoted in *The Irish Catholic*, 25 May, 2006
43. 'Towards an ethic of sport in contemporary culture', 41-2

is increasingly a cause both for concern and comment. The wearing of various forms of protective gear has become commonplace in a spectrum of sports ranging from cricket through hurling to rugby. A challenge by the Bury goalkeeper Chris Harker cost the England international striker (and later successful club manager) Brian Clough his promising career, while the collision between Chelsea goalkeeper Peter Cech and Reading striker Stephen Hunt resulted in a depressed skull fracture for the former and, after his lengthy recuperation, the necessity of continuing to wear protective headgear. A photograph of the incident carried the headline 'Endangered Species'.[44] The question of moral involvement by medical practitioners in sports involving a high degree of physical interaction and impact is raised by journalist Chris Hewitt: 'It does not fit easily with the wider doctrinal thrust of the Hippocratic Oath, this preparation of men for the slaughter, but the big question must surely occur once in a while. Is rugby union sustainable at the top level, given the increasingly high risk of injury and seasonal casualty lists running into the thousands? Is it ethically sound for a doctor to associate himself with so perilous a game?'[45] Dr Simon Kemp, the head of sports medicine at the RFU and England team doctor, responds that best quality care of players seems to him 'to be entirely consistent with the values of my profession'.[46] The gladiatorial nature of some sporting contests is enhanced, if not exaggerated, by some of the protective gear players wear. However, Kemp notes that such apparel may add to the risk of injury through the mistaken perception of players that they are adequately protected.

'There Will Be Blood'

While many high impact sports involve teams, the issue of injury is particularly important in the one-on-one contest that is boxing. In the wake of the death of American fighter Levander Johnson in September 2005, an extensive editorial in the Jesuit Italian publication *La Civilta Cattolica* (popularly characterised as carrying at least Vatican semi-approval) questioned the

---

44. *The Independent*, 17 October, 2007
45. 'Facing up to the Big Hits', *The Independent*, 5 October, 2006
46. 'Facing up to the Big Hits'

morality of professional boxing.[47] Noting that more than 500 professional fighters had died in the previous 100 years as a result of injuries incurred in the ring, the leader laments that 'the dead in boxing count for nothing'.[48] After describing the aggressive and vicious nature of such contests and delineating their dangerous consequences for life and limb, both immediately and in the long term, the editorial evaluates the engagement under the natural moral and divine precept of the Fifth Commandment, that is, not to kill by consciously and voluntarily inflicting such wounds that lead to death of another. Its grave and absolute negative evaluation is exacerbated by economic considerations: 'In reality, professional boxing is manipulated by powerful economic organisations, often cold-blooded and ruthless, for whom the fighter is not a "man" but only a machine for making money.'[49] The association of avarice and angry, aggressive encouragement of fans in the arena with the apparent risk(s) to the health and life of fighters amount to the writer's condemnation and refusal 'to be silent before such aberrations that are contrary to human and Christian morality, which are gravely detrimental to human life and dignity'.[50] In contrast, the American academic Carlo Rotella analyses the appeal of blood letting in boxing: 'When blood from a serious cut finds its way into the lights, everything seems to change: it's cut time ... Spectators, shamed and fascinated, plunge headlong into cut time. What was inside and hidden, implicit in the fight, has come outside.'[51] Ironically, it is vicarious viciousness rather than any sense of sporting enjoyment that may be expressed in and emerge from emotive engagement with the exhibition of grown men gorily beating each other in a grotesque parody of athletic prowess. The Oscar winning film *Million Dollar Baby* explores the effect of serious injury on women boxers and wider moral issues, including euthanasia.

---

47. '*Immoralita Del Pugilato Professionistico*', quaderno 3728/15 October 2005, 107-112

48. '*Immoralita Del Pugilato Professionistico*', 107. (Translation by author.)

49. '*Immoralita...*', 111

50. '*Immoralita...*', 112

51. *Cut Time – An Education at the Fights*, reviewed in *The Daily Telegraph*, 19 January, 2006

A television programme about professional bull-riding, *Bull Trouble*, describes the fastest growing sport in the United States which attracts 1.7 million fans to its shows and television audiences of up to 100 million. Director Marion McKeone states that 'the sport is as simple as it is dangerous' and 'that the danger, the possibility of a blood-and-gore spectacle as much as the skill that hooks the fans'.[52] Bull rider Justin McBride declares that 'Of course the fans pray we won't get gored, but they pray they won't miss it if we do.' Allied to this extreme sporting activity is bull fighting, which was famously celebrated in the writings of Ernest Hemingway. (Interestingly the opening chapter of John Carlin's insider account of Spanish football team Real Madrid is entitled 'Matadors and Bulls').[53]

The spectacle of such offering, its connotation of sacrificial offerings and connection with the death of Christ is a practice that could prophetically, if not quite profitably, be pursued by theologians both in terms of morality and spirituality. More immediately it raises the issue of the impact on and interpretation by society of such bloody contests involving humans and animals. The words of classical scholar Simon Goldhill offer wise counsel in this context: 'The gladiatorial games, these archetypal entertainments of Greece and Rome, are very much still inside us … They turn out to be a particularly valuable route in reflecting critically on what we do. They give us a necessary vantage point to see ourselves. If you want to know what you think you are doing, the games are a good place to do that thinking from.'[54]

Hooli-fans
Soccer hooliganism in particular can take on political, sectarian and cultural attitudes and aspects, as Franklin Foer shows in his study of the game in the former Yugoslavia between Croatia and Serbia and in Glasgow between Celtic and Rangers, with overt Christian (Catholic, Orthodox and Protestant) references often

---

52. Marion McKeone, 'Where the bull is boss', *The Irish Times – Weekend Review*, date not available
53. *White Angels*, London: Bloomsbury, 2005
54. Quoted by Enda McDonagh, 'Theatre, Tragedy and Theology' in *Recognising the Margins*, eds. Werner G. Jeanrond and Andrew D. H. Mayes, Dublin: The Columba Press, 2006, 215-228 at 217

on display.[55] In the latter decades of the twentieth century the excesses of soccer fans throughout the world, which erupted from time to time into extreme acts of violence, led sociologists to explain the phenomenon in terms of personal and political identities involving economic and ethnic issues. As Foer notes, 'They have written about down-sized men, the ones whose industrial jobs were outsourced to third-world labour. Deprived of traditional work and knocked off patriarchal pedestals, these men desperately wanted to reassert their masculinity. Soccer violence gave them a rare opportunity to actually exert control. When these fans dabbled in racism and radical nationalism, it was because those ideologies worked as metaphors for their own lives. Their nations and races had been victimised by the world just as badly as they had been themselves.'[56] During this period the behaviour of English soccer fans at European club and international fixtures became a matter of concern and comment in the context of European political and economic integration. The profile of such hooli-fans defy characterisation in traditional class terms, with followers from professional sectors being found guilty of crimes alongside blue-collar workers and unemployed. In January 2007 the killing of a policeman during rioting by rival Catania and Palermo fans resulted in the cancellation of all the country's League fixtures and an international match against Romania, with a call from the president of the Italian players' association, Sergio Campana, for a year's moratorium on matches: 'I want my proposal taken seriously that football should stop for a year in order to reflect on the evils that exist.'[57]

Ironically, in this period the traditional composition of club teams such as Arsenal, Chelsea, Liverpool and Manchester United from the so-called 'home' countries (England, Ireland, Scotland and Wales) underwent dramatic and drastic change with an influx of players from other parts of the world, including Africa and Asia. Violence at home football games, particularly involving 'derbies' (matches between local rivals) involve

---

55. *How Football Explains The World,* London: Arrow Books, 2005
56. *How Football Explains The World ,* 13
57. 'Game in Crisis', *The Independent on Sunday,* 4 February, 2007

issues of representation and resentment at the success of the 'old enemy'. Dynamics of scapegoating and demonising opponents (players and fans) include anthropological and ethical dimensions. In sports other than soccer, hooliganism can be hidden in more subtle forms of behaviour, though in many codes rivalry between clubs, counties and countries has become routinised in friendly stereotypes and banter, leaving the players to do 'battle' on the field of play and leaving it there after the match. Examples of such neighbourly needling are expressed in the traditional rivalry of Cork and Tipperary hurling with their respective claims and catchcries of 'The Rebel County/Republic of Cork' and 'Hay saved, Cork bet'. (Adoption of the American Confederate flag by some Cork fans in recent years lends an edge to such 'tribal' expression, something to be yet exploited by the opposition.)

Fielding Justice

Cheating in competition(s) cannot be separated from a culture of corruption which is carried out at various levels, from single match or race fixing and the manipulation of results over a series or even a whole season through financial inducements involving players, their agents and managers (including the buying and selling of players which brings a 'bung' to the back pockets of managers), to scandals which implicate officials and administrators. As the 2005-6 Italian *Serie A* season drew to a close, a concatenation of charges – including the fixing and throwing of games, fear of violence, blackmail and illegal betting involving players, referees, managers and administrators – embarrassed what many consider to be the most entertaining soccer championship in the world with its highly esteemed prize, the *Scudetto*. As the head of the Olympic committee Gianni Petrucci claimed that the sport needed to regain credibility, the suspicion surfaced that the problems were not singular but systemic. In a country where the biggest daily selling newspaper devotes most of its copy to coverage of the sport, and one of the greatest clubs is owned by a former Prime Minister, the comment of a reviewer of *Calcio: A History of Italian Football* seemed prescient a month before the latest revelations: 'Sometimes it feels as if Italian football is staggering toward its end, overwhelmed by cynicism, scandal, violence and exhaustion.'[58] While 'the last days of Rome' may seem a somewhat premature scenario for the state of soccer in Italy, the most recent scandal shows up the structural dimensions and dangers inherent in a sport where mass appeal, marketing and media interests intertwine.

Under its headline 'Gambling Nation', *The Independent* reported the following statistics for Britain: £50 billion spent on betting in 2005; 700% increase in the average amount gambled in the previous five years; 370,000 problem gamblers, which is expected to double in the following five years; the 2006 soccer World Cup expected to be the single largest gambling event in history.[59] Professor of Gambling Studies, Mark Griffiths, notes that 'there has been no great public push to liberalise [gambling], it has come from the gaming industry and the Government'.[60] The expansion of betting and gambling via the Internet and in super-casino(s) is not only an economic matter but an ethical one as well. Betting and gambling can give rise to personal, familial and social problems and the role of the state in liberalising access raises not only legal but also moral questions. As a voluntary form of taxation, betting on sports events contributes to the common purse and the common good, helping to create a climate of recreation and participation for punters unable to attend matches or meetings. However, both the addictive nature of the activity and the added emotional and financial burdens for families in particular are matters not to be lost sight of in the lure of bronze, silver and gold which are monetary rather than medallic in nature.

At the heart of the concept of fairness is equality. Frances S. Adeney identifies gender equality as a universal value that requires to be recognised, respected and realised.[61] Gender issues in terms of participation and prize money arise in the sporting

---

58. John Tague, *The Independent on Sunday*, 23 April, 2006. An account and analysis of Italian soccer's scandal is articulated, after the success of the country in the 2006 World Cup, in 'Paradiso to Inferno – After The Glory, The Shame', *The Observer Sport Monthly*, August 2006
59. 25 May, 2006
60. Idem
61. See her 'Contextualising Universal Values', *The International Bulletin of Missionary Research*, 31 (January 2007):33-37

arena and associated areas such as advertising. The exclusion of women from playing on the Augusta National course (though not from paying for entry to the game's first Major of the season) was dramatically highlighted a number of years ago with the question of whether Tiger Woods would continue to participate in the event given the gender based and biased prohibition. The issue of 'fair pay for fair play' is cleverly caught in the caption, 'Serve and volley, women are worth the same lolly', where columnist Sue Mott raises the question of paying men and women winners in tennis the same prize money.[62] Noting that sports equality is enshrined in American law and that Australia accepted the norm in 2001, she argues that the issue involves a fundamental matter of justice. On this question Women's Tennis Association Tour chief executive Larry Scott stated in 2006: 'In the 21st century, it is just morally indefensible that women competitors in a Grand Slam tournament should be receiving less prize money than their male counterparts. Women got the vote in Britain in 1918, and the Sex Discrimination Act has been in force for over 30 years, yet Wimbledon continue to take a Victorian view when it comes to pay'.[63] In February 2007 Wimbledon followed the practice of the other Grand Slam events and announced that the principle of prize money equality would be extended to both male and female competitors. Scott said that he was 'very pleased Wimbledon has made the decision to go all the way to equality', a decision which he described as both 'poignant and symbolic'.[64] Chairman of the All England Club Tim Phillips stated that the decision would be good for tennis, good for women players and good for Wimbledon, while former multiple Wimbledon winner Billie Jean King said it was the right thing to do for the sport, the tournament and the world.

The question of equality in sport, both professional and amateur, also embraces issues of racism and homophobia. Racism rests on defining human beings and groups on the basis

---

62. *The Daily Telegraph*, 25 April, 2006. In the context of women's tennis she also takes the opportunity to criticise the Fatwa issued by a Moslem cleric against Sania Mirza (ranked 40th in the world) for the indecency of her sportswear and for playing doubles with a Jewish partner.
63. 'Sport Quotes of the Year', *The Sunday Tribune*, 31 December, 2006
64. Quoted in *Irish Examiner*, 23 February, 2007

of diversity – ethnicity, physical characteristics, culture, religion – in a manner which both denigrates others and denies their intrinsic, inalienable dignity.[65] Allegations of racist taunts against and treatment of players of African origin in Europe's soccer leagues have accumulated in recent years, while in the French rugby championship, Pau's black lock forward Guy Jeannard left the field in anger after an altercation with Toulon and former Free State (South Africa) player Charl van Vliet, claiming that he had been subjected to 'intolerable racist insults on the field'.[66] After Barclays Bank had bought the rights for more than $300 million to name the new stadium for baseball's New Jersey Nets 'Barclay Center', allegations about its past profits from slavery and links to the apartheid regime in South Africa surfaced, which a spokesperson for the Bank denied though this was rejected by a Brooklyn council member Letitia Jones: 'Brooklyn has been described as the 'black belt' of New York City, and because of their past practices, I do not believe it is appropriate that this deal goes ahead. We've no legal grounds to stop it, but we will be putting moral pressure on the shareholders and investors in the development project.'[67] Muhammad Ali rejected Cassius Clay as a slave name and became, in the words of Keith Duggan, a 'wondrous, scarcely believable figure to black Americans struggling for equality'[68] in the era of struggle for civil rights. *The Times* columnist Simon Barnes examines the issue of homophobia in sport, particularly soccer, in a provocatively titled piece, 'Football destined to remain the last bastion of homophobia – that's the straight, naked truth'.[69] The cautioning by the Crown Office of Polish-born Glasgow Celtic goalkeeper Artur Boruc for a breach of the peace after he had blessed himself in a derby game against Rangers in 2006 raises questions of religious prejudice, as does the widespread singing of sectarian chants.

65. See 'The Church and Racism', Pontifical Commission for Justice and Peace, Vatican City, 1988
66. Quoted in Johnny Waterson, 'Race runs through sporting boundaries', *The Irish Times*, 23 December, 2006
67. 'Black leaders erupt over Barclays sports deal', *The Independent*, 2 February, 2007
68. *The Irish Times*, 20 January, 2007
69. *The Times*, 6 October, 2006

With their origin in the arena of sporting activity, the terms or titles 'good sport' and 'spoil sport' have become expressions of both emotive experience and ethical evaluation. Sport is sometimes seen as a metaphor for life and interpreted in moral terms, with an encouragement to imitate ethical standards shown in the performance of sporting prowess and search for success. However, this is often sadly not the case, as many of the examples cited above show. In this regard sport may be more mirror than metaphor.

In his article on sport in *The Columbia History of the Twentieth Century*, Jean-Marc Ran Oppenheim asserts that 'sports and the games from which most derive have, throughout human history, reflected the structures and the aims of the societies in which they were practised [and] this has been true in the twentieth century as in any other.[70] This interpretation is supported by the view of Marshall McLuhan who, according to Carlo Nanni, 'advances the thesis that one discovers the code to a culture by looking at the way a whole generation plays its games'.[71] Calling to mind McLuhan's 'global village', the contemporary context for considering and evaluating sport is that of globalisation. In response to the question 'Is there any cultural practice more global than football?', David Goldblatt points to the fact that 'In an epoch characterised by unprecedented global interconnectedness, the most universal cultural phenomenon in the world is football.'[72] Globalisation has brought sport to the proverbial ends of the earth.

As Bishop Stanislaw Rylko points out, 'Sport's capacity to engage huge crowds of people on a planetary scale, and to straddle geographic, social, economic and language barriers makes it one of the most universally recognised components of popular culture'.[73] In this sense 'global games', such as the World Cup (soccer) and the Olympics and to a lesser extent the rugby and

70. 'Athletics: Play and Politics', New York: Columbia University Press, 1998, 102-126 at 102
71. 'Sport and the educational emergency', *L'Osservatore Romano*, weekly English edition, no 48, 26 November, 2008
72. *The Ball Is Round: A Global History of Football*, London: Penguin Books, 2007, xii.
73. *The World of Sport – A Field of Christian Mission*, 5

cricket world cup competitions, generate important moral implications and issues through their global involvement with international communication and commercial interests.

The investment of global business in sport through advertising, sponsorship and marketing makes the intertwined issues of investigation and evaluation an ethical imperative, a task that the media seems somewhat reluctant to undertake.

A recent editorial in the Jesuit weekly magazine *America* expresses the moral dilemma at the heart of sport and the dimension of ethical exemplarism it can play: 'Sports reflect the society we live in, and our world is both violent and, as the past few weeks have shown, greedy. We would like to think, however, that sports can and should be the exception and the model. We believe deep down that we are much better than the violence, the cheating, the greed or the win-at-any-cost attitude.'[74] The moral evaluation of sport means the commensuration of Orwell's statement about serious sport being seen as war without shooting with former American Secretary of State Condolezza Rice's comparison of (American) football to war: 'What you are doing in both arenas is taking and yielding territory, and you have certain strategies and tactics.'[75]

---

74. 'The Sporting Life', 20 October, 2008
75. Quoted in Alice Thomson, 'Which one makes her country proud?', *The Daily Telegraph*, 2 August 2006

CHAPTER SEVEN

Sport and Redemption

'The Irresistibe Danny Cipriani – The Second Coming of the Saviour of English Rugby.'[1]

'Talk of sport offering "redemption as well as rebirth into a new type of reality, separated from ordinary reality by its sense of being permeated with ultimacy and holiness" cannot be accommodated in a Christian worldview. When scholars suggest that sports can offer "redemption", "rebirth" and easy access to God's throne of grace, it is at this juncture I feel they have done a grave disservice to both believer and non-believer.'[2]

In the Name of the Cross

Near Eastern and New Testament scholar Sean Freyne concluded his recent book *Jesus – A Jewish Galilean* with the death of Jesus of Nazareth in Jerusalem.[3] The earliest formed part of the canonical gospels focused on the passion, crucifixion and death of Jesus for the apologetic purpose of explaining that the Christ had been unjustly condemned and to avoid the impression that the story of his resurrection from the dead was merely the account of another redeemer myth without any historical connection to the cause and course of his ministry which culminated in the cross. (In time, the formation of the gospel tradition tried to bridge the gap that the article of the Apostles' Creed gives rise to in leaping from Jesus' birth 'from the Virgin Mary' to his crucifixion, death and burial 'under Pontius Pilate'.) Jesus' execution resulted from the rejection of his mission to renew Judaism through his proclamation and praxis of God's Reign. However, a purely

---

1. Cover caption of *The Observer Sports Monthly*, October 2008
2. Nick J. Watson, 'Nature and transcendence: the mystical and sublime in extreme sports' in *Sport and Spirituality*, 95-116 at 113
3. London: T&T Clark, 2004. The 'classic' commentary on the passion narratives in the gospels is Raymond Brown's two-volume *The Death of the Messiah*, New York: Doubleday, 1994. A shorter study is Geza Vermes' *The Passion*, London: Penguin Books, 2005

'religious' interpretation of his fate fails to take account of the complexity and conspiracy of institutional constituencies which centred on the Roman Empire and local political enclaves as well as the Temple. The need for a broader historical (and human) interpretation is contained in the fact that the inscription put on his cross 'was written in Hebrew, in Latin, and in Greek' (John 19:20). The cross of Jesus counts the various establishments – political and social, religious and military – which meted out to him a most violent and vicious form of dying. Often classified as the central symbol of Christianity, the cross condenses the history of human contradiction, cruelty and conflict that has accumulated through the centuries. However, as the bridge connecting the particulars of his historical words and works with his universal post-resurrection presence, the cross holds out the hope that the horizon of human history is marked by the wounds of the One through whom redemption, both in terms of earthly liberation and eternal salvation, reaches out to all people.

The symbolic representation and moral-spiritual participation of Christian believers in the *Via crucis* of Christ through the enactment of the passion play – the most famous of which is at intervals of a decade (except for the two World Wars) in Oberammergau in Bavaria – and the devotional Stations of the Cross throughout the liturgical season of Lent establish a mode of theological evaluation for the language and imagery of the events of Jesus' final days and hours on earth. An added aesthetic standard for accessing and assessing the crucifixion of Christ is heard in the multiplicity of classical and contemporary musical settings of the passion story, most magnificently in the Saints Matthew and John pieces by J. S. Bach. The language and symbolism of Christ's final days are caricatured in lines such as 'Carrying the Cross'/'Rewarding Cross to bear'.[4] This play on words cleverly refers to the Gaelic football fortunes of champion clubs Crossmaglen Rangers and Crossmolina in their respective counties of Armagh and Mayo. A similar sentiment is shared in the caption covering Munster's rugby victory over Welsh side

---

4. *The Sunday Times*, 20 February, 2005/*The Irish Times*, 5 November, 2005.

Neath in the Celtic League final – 'Bearing the Celtic cross'.[5] These underlying themes of suffering and victory recall the Latin sayings *per crucem ad gloriam* (through the cross to glory) and *in hoc signo vinces* (in this sign you will conquer). The theme of victory (and defeat) is explicitly captured in 'Liverpool's passion play shatters Chelsea's dream.'[6] Moreover, the association of the cross with victory in sport is conveyed and coined in the emblem of All-Ireland medals in the codes of Gaelic football and hurling. However, a more fitting historical analogy for sporting engagement and entertainment might be the spectacle of *panem et circenses*[7] regularly presented by the spin *magistri* of the Roman Empire. In this context the chilling comment of Thomas Boswell on the American Super Bowl contest captures the relegation of assassination, to say nothing of redemption, in the arena and assessment of sport: 'Nothing stops, or even deflects, the NFL – which did not cancel a single game the week President John F. Kennedy was shot – from fulfilling its self-appointed role as national purveyor of bread and circuses.'[8]

Faith from Easter

The resurrection of Jesus is the central claim and confession of Christian faith and the church stands or fall by virtue of its validation and verification, a view clearly expressed by Paul: 'If Christ has not been raised, then our preaching is without substance, and so is your faith. What is more, we have proved to be false witnesses to God, for testifying against God that he raised Christ to life when he did not raise him.' (1 Cor 15:14-15) For Paul the stakes could not have been higher, as the truth of Jesus' resurrection and its corresponding christology concerns the very credibility of God. While belief in the resurrection of Jesus raises many philosophical and theological questions, worship of

---

5. *The Sunday Tribune*, 2 February, 2003

6. *The Irish Independent*, 4 May, 2005. Also 'Rooney primed for passion play', *The Irish Independent*, 21 May, 2005

7. *Duas tantum res anxius optat panem et circenses* – [The people] eagerly long for two things, bread and circuses, Juvenal (c. 60-140 AD), *Satires* X, 79. cf www.the latinlibrary/juvenal.

8. *The Washington Post*, 22 January, 1989. (Quoted in Elizabeth Webber & Mike Feinsilber, *Dictionary of Allusion*, Springfield, Mass: Merriam-Webster, 1999, 82

it and witness to its factuality is the foundation of Christian faith. In the succinct statement of prominent scripture scholar Joseph Fitzmyer, 'not to admit the resurrection of Jesus means that one is not a Christian'.[9]

Easter faith emerges from the experience of the disciples of Jesus encountering him as the Risen Christ. These events, and the evidence of his empty tomb, are expressed in the different and somewhat disparate narratives of the gospels primarily, and to a lesser extent, in the letters of Paul. The New Testament does not attempt to give account of the resurrection-event itself, a fact that the newly found and founded faith of the disciples, both men and women, were happy to accept as they were both comforted and confronted by the One who came to be called Christ, Lord, Saviour, Son of God, God. Both the origin and objective of Christian faith come from the claim and confession that the crucified Jesus was raised to be exalted and revealed in divine glory which entailed the experience of his return from the realm of the dead.[10] The interrelationship and interdependence of creed, church and canon is crucially captured in the conclusions of historian John C. Moore: 'As an artefact, the Bible gives us solid information about the faith of the early church, but the faith of the living church makes the Bible more than an artefact. The authenticity of the Christian church does not depend on the Bible as sacred text; the authenticity of the Bible as sacred text depends on the Christian church, the people of God. And at the core of their faith is their belief in the resurrection.'[11]

The meaning and message of Easter can be explicated and explained as a four-fold event – eschatological, salvific, theological

---

9. *A Christological Cathechism*, New York: Paulist Press, 1991, 86

10. Literature on the resurrection is vast and varied in value. For an excellent exposition and exploration of the scriptural material with extensive bibliography see N. T. Wright, *The Resurrection of the Son Of God*, London: SPCK, 2003. An account of methodological approaches within theology to the resurrection is articulated in Kenan B. Osborne, *The Resurrection of Jesus*, New York: Paulist Press, 1997

11. 'The Resurrection, the Church and the Bible', *America*, 10 April, 1993. Moore's earlier summary of the scriptural testimony is magisterial: 'For most secular scholars the resurrection did not happen simply because it could not happen. Even some Christian scholars understand the resurrection figuratively, not literally. But nothing in the New

and revelatory.[12] Firstly, the resurrection is not a reward for the figure of Jesus who remained faithful to the will of God the Father but the realisation of the mission that animated his ministry which he articulated and attempted to actualise as the symbol 'kingdom' or 'reign of God'. As the eschatological prophet of God's purposes for the world, Jesus embodied and expressed God's intention for Israel which would become extended in the scriptural phrase 'to the ends of the earth'. To paraphrase Paul, the resurrection is the first fruits of the kingdom proclaimed and made present in the person of Jesus. The vindication of Jesus means the victory of God's Reign: Jesus is not destroyed through death. In the resurrection Jesus does not return to an earthly existence such as he embodied prior to his crucifixion. His exaltation is experienced as eschatological, exhibiting the 'end time', the eternal age that humanity still awaits but can anticipate on account of and through Jesus. Secondly, the resurrection cannot be reduced to a (mere) apologetic argument or even proof for the divinity of Jesus of Nazareth. The 'victory' of Jesus over sin and death, evil and the powers of this world unveil the understanding that the resurrection is an event of cosmic significance and salvation. The Christ-event, that is, the totality of Jesus' life, death and resurrection, is both the cause and effect of what Paul called the 'new creation' and the hope of resurrection-destiny for the whole of humanity. Thirdly, the resurrection is not reducible to some interior event or effect in the experience of Jesus' first followers. It emerges from the energy of God to ex-

Testament is better documented than the story of the resurrection. It is assumed in those letters of Paul that are the earliest of the New Testament texts, and it is central to all four gospels and Acts. It is not an account that arose long after the life and death of Jesus ... The resurrection story was there from the beginning. Some of Jesus' followers claimed to have been eyewitnesses of the Risen Lord, and they were in Jerusalem to be questioned by the other first Christians. It seems very likely that the demoralised disciples would have returned to their homes and trades had they not been convinced that Jesus had risen and spoken to them. Their behaviour is scarcely comprehensible apart from their faith in the resurrection.'

12. In this I am relying on Brian McDermott, *Word Become Flesh – Dimensions of Christology*, Collegeville, Mn: The Liturgical Press 1993, especially 'The Meaning of Easter',118-23

hibit who God is, the creative power of God who can not only bring light out of darkness but life from death through love. Fourthly, the resurrection relates both God and Jesus in an event which finally and fully reveals who Jesus is. Jesus is disclosed as being totally with God, filled with God's power and life. In the wake of the resurrection Jesus' identity in human and divine indices is completed in the experience and expression of those who have faith in him. No longer restricted in time and space Jesus, in the power of the Spirit, can be encountered 'to the ends of the earth'. Through the light and lens of Easter faith the early disciples of Jesus came to believe and broadcast that the end of history is the establishment of God's kingdom 'of righteousness, and peace and joy in the Holy Spirit' (Rom 14:17).

Resurrecting Sport

In the 1970s Leeds United were one of the most famous and feared football clubs in English soccer. For some they were the finest first eleven to have played, if not quite graced, the not so beautiful game in the former First Division Championship, a claim hotly disputed by fans from other clubs. 'Blackwell believes in resurrection.'[13] This refers to the conviction of Leeds manager Kevin Blackwell that the club could make it to the Premiership after their 3-0 defeat by Watford in the 2006 second tier Championship play-off final. The irony of this is intensified by the fact that, a season later, the club was relegated a further division to the Coca-Cola League One. Relegation as a result of failure rather than resurrection through success has formed the fate of the club and the feelings of its followers who yearn for the halcyon days when a host of international stars played for Leeds. 'A 19-point margin for the resurrection men.'[14] In recent years the efforts and exploits of the Waterford senior hurling team have both fascinated and frustrated both their own fans and followers of the game from other counties. This reference to Waterford's resurgence and victory over Clare a week after they were described as looking 'sick and indigent' in the League final (which they lost) raises the prospect more of reinvention rather

---

13. *The Observer*, 21 May, 2006.
14. *The Irish Times*, 19 March, 2005

than resurrection, a point pathetically underlined by their performance in the 2008 All-Ireland final. The adoption of the language (and life) of resurrection is most obvious in 'Saints rise
from the dead through touch of Drahm',[15] a reference to the 17
points scored by Northampton's Shane Drahm in their 22-20 victory over Harlequins in the English rugby Premiership. Reliance
on the cultural capital of the Christian creed completely outside
the context of conversion and the church's liturgical celebration
carries the considerable risk of reducing such confession and
theology to the level, at best, of stock phrases and clichés.

Explicit mentions of Easter include 'Reds enjoy Easter rising' /
'Easter arrives to resurrect Saints'/'No Easter resurrection as
Kingdom eludes Dubs'.[16] These refer respectively to Manchester
United's 4-3 victory over Leeds (then in the Premiership), to the
last minute try by the propitiously named Northampton player
Mark Easter in the 24-21 victory over Bath and to Dublin's failure to defeat All-Ireland champions Kerry on an Easter Sunday
contest which confirmed Kerry's League Division One status,
which involved Dublin dropping a division as a result. A variation on the theme is *Passion Plays – The Resurrection of Munster
Hurling*, a double DVD set produced to portray the resurgence
of certain counties in the Munster Hurling Championship during the decade 1994-2004.[17] The value of such references depends on their religious significance – medieval dramas, Easter
event and resurrection – and their continuing resonance in the
consciousness of readers and listeners. Notwithstanding their
cultural residue, the spiritual meaning of such specific symbols
and doctrines and their significance for sport call into play the
broader question of the relation between faith and culture,
which carries deeper issues of communication, comprehension
and conviction. Moreover, the vagueness, if not indeed the
vacuity, of such references and resonances is less than veiled by
designations such as 'the latest resurrection of Manchester

---

15. *The Observer*, 27 March, 2005
16. *The Sunday Independent*, 31 March, 2002/ *The Observer*, 9 April, 2006/
The Irish Independent, 9 April, 2007
17. *GAA Classics 2*, Dublin: Sideline, in association with RTÉ, 2007

United, a resurrection of sorts'.[18] The spiritual and theological meaning of resurrection, both in relation to the original unique Easter event and the universal hope of human resurrection from the dead which it offers does not admit of degrees, either in temporal or qualitative terms.

Sporting salvation
Appendix A displays a number of references in recent years in the media to the language of salvation, redemption and atonement across a range of sports from cricket and Gaelic games through golf and racing (both by humans and horses) to rugby and soccer. A representative sample reveals recourse to the traditional terminology of Christian faith and theology which tells of the deliverance and destiny of humanity through the divine intervention and invitation of God through Israel which culminates in the incarnation and contains both the healing of history and the eternal hope of heaven. 'Saviour [Shane] Warne – Australia avoid the follow-on as rain disrupts Old Trafford Test.'[19] In the past two decades the figure of Shane Warne has been both a formidable opponent and controversial character, both in his native Australia and throughout the cricketing world. The reference here to his role in one of the games during the 2005 Ashes series against England is representative of the esteem and effectiveness of his bowling skills and successes. Attribution of the title of 'saviour' to an individual involved in a team sport is significant, though not unusual in the hype, if not indeed the hysteria, that singles out players for their performances in particular games.

'In dire need of redemption';[20] 'An indispensable figure in their redemption was their captain';[21] 'I was hoping we would redeem ourselves. But, it was even worse.'[22] These three references to the fortunes (and figures) of the Tipperary senior hurling team are situated against the background of the last All-Ireland championship victory by the Premier County in 2001.

18. James Lawton, *The Independent*, 8 November, 2005
19. *The Sunday Times*, 14 August, 2004
20. *Sunday Independent*, 6 June, 2004
21. *Sunday Independent*, 20 November, 2005
22. *Irish Examiner*, 1 March, 2006

After almost two decades in the berated (though not biblical) wilderness from 1971 to 1989, Tipperary returned to the game's grand circle under the astute management of one of its former greats, Michael 'Babs' Keating, a hurler of the heart, to paraphrase the cricket commentator John Arlott. Restored to the helm in time for the 2005-6 season his nuanced reference to the need for a 'form of redemption' is interesting and even ironic when interpreted in light of the decision during the 2006 championship to remove the 'indispensable' Thurles Sarfield player Ger 'Redser' O'Grady from the squad after a well-publicised incident involving indiscipline off the field. 'Redeemer seeking one more miracle.'[23] Drawing on the biblical motif of 'turning water into wine' *Irish Times* journalist Tom Humphries refers to the pivotal role Brian McEniff played, as both player and manager, in the successes of the Donegal senior football side over a period of five decades. The juxtaposition of one out of the many miracles in the ministry of Jesus with the status of redeemer raises the question of whether there is more than a single saviour figure in Gaelic football. Could every successful All-Ireland winning manager be manifested not only as a miracle worker but also made out to be a saviour? Players and fans could equally claim the title for their victorious coach.

'Watching David Duval snaphook his drive into the stream that runs alongside the second hole of the TPC Sawgrass course, it was never more apparent that, in golf, redemption is a lot harder to find than par';[24] 'Last week's French Open end may have been darkly familiar for Jean van de Velde, but it brought a long-awaited redemption.'[25] The fate of former British Open champion David Duval has been the source of much commentary and speculation since his spectacular slide down the world ranking of golf in recent years. Considered one of the more talented exponents of the game, his demise has coincided with the rise of Tiger Woods to the top. Reference to the achievement of redemption in the game is highlighted by the fortune of Frenchman van de Velde who, in contrast to Duval, lost an Open championship when he drove his second shot at the last hole

23. *The Irish Times*, 30 August, 2003
24. *The Guardian*, 26 March, 2005
25. *Sunday Tribune*, 3 May, 2005

into the water and squandered a seemingly unassailable lead. Ten years later, with the Open championship due to return to Carnoustie, van de Velde disclosed a degree of detachment that focused on his own failure rather than on faith: 'God would have had more important things on his hands than whether or not I was winning an Open.'[26] The absurdity of articulating 'golfing redemption' is well illustrated in the remark of Scot Colin Montgomerie on the rotation of the event to Carnoustie, the venue dubbed 'Carnasty' on account of the conditions encountered there in 1997: 'It can redeem itself and it will. It's a great course and one which speaks for itself. They don't need to trick it up.'[27] Moreover, if redemption for golfers is reckoned in terms of score(s) attained and success achieved, it raises the spectre of damnation for many who attempt to play a game that calls for an amalgam of athleticism and ability actualised by a few, and not always available even to them, because of injury and other factors outside of human control, including the weather.

'Nobody has been a more influential presence on the world rugby stage over the past 15 years. Henry was coach of Auckland when they were quite the most formidable sub-international side in the game. He redeemed Wales and coached the Lions in the thrilling series of 2001.'[28] The contrasting fortunes of Graham Henry, from setting the stage and strategy for Wales' proverbial rise from the ashes to achieve a European grand slam success under his successor to the loss by the Lions touring side to Australia in 2001 and masterminding the victory of New Zealand over them in 2005 relativises the notion of redemption

---

26. Quoted by Lewine Mair in *The Daily Telegraph*, 20 April, 2007
27. Quoted by Mair in *The Daily Telegraph*, 31 January, 2007. This naturalistic sense of redemption stands in marked contrast to the moral conception contained in the comment of William Fotheringham concerning cycling's Tour de France: 'The vastness of the drug scandals – Festina in 1998 during the race, the blood-boosting ring this year, just before the start – was such that it induced an intense need for something and someone to restore belief, to redeem the event'. 'Landis case erodes all trust in Tour', *The Observer*, 30 July, 2006
28. *The Observer*, 17 April, 2004

in rugby.[29] Shifting between (potential) saviour and actual scourge of the British and Irish Lions in the space of four years Henry might have more profitably been hailed as gamekeeper turned poacher. 'Blower saviour for Christians'[30] is a clever caption which captures the imagination of the so-called rugby faithful with its reference to the only score, a try, in the 2004 Munster Schools Senior Cup competition between Christian Brothers' College and Ard Scoil Rís. In the fervent atmosphere of the provincial school arena the appellation of 'saviour' is appealing and adulatory. However, its apposition alongside 'Christians' is seemingly tacky, in theological terms and taken from the angle of Christian education raises issues of ethos and evangelisation. 'He is hardly in the messianic category yet. The worrying part is that we need a saviour in the first place.'[31] This reference to Shannon player and tight head prop forward Tony Buckley highlights the critical, literally pivotal, role of players in that position and the dearth of talent to occupy it, especially at the higher levels of club and international competition, a fact highlighted by the offering of large contracts to successful candidates. This conflation and corruption of christological title and soteriological function in sporting commentary is a cause of concern for the Christian community. '*Bloody marvel* steers Sweet Chariot on road to redemption.' Wilkinson scored twenty-seven points in the 42-20 defeat of Scotland which was seen and presented as not only a vindication of his selection but a celebration of his courage and competence after copping an injury in the course of the game which required stitches. Hope turned to

---

29. The relativitism of reckoning redemptive success in sport is reflected in Donald Trelford's reference to Henry's opposite number in the 2005 series: 'What is it about Sir Clive Woodward that causes mayhem wherever he goes? He has already stormed out of Twickenham, his World Cup triumph having gone sour, made a hash of the British [and Irish] Lions tour, failed in his promised revolution at Southampton, and failed again in his comeback bid for English rugby's top job. Now he emerges, as if by magic, as the would-be saviour of Britain's Olympic prospects, splitting the world of athletics in the process.' 'Woodward already ruffling feathers as Olympic saviour', *The Daily Telegraph*, 12 September, 2006
30. *Irish Independent*, 11 February, 2004.
31. *The Sunday Times*, 20 March, 2005

hype both in the stands and in the media with the English ruby anthem – the spiritual 'Sweet Chariot' – and its association of the coming of salvation being connected to Wilkinson's wondrous footwork, even if the try he scored was illegal. Redemption is again seen as an achievement, associated with human success. However, the season revealed that, even in these terms, such salvation was short-lived. Conversion rather than redemption might be a more appropriate description of such life-changing moments in Wilkinson's contributions to the fragile fortunes of his country.

'Rail Link on track to redeem unlucky sire.'[32] Rail Link's victory at the blue riband stage of Group One racing is presented as a form of redemption for the failure of his sire Dansili to deliver at this level. Attribution of a redemptive ability to an animal transcends the anthropomorphism that increasingly characterises the description of horses involved in racing. In this case salvation of one's sire marks a new high (or low) in the spiritual status of the so-called king of the track.

'Radcliffe takes another big step on road to redemption';[33] 'Radcliffe finds redemption.'[34] After her defeat and distress in the Athens Olympic marathon the English athlete's success in the London event is hailed as a step towards finding salvation in her sport while her victory in the marathon at the World Championship in Helsinki a few months later is reckoned as her having reached redemption. The logic of such assertions belies belief in the meaning of sporting achievement.

The majority of sporting references to salvation and redemption involve soccer. The former chairman of Chelsea football club, Ken Bates, is described as a 'self-made saviour' which is a contradiction in terms as salvation, in whatever shape or form suggested, is a state that is given and received rather than earned or attained. (In this context RTÉ commentator Bill O'Herlihy's remark about Brazil and their star player Ronaldo 'earning' redemption in their 2002 World Cup victory is not only reductive but redundant.) Ironically Chelsea's phenomenal success in the English premiership in recent years occurred after

32. *The Independent*, 21 July, 2006
33. *The Daily Telegraph*, 18 April, 2005
34. *The Irish Times*, 15 August, 2005

Bates' departure from the club. 'Punters put faith in the Geordie saviour'[35] The former Liverpool and Real Madrid striker Michael Owen surprised many commentators and fans with his move to Newcastle United at the beginning of the 2005-6 Premiership season. The fervour of Magpie fans – the so-called 'Toon Army' – has often been likened to religious faith, not always favourably.[36] Within a few months, however, their faith in Owen owned little hope, not least for the manager who signed him and who was sacked – 'Owen now unable to save [Graham] Souness.'[37] Moreover, a serious injury incurred during England's 2006 World Cup campaign ruled Owen out for the following season which saw the club's fortunes fade without a first-class striker to replace the legendary Alan Shearer. 'Saviours' days.'[38] The spectrum of famous' goalkeepers here ranges from the revolutionary Che Guevara through the Algerian-born French existentialist philosopher Albert Camus to Pope John Paul II and England World Cup winning number one Gordon Banks. This erstwhile ensemble of goalkeepers raises the spectrum of Camus and John Paul discussing different views of philosophy and the Pope and Che Guevara talking about liberation theology. The novelty of assembling them as one-time soccer goalies highlights the differences in the various positions defended by them on religious and political questions.

'England hold heads high after tour of redemption.'[39] This reference to England's cricket series win over India brings to the fore the question of the meaning of redemption in the wake of the Mumbai massacre. Angus Fraser states that 'in the build-up, greater attention had been paid to the safety and security of the players than the quality of the cricket being played'. Perhaps salvation here refers more to such safety and security off the field rather than scores and success on the pitch. Moreover, the subse-

---

35. *The Racing Post*, 31 August, 2005

36. 'For them, as for other weird religious cults, salvation is always imminent' – a reference to the perennial and perpetual expectation of Newcastle United supporters for trophy success after a gap of thirty seven years. *The Sunday Telegraph*, 5 February, 2006

37. *The Irish Times*, 2 January, 2006

38. *The Times*, 31 March, 2006

39. *The Independent*, 24 December, 2008

quent resignation of England team captain Kevin Pietersen and sacking of coach Peter Moores suggest that behind the scenes chaos and conflict rather than order and harmony were the dominant forces at play. The fact that England face Australia in the Ashes in 2009 makes reference to redemption all the more futile and facile.

The God Who Saves

'The primary statement that needs to be made is that the doctrine of redemption concerns what God has accomplished for us in the life, death and resurrection of Jesus Christ, namely the removal of the obstacles lying between God and us, and the offer to us of participating in God's life. In other words, redemption is about God – as the author of our redemption – before it is truly about us, and it is only because this is so that redemption can truly mean liberation for us and can be for all time and all times the good news of salvation.'[40] This summary statement, from the Vatican International Theological Commission, sees redemption as a revelatory activity of God realised in the paschal mystery of Jesus Christ. Its emphasis on the fact – and faith – that redemption results from God's intervention and involvement in human history is essential for the theological effort to explain both its exercise and effects. Redemption is from God, revelatory of who God is and realised in those who receive it. Redemption is 'from above', gratuitously given from the side of God. The human reception of redemption is experienced and enjoyed in both earthly and eternal modalities and 'moments': 'Redemption in the theological sense must be the liberation of

---

40. 'Select Questions on the Theology of God the Redeemer', *Communio*, 24 (Spring 1997) par 1, 161. Traditionally Christian theology tended to treat firstly the person of Christ – christology – then the redemptive work of Christ – soteriology. However, as Walter Loewe has noted, 'in modern theology the common, even predominant, practice has been to reverse the sequence, placing some prefatory notion of salvation before the treatment of Christ [which] reflects the Christian community's struggle to respond to the scepticism of modern western culture by demonstrating, in one fashion or another, a need for Christianity'. 'Christ and salvation', in Kevin J. Vanhoozer, ed, *The Cambridge Companion to Postmodern Theology*, Cambridge: University Press, 2003, 235

human existence in its concrete totality, i.e. both historical liberation and eschatological salvation in intrinsic and mutual mediation.'[41] Articulated as both 'the removal of obstacles' and 'the
offer of participating in God's life' this redemption is revealed in
two distinct but not separate modes, the realisation of atonement between God and people and their resulting adoption.

This double dimension of redemption dovetails in liberation
from and salvation *for*. People are liberated from a spectrum of
conditions and causes, internal and external, individual and collective. Redemption as liberation *from* reflects a range of human
and historical experience that extends from the limitation of finite life with its inherent physical frailty and psychological
fragility to the moral failure that is found at the root of evil and
sinfulness. Liberation looks both to freedom from the human
condition with its vast array of abuse of freedom and the hope
that such abuse will not amount to a cumulative catastrophe. If
the need for liberation necessarily focuses on the shadows and
darkness of historical diminishment, destructiveness and death,
salvation sees that we are saved *for* something that is positive,
the light that transcends tragedy and illuminates the truth of
human dignity, decency and dreams. Liberation issues in deliverance, salvation intends destiny.

Redemption results from the incarnation of God in Jesus
Christ which, in theological terms, is interpreted as an invitation, not an imposition. Therefore, the economy of redemption
is expressed in both the divine necessity for such an offer and
the human need for openness to accept it. A recent International
Theological Commission document speaks of the 'fundamental
truth of the "absolute necessity" of God's saving act toward
human beings: No human being can ultimately save him/her-
self. Salvation comes only from God the Father through Jesus
Christ in the Holy Spirit.'[42] Underpinning this re-affirmation of
Jesus Christ as the unique Redeemer is the revelation of the universal extension of the economy of redemption, enjoined in the

41. Anselm K. Min, *Paths to the Triune God – An Encounter between
Aquinas and Recent Theologies,* Notre Dame: University of Notre Dame
Press, 2005, 333
42. 'The Hope of Salvation for Infants Who Die Without Being
Baptized', *Origins,* 36 (April 26, 2007), 735

absolute embrace of humanity and history in the Christ-event.[43] God's universal outreach is offered in the uniqueness of Christ. The engagement and involvement of human freedom implies the possibility of the rejection of redemption, either as freedom *from* and *for* or even both. Nevertheless, revelation attests to God's universal redemptive will eternally.

If, as Roger Haight claims, 'salvation [is] the deepest and most central question that Christanity as a religion addresses'[44] the corresponding answer is contained in the confession that Jesus of Nazareth is the 'absolute messenger of salvation'.[45] For Christian faith there is no gainsaying the gospel proclamation that the Absolute has appeared and acted in history. However, belief that Jesus is the absolute messenger of redemption brings the issue of interpreting the means of this redemption to the fore.[46] This question is clearly stated by Gerald O'Collins: 'How has Christ made an essential difference for us, as individuals, as a human community, and as a whole created world? In other words, in what ways does a past event of redemption or set of such events work, both here and now in the future, to save human beings and their world?'[47] The means of our redemption

---

43. Thus the document affirms as a fundamental and central principle of Catholic conviction and attitude the assertion that 'the universal salvific will of the one and triune God is offered and accomplished once and for all in the mystery of the incarnation, death and resurrection of the Son of God'. Par 52, 736

44. *The Future of Christology*, New York: Continuum, 2005, 8

45. The theology of Karl Rahner, for example his 'Christology Today', *Theological Investigations*, Volume XXI, New York:Crossroad, 1988, 220-7

46. 'The meaning of Christian redemption did not receive clear doctrinal formulation, as did the Person and natures of Christ. Nevertheless, the concepts of salvation were both implicit and explicit in the arguments concerning the christological assertions. In many cases, those concepts were the theological reasons adduced for the christological affirmations'. Paul Joseph LaChance, 'Christ Our Salvation: An Intersection of Christology and Soteriology', *Josephinum*, 12 (Winter/Spring 2005), 2

47. *Jesus Our Redeemer*, Oxford: University Press, 2007, v. Thus Colin Gunton states that 'the New Testament uses a range of ways, from the pictorial to the more conceptual, on which theology has drawn to build up a broad range of articulations by which a human being called Jesus both embodied and achieved what is called salvation.' *The Christian Faith: An Introduction to Christian Doctrine*, Oxford: Blackwell, 2002, 72

and its meaning – as past event, present experience, future expectation – are inseparable.

While a focus on the final harrowing days and heart-rending hours of Jesus' life has facilitated an awareness and articulation of atonement as deliverance from the evils of sin, suffering and death, a major feature of such a cross-centred approach has allowed the development of a theology of satisfaction. In this approach atonement is vicariously achieved through Jesus' act of abandonment that amounts to a ransom that satisfies Satan or appeases a God-figure that is altogether other than the Abba revealed as the beloved Father of Jesus the Word made flesh.[48] Laying aside the mercantile terms of such an approach to atonement – paying debt (s), seeking satisfaction, making sacrifice, providing pedagogy – the means of redemption appears reduced to human and historical agency where Jesus merely allows and accepts what is done to him, albeit in mysterious obedience to the will of God. Without connection to the course and cause of his public ministry which preceded and pointed to his 'termination with extreme prejudice' by a conspiracy of political and religious interests, the crucifixion of Jesus runs the risk of amounting to not only a denial of his divinity but also a dilution of his humanity. The means of our salvation must also take account of what happened after Jesus' crucifixion, namely, his resurrection. As the Australian theologian, Anne Hunt, has pointed out, 'The good news of salvation and liberation is revealed to us in the person of Jesus, in his teaching, his life, and pre-eminently in the Paschal Mystery of his death and resurrection.'[49] To borrow a scriptural image, the 'seamless garment' of the life, death and resurrection is the mantle of our redemption. Atonement

48. In an article that he claimed could have been called 'Saved from Atonement' Robert Daly stated that 'the logical implications of some of the classical Christian atonement theories have Christians imitating a violent God whom they perceive as arbitrary, or impotent, or deceitful'. 'Images of God and the Imitation of God: Problems with Atonement', *Theological Studies*, 68 (2007), 39

49. 'The Trinity and the Church', *The Irish Theological Quarterly*, 70 (2005), 235. Moreover, Hunt points out that 'it is in his Paschal Mystery that the mystery of the Trinity is revealed to us and for us and for our salvation and where our understanding of this great mystery of our faith is grounded'.

takes account of what Jesus said and did, suffered and experienced at the first Easter. If Christian redemption leads to the 'removal of obstacles' from the whole of human life, and not only death, theology must attend to the seamless story of Jesus as the means towards this end, both earthly and eternal.

Where redemption as liberation examines the past and present experience of the faith of Christians, redemption as salvation explores its present and future elements. Salvation sees adoption as both the means and end of Christian existence, a sharing in the resurrection-destiny that Jesus both enjoyed and exhibited in the first Easter. Through a series of images and concepts – complementary to those concerning atonement and liberation – the letters of Paul and the Gospel of John in particular present freedom, communion, glory and sanctification as the state of present existence and future enjoyment. The love of God revealed and realised in the process of human redemption produces an intimacy between Creator and creature that can only be characterised in the language and life of familial relations, where God the Father and Jesus the Son and Brother belong inseparably to all those who accept the invitation to redemption in the bond of the Holy Spirit. The present grace and goal of salvation aims, as the Eastern theology has always emphasised, at human participation in the divine life, a process and state described as deification or *theosis*. At the same time this tradition serves as a vital reminder that the mystery of redemption, while affording an understanding in terms of atonement/liberation and adoption/salvation, must finally admit an apophatic dimension, that is, in the words of Nicholas Boyle, 'an attempt, which knows it must fail, to be the adequate response of human understanding to God's gift and redemption of the whole wide world'.[50]

Endgame

Eschatology is the endgame of human existence explored in faith and expressed in hope. Euphemistically Brian Daley describes eschatology as 'faith in final solutions'.[51] Focused on the

---

50. 'Truth believers', *The Times Literary Supplement*, n 5247, 6 April, 2007
51. *The Hope of the Early Church – A Handbook of Patristic Eschatology*, Peabody, Mass: Hendrickson, 2003, p.- 1. For a contemporary treatise see Zachary Hayes, *Visions of a Future – A Study of Christian Eschatology*, Collegeville, MN: Michael Glazier, 1989

so-called 'final things', it flows from the belief in God's full involvement with the history of humanity, from beginning to end, from creation to consummation in Christ. The counsel of one of the advisers of King Edwin in the seventh century, as recounted in the Venerable Bede's *Ecclesiastical History of the English Speaking People*, situates the search for such solutions: 'Your majesty, when you sit at table with your lords and vassals, in the winter when the fire burns warm and bright on the hearth, and the storm is howling outside, bringing the snow and the rain, it happens of a sudden that a little bird flies into the hall. It comes in at one door and flies out through the other. For the few moments that it is inside the hall, it does not feel the cold, but as soon as it leaves your sight, it returns to the dark of winter. It seems to me that the life of man is much the same. We do not know what went before and we do not know what follows. If the new doctrine can speak to us surely of these things, it is well for us to follow it.'[52]

Eschatology is an extrapolation from and extension of the Christian experience of faith in the church and world beyond the historical horizon of human existence, that is, from earth to eternity. As such eschatology is the supreme evocation of the theological virtue of hope. This hope concerns human life (both individual and communal) and its need for healing, the longing for loose ends to be tied up, for tears to be dried up, for ruptures to be reconciled, for sin to be forgiven. As the exploration of 'the hope that springs eternal', eschatology expresses the human desire that the patterns, process and purpose of personal and social existence will be drawn into and perfected in the presence of the living God. However, eschatology does not simply project an earthly utopia onto a heavenly screen and imagine that God is simply the guarantor of human goodness. A Christian perspective on the end state of human existence exercises equanimity: partly seeing the 'final things' in terms of fulfilment, partly in terms of forgiveness. An 'eschatological reserve' cautions against any attempt to articulate 'what no eye has seen, nor ear heard, nor the human heart conceived, what God has prepared for those who love him' (1 Corinthians 2:9). Commenting on the

---

52. Quoted in *The Dutch Cathechism*, London: Burns & Oates, 1967, 3

exposition of eschatology in *The Cathechism of the Catholic Church*, Brian E. Daley states that 'unlike many works on Christian hope composed in earlier times [it] seems deliberately to avoid presenting its readers with what might be taken as a treatise on human nature, a scenario for the final conflicts of human history, or a map of the "world beyond".'[53] While focused on the end-time, eschatology also emphasises earthly experience as an anticipation of 'things assured' (cf Hebrews 11:1), an anticipation that is both an interim enjoyment and an impetus towards the end.

Traditionally, eschatology has treated the four 'final things', that is, death, judgement, heaven and hell, though the end of the world, limbo and purgatory have been appended to these and also articulated as part of the mortal and post-mortem human condition. As embodied, finite beings humans experience well-being and sickness, growth and diminishment, life and death. Human existence extends from birth to death in the passage of time and through space perceived as place, like the bird entering and exiting the hall in Bede's image. As an inevitable and universal prospect for humanity, contingency offers little comfort. In Heidegger's words, often presented ironically as immortal, we are all 'beings-unto-death'. Death is experienced, both individually and in relation to those dear to us, as an existential, personal process rather than as a biological, physical reality. Despite the scientific-technological promise of prolonging life, the necessity of the ageing process and the prospect of the approach of death cannot be postponed indefinitely. Death denies the dominion of absolute autonomy over human life and demands that people face it immediately and ultimately, that is, in terms of both the manner of dying and the meaning of death. In the face of sickness, suffering and separation Christian faith offers the hope of redemption, both as liberation from the limitations of the human condition, including sinfulness, and salvation interpreted as a resurrection-destiny.

In its 1979 Declaration, *The Reality of Life after Death*, the Congregation for the Doctrine of the Faith declared that the church's belief in the resurrection of the dead referred to 'the

---

53. 'Eschatology' in *Commentary on the Cathechism of the Catholic Church*, ed Michael J. Walsh, London: Geoffrey Chapman, 1994, 205-224 at 207

whole person. For the elect it is nothing other than the extension to human beings of the resurrection of Christ itself.'[54] While recognising a continuity between earthly and eschatological existence there is also a 'radical break between the present life and the future one, due to the fact that the economy of faith will be replaced by the economy of fullness of life'.[55] An eternal economy eschews a dualism or division of corporeal and spiritual dimensions, that is, the resurrection of the dead involves a resurrection of the body. However, the phrase 'for the elect' raises the question of examination or judgement and salvation or damnation. The classical expression of the eschatological judgement scene is the fresco by Michelangelo found in the Vatican's Sistine chapel which calls to mind chapter 25 of the gospel of Matthew. Jesus' greeting of 'the sheep at his right hand' as those 'blessed by my Father' with his gathering them into 'the kingdom prepared for you from the foundation of the world' and his cursing of 'the goats at the left' with his casting them 'into the eternal fire prepared for the devil and his angels' represents, in a sporting metaphor, the final whistle. Eternal salvation of the elect is expressed in *The Cathechism* as entry into heaven, the 'ultimate end and fulfilment of the deepest human longings, the state of supreme, definitive happiness' enjoyed in a communion of life and love with the Triune God, the saints and the blessed, that is, all those who are saved and share in the final form of graced eternal existence.[56] Hell, on the other hand, is the eternal state of separation, 'definitive self-exclusion from communion with God and the blessed'.[57] After the 'particular' post-mortem judgement of each person's life there is a possibility of a period and process of purification or purgation in which people who have not died in the state of mortal sin are afforded through grace and the

---

54. *In Vatican Council II – Volume 2*, ed. Austin Flannery, Dublin: Dominican Publications, 1982, 501
55. Ibid, p 503
56. Dublin: Veritas, 1994, par 1024, 234
57. *The Catechism*, par 1033, 236. Daley comments that 'final salvation or damnation are not presented primarily as the success or failure of individual lives, but as inclusion in – or exclusion from – a community of salvation, whose life is already anticipated in the sacramental life of the church'. *Commentary*, p 208

intercession of others including those on earth, as it were, extra time to exhibit that total conversion of heart which is required for entry into union with God, the saints and the elect.[58]

In the Christian creed the final judgement of those still living and the dead is linked to the *Parousia* or Second Coming of Christ 'in glory'.

The Final Score

The sudden death of former player and manager Alan Ball in April 2007 sent a shock through the close knit soccer community in England, especially the generation that was both involved in and remembered the country's 1966 World Cup victory when Ball was the youngest and, for many, the best member of the team which defeated West Germany in the final. Twice the most expensive transfer in the history of English football, his energy and enthusiasm for the game was evident up to the time of his death. Soccer commentator Patrick Barclay praises his selfless spirit in the commitment to the common cause that constituted him as a true team player which earned him the deep admiration of football fans everywhere, 'even north of the border: the Scots appreciated the way that, in taking the trouble to sneer at them, Ball paid respect to the game's oldest international rivalry'.[59] At his funeral service in Winchester Cathedral, Canon Michael St John-Channell contrasted Ball's common touch and down-to-earth quality with the 'pampered superstars of the Premiership'. As memories of the World Cup final in which Ball starred were to the fore he included the closing lines of match commentator

---

58. 'As Protestant theology has constantly pointed out, the idea of purgatory is not found in the scriptures ... There seems to be no reason in the nature of the case or in the tradition for insisting that purgatory means in the literal sense an extension of quasi-time outside worldly time, extended beyond the moment of death. The possibility of the imagery of purgatory representing another aspect of death as the divine judgement, demanding a refocusing and reordering of all aspects of the person's expectations and relationships, seems strong, credible, and intelligible.' Monika K. Hellwig, 'Eschatology' in Francis Schüssler Fiorenza & John P. Galvin, eds, *Systematic Theology – Roman Catholic Perspectives*, Volume 2, Minneapolis: Fortress Press, 1991, 369.

59. 'If only today's England players had Alan Ball's selfless spirit', *The Sunday Telegraph*, 29 April, 2007

Kenneth Wolstenholme in his homily: 'Remember those famous words: "They think it is all over, it is now." Not for Alan. For him it is a new beginning.'[60]

The personal poignancy and proclamation of Christian faith in hope for a great player contrasts with the tribute to a television programme contained in Tony Francis' piece 'A fond farewell to an old and outdated friend'.[61] BBC *Grandstand* started in 1958 with a promise of presenting 'Saturday's new style, non-stop parade, featuring sports and events where they happen, when they happen'. After more than 3,000 programmes *Grandstand* gave way in 2009 under the weight of a number of factors: the pressure coming from commercial coverage of fixtures, the loss of revenue and access to core competitions and events, the changing formats of coverage, particularly those that concern Saturday soccer. With its familiar signature tune it seems to many that another venerable institution has again yielded to the vagaries of time and the fashions of sporting fans. A former presenter opens his paean for a programme presented as an obituary with the following observation: 'Next to the Catholic cathedral on Derby Road was a shadowy squeeze of a building which became a temple of sport on Saturday evenings in the winter.'[62] 'Evenings in the winter' echoes Bede's image of the king and his advisers sitting in hall in their quest for meaning, though here it expresses the search and desire for entertainment and enjoyment.

Belief that the meaning of sport is reflected in the moral and metaphysical issues and questions of life and death is recorded in a memorable quote given to sportswriter David Walsh by former Dublin Gaelic football captain Tony Hanahoe: 'The census forms come round and there is a question which asks, 'When did education cease?' I answer, "death". All the factors you face in sport recur throughout life. I would look askance at those who see futility in the pursuit of a leather bag of wind.'[63] Indeed

---

60. *The Guardian*, 4 May, 2007

61. *The Daily Telegraph*, 26 April, 2006

62. *The Daily Telegraph*, 26 April, 2006

63. Quoted by Daire Whelan in 'The Afterlife', *Village*, 12-18 August 2005. This article remembers and reflects on some of the members of the Dublin team which reached six All-Ireland finals in a row in the 1970s.

sport has often been associated with death through accidents and disasters which have resulted in the loss of life by both players and spectators, individually and in groups. The Heysel and Hillsborough tragedies that involved Liverpool and their fans serve as a stark reminder that events off and around the field of play often end in death on a large scale, a situation which sees the pastoral and theological ministry of the Christian churches supplying comfort and hope, a need which the media cannot supply. In this context there is a chilling ring to the remark of Steve James about the crisis in English cricket at the start of 2009: 'This week might have been a mess, but it has certainly been no disaster. Such a word should rarely be attributed to sport. Life goes on. England play cricket again in a fortnight. And it might just be that they have a better captain than the last time they did so.'[64]

Catholic faith, teaching and theology concerning post-mortem existence were often exercised by the question of limbo and purgatory. These too have found their way into the arena of sporting analysis. 'Campbell stuck in limbo as Eriksson wavers on line-up',[65] a reference to the indecision of the English football manager whether to play Arsenal player Sol Campbell or not. Called into theological question in recent decades, the concept became officially redundant with the declaration that 'in the context of the discussion on the destiny of those infants who die without baptism the mystery of the universal salvific will of God is a fundamental and central principle' which affirms the eschatological hope that redemption can be extended to all, including infants who have died before baptism.[66] It requires a considerable extension of the category to imagine that indecision about picking an individual to play a particular game or not is somehow equivalent to the shadowy state of existence symbolised by limbo. The analogy limps at best, not least because to qualify for a limbo-like level in international sport presupposes a life of considerable duration, development and display of skills not associated with infants or children. Furthermore, the idea that the manager is invested with powers of redemption to

64. *The Sunday Telegraph*, 11 January, 2009
65. *The Times*, 6 September, 2005
66. See *The Hope of Salvation*, pars 43 and 68

release the player from limbo is incredible, if not indeed idola-
trous.

'Faldo happy to steer clear of the purgatory of Pinehurst'. In
2005 six times major winner Nick Faldo decided to decline the
opportunity to play at the US Open in favour of fishing, declaring that the venue 'will definitely be the hardest course of the
year' and that he 'just didn't enjoy it when I played it as I found
it has 17 greens that are cupcakes and one, the 17th, that is a
saucer'.[67] The metaphor of purgatory for golf depends on the
meaning of suffering that is both self-inflicted and deserved.
While many may sympathise with this view of the game at
times, enjoyment rather than mere endurance is the over-riding
motive for participation, whether as players or spectators.
Moreover, belief in the state of purgatory is the basis for the possibility of purification and eternal perfection. Applied to the
earthly exercise of golf or any other game that requires high levels of skill and strength, such a process is a prerequisite not only
for ultimate success but also for the possibility of staying the
course. While former champions may imagine that they have a
right to immediate entry into a golfing heaven, Christian faith
insists that purgatory is a process of post-mortem purgation for
serious sin(s) that bear no similarity to the ups and downs of a
round of golf.

'Football's eternal mysteries continue'[68]

The media have not been averse to attributing the power of resurrection to managers and others administering sport, as in the
opening line of Kevin McCarra's preview of the Charity Shield
game between Arsenal and Chelsea: 'Arsene Wenger prepared
for the new season by raising the dead', a reference to the
Amsterdam tournament where 'Arsenal's games leapt to life
and comatose armchair viewers lifted their heads from their
chests'.[69] Reduction of resurrection to revivification of players
and resuscitation of television viewers, to say nothing of the reaction of spectators at the matches, is a ridiculous representation

---

67. *The Irish Independent*, 31 May, 2005
68. *The Irish Times*, 8 June, 2002. Caption of piece by Tom Humphries
covering Argentina's 1-0 victory over England in the World Cup.
69. *The Guardian*, 6 August, 2007

of the religious concept and reality. The resurrection of Jesus did not entail a return to the earthly existence that he enjoyed prior to his passion, crucifixion and death, nor can it be equated to an effect in the experience of the disciples who had been with him throughout the last years of his earthly life. The resurrection remains in the realm of mystery and cannot be reduced.

Sporting references to heaven (and hell) run from basketball to cricket through Gaelic games to soccer. One that managed to combine both was the headline 'Cook finds heaven after his Ashes hell.' After the ill-fated Ashes series in Australia which Cook described as going through hell, his fifth Test century at the appropriately named Lord's cricket ground only serves to heighten the drama in drawing on eternal states of existence. Here heaven and hell are squeezed into insignificant interpretation. In 'Heavens above, what have I done?',[70] Simon Hattenstone imagines himself intervening to influence the fortunes of English cricket: 'But – and I know this sounds a tad messianic – I think I might have a direct line to him (or her) upstairs.' An accompanying drawing depicts a figure like God the Father above the clouds, attended by angels and holding the sports section in his right hand, while his left hand directs a bolt which bowls out (another) English player. However, the illogic of his imagined intercessory power is illustrated in his claim that 'sport and superstition have long gone hand in hand, and cricket is particularly susceptible to irrational belief systems'.[71] Eternal verities and the vagaries of English cricket are clearly not commensurable.

'Six trips to heaven.'[72] Simon Lewis lists a number of sporting events and venues in 2009 which include the Iditarod trail Sled Dog Race in Alaska, the Italy versus Republic of Ireland World Cup qualifier and the Athletics World Championships. The British and Irish Lions Tour 'offers the chance of redemption after the misery of the 2005 Test whitewash in New Zealand', which is infelicitous, if not insulting, in the face of opponents and hosts, South Africa and the author's advice to travellers to visit the Apartheid Museum in Johannesburg, the

70. *The Guardian*, 23 November, 2005
71. *The Guardian*, 23 November, 2005
72. *Irish Examiner*, 10 January, 2009

venue of the third Test. However, an accompanying word of warning (and wisdom) could well include the lines of Jerry L. Walls in the opening paragraph of his article on heaven: 'The highest happiness available is not limited to whatever pleasure and satisfaction we may enjoy in this life, either because of good fortune or our own successful efforts in pursuing and achieving it. Happiness so understood is very much a hit-or-miss affair, subject to the caprice of health, accidents, and the whims of others. At best, it is sporadic and partial.'[73]

Tom Humphries' reference to soccer's 'eternal mysteries' is echoed in many captions and comments concerning clubs and countries. The likening of Glasgow Celtic's achievement of a lucrative place in the play-off stages of the Champions League in 2007 to paradise is perceived and presented more in terms of reaching the promised land rather than resting in a state of eternal happiness and holiness. On the day of the 2007 FA Cup Final *Racing Post* placed an image of Wembley as 'Football Heaven' above pictures of Manchester United's Alex Ferguson and his Chelsea counterpart Jose Mourinho with their arms raised towards the sky as if in intercession or thanksgiving. Ironically the rivalry between the two clubs and their managers did not presage or promise peace, a value particularly associated with heaven. Indeed, following Chelsea's victory, their 'Blue Heaven' resonated with and reinforced the 'Red Devils' nickname of the team they had defeated.

Notwithstanding the difficulties inherent in interpreting 'the eternal mysteries' in sporting terms, the issue of sport in heaven (and hell) is not without worth. (While many might consider the question ludicrous, that is, incurring ridicule or laughter, it is worth recalling that the roots of the word, the Latin *ludus*/game, *ludere*/to play.) The English journalist, novelist and poet John Oxenham believed that there would be 'athletics of all kinds', boating, cricket, rugby, soccer and tennis as active, participatory sports in heaven though he denied any place for spectators, which may reflect the fact that he died in 1941 when television

---

73. In *The Oxford Handbook of Eschatology*, ed. Jerry L. Walls, Oxford: University Press, 2008, 399-412 at 399

was still in its developmental stage.[74] On the question of competitive sports in heaven the opinion of the grandchild of Lamar Hunt, creator of the AFL Super Bowl and called 'Games' since high school because of his devotion to sport, is worth offering: 'In his final illness, one of his grandchildren is said to have wondered whether there were football teams in heaven. "If there isn't", the little boy concluded, "I know Pappy will start one".'[75] The heavenly idea of sport may serve to emphasise intrinsic enjoyment and efforts at achievement, thus purifying it of aggression and advancing its appeal. Shorn of ideological interpretation and excessive economic interests, sport may be seen in aesthetic and idealistic terms, as the view of theologian Jurgen Moltmann suggests: 'Athletics have their own worth and meaning in themselves. In athletics and games one attempts not to make something but to present oneself. Athletes and players are not technicians but artists. They do not produce something that someone can use; they produce something at which one can rejoice ... Sports in service of country, sports in honour of socialism, sports as the greatest product of a capitalist, production-oriented society – these are the alienation, abuse, and destruction of the naturally human and thereby truly religious dimension of athletics. Whoever rides a horse should not ride for Germany but because he or she likes to ride and ride well.'[76] Freed for enjoyment and entertainment, the redemption of sport may result in it being included in the inexhaustible index of heavenly pleasures. On the other hand, a sporting hell might be interpreted in terms of an image supplied by the French existentialist writer Albert Camus, who once stated that everything he knew about morality he learned from football. In *The Myth of Sisyphus*, Camus views human existence in terms of the Greek myth about the fate of a former king of Corinth. His punishment in Hades for misdeeds on earth consists in the incessant rolling of a heavy stone up a hill. Every time he reaches the top the stone eludes his grip and rolls back to the bottom, only for Sisyphus to begin the

74. See Colleen McDannell and Bernhard Lang, *Heaven – A History*, New Haven: Yale University Press, 1988, 299-300
75. Rupert Cornwell, Obituary, *The Independent*, 15 December, 2006
76. *On Human Dignity*, London: SCM Press, quoted in *The Furrow*, 35 (December 1984), 751

inexorable process again. The futility and frustration of eternally finding that a putt rolls only to the edge of the cup, of a ball that always stops on the goal line, of shots that never become scores, to say nothing of relentless rows and fights on the field, are indeed intimations of immortality in a sporting hell.

Second Coming or Second Wind?

In churches across the world each Sunday Christians make their profession of faith popularly known as the Creed. Consisting of a series of articles, it articulates and asserts their faith convictions concerning God the Father, Son and Holy Spirit, Creator, Redeemer and Sanctifier, the church, resurrection of the dead and eternal life in 'the world to come'. The Creed consists in confessing belief, in summary form, in the core revelation of Christian faith concerning God's commitment to humanity and its history constructed on the cornerstones of creation, incarnation, resurrection and eschaton. Thus, the late eminent theologian and historian of Christian doctrine Jaroslav Pelikan declares, in his *magnum opus* that 'one of the most persistent features of all creeds and confessions of faith – so persistent as to be obvious and therefore in danger of being overlooked, especially in the aftermath of the modern controversies over liberal theology – is the utter seriousness with which they treat the issues of Christian doctrine as, quite literally, a matter of life and death, both here in time and hereafter in eternity.'[77] The seventh and final christological article of the Nicene-Constantinopolitan Creed confesses faith in Christ's second coming, which is linked to the eschatological judgement of those still on earth and the dead.

A difficulty with speaking of the second coming of Christ (in Greek *Parousia*) is the danger of seeing it separate from the incarnation. The image of the 'seamless garment' in the gospel of John (19:23) indicates that the Christ event is the complete (and completed) mystery of redemption which cannot be divided into discrete moments. As Zachary Hayes notes, 'In reality the parousia emphasises the saving presence of Christ to history, and the completion on a cosmic scale of the process begun in the

---

77. *Credo*, New Haven: Yale University Press, 2003, 70

incarnation, death and resurrection of Christ.'[78] Indeed a respectable theological tradition which enjoys solid scriptural basis (associated with Scotus) sees Christ as the crown of creation, the *parousia* as the perfection and fulfilment of God's plan from the beginning. In this theological trajectory the mystery of redemption in Christ unfurls from creation to the consummation of the world, covering that which both firstly comes forth from God and also that which returns to God. Thus, Andrew Chester states that 'The overriding perspective for Christian eschatology will be the recognition that the whole future and all time are set within God's control and his good purpose, and that this entails his bringing all human life, both individually and collectively, and the whole created order, to its true end, and liberating it from whatever holds it from its true fulfilment.'[79] Through this perspective the paschal mystery and *parousia* are, as it were, two sides of the one coin. There is one 'mystery', the saving plan of God and talk of 'eternal mysteries', in terms of faith or football, is theological denial.

In the space of a month in 2005 two Irish newspapers spoke of the 'second coming' in three different contexts involving the All-Ireland football championship: firstly, the semi-finals involving counties Cork, Dublin, Kerry, Tyrone; secondly, the replay of the Armagh versus Tyrone semi-final; thirdly, the final line-up between Kerry and Tyrone.[80] This sequence of references to second coming is more than stretching a point, a repetition which makes it meaningless. In relation to the Armagh versus Tyrone replay Eamon Sweeney invokes W. B. Yeats' poem *The Second Coming* in the hope that history would not repeat itself: 'Things falling apart – check. Mere anarchy – check. Worst full of passionate intensity – check. However, Yeats could be a hopeful old cove at times and the next part of the poem begins, "Surely some revelation is at hand; Surely the Second Coming is

---

78. 'Parousia' in J. Komonchak, M. Colllins, D. Lane, eds, *The New Dictionary of Theology*, Dublin: Gill and Macmillan, 1987, p 743

79. 'Eschatology', in Gareth Jones, ed, *The Blackwell Companion to Modern Theology*, Oxford: Blackwell Publishing, 2007, 256

80. 'Second Coming', *Irish Independent*, 27 August, 2005: 'The Second Coming of Tyrone and Armagh', *Sunday Independent*, 4 September, 2005; 'A Second Coming', *The Sunday Tribune*, 25 September, 2005

at hand." Which is what we have today. The second coming of Tyrone and Armagh. And do you know what? It doesn't seem so bad after all. Changing circumstances mean people are actually looking forward to it, thinking that it could well be the polar opposite of the last day out.'[81] Sweeney's references to 'changing circumstances' is the Achilles' heel of his analysis. In the colloquial language of sport a replay represents a whole new ballgame. Furthermore, if the first outing of the old opponents was a 'pretty dreadful spectacle', what reasonable prospect is there that the second coming together of the teams at this stage of the competition would be any different? The reduction of Yeats' poem with its apocalyptic overtones to the outcome of a football match represents more than a touch of journalistic licence. In addition to the obvious Christian reference, Sweeney includes Islam in his send-up of the television commentators as 'the Three Wise Monkeys of The Championship on Al-Jazeera.'[82] Having robbed Christian revelation of any relevance, this latter reference only serves to render the sense of *reductio ad absurdum* replete.

In the 2006-7 football season David Beckham hit the headlines for different reasons. After a much publicised transfer to the Los Angeles Galaxy side for the MLS season (set to begin in summer 2007) Beckham finished his career with Spanish side Real Madrid with a series of fine displays which served to restore the fortunes of the famous club, at least at national level. After being ignominiously dropped from the England squad for the 2008 European qualifiers after the country's exit from the 2006 World Cup finals, it was generally assumed that his international career was over. However, manager Steve McLaren recalled him to the squad and side for friendly and competitive

---

81. 'Forward thinking offers hope', *The Sunday Independent*, 4 September, 2005.

82. 'I use the term "Al-Jazeera", because to see these boys commenting is to experience the queasy sensation Salman Rushdie feels when the continuity announcer says, "And now, it's time for the Islamic Fundamentalist book review programme". The grave seriousness with which they take their subject (and more importantly themselves), their oracular delivery and sense of a hostile world, it's Mullah time alright.' *The Sunday Independent*, 4 September, 2005

fixtures in June 2007. Henry Winter summed up much of the press and public reaction with the caption 'McLaren slips up again in turning to a faded idol'.[83] On the same day Winter's colleague Sue Mott also considered Beckham's changed status with a photograph portraying Beckham with arms raised looking skywards with the caption 'Pray for a result', referring to his return to international duty in the following terms: 'The second coming of David Beckham is being treated like the Second Coming. Disciples on one side, non-believers on the other, exchanging hyperbole and spite respectively ... [with] David a) the saviour of England or b) falls short of his trumpeted genius.'[84] Believing that his recall only served to highlight the straitened state of the English football side, Mott concluded that the country needed a team, not an individual.

Beckham played a key role in both England's 1-1 draw with Brazil and their 3-0 defeat of Estonia with the quality of his trademark crosses which were converted into goals by his colleagues. Hailed as a hero who had assured his international future, whose 'latest resurrection is complete', Beckham's restored self-confidence was blazoned by the headline 'I can play on for years, says reborn Beckham.'[85] Given Beckham's celebrity status, counted in his capacity to capture column inches through public devotion to consumerism and his classification in messianic, salvific and iconic categories, it is not surprising that his return to international ranks should be interpreted in eschatological terms, though this expectation of the English team tends to end in tears rather than triumph. Reference to him as the 'soccer-Christ'[86] beggars belief in the Davidic genealogy that grounds much of the christology of the New Testament.

'Out of the darkness ... and into the light'[87]

These paragraph headings from a piece by Kieran Shannon on Tipperary's defeat by neighbours Waterford in the quarter-final

83. *The Daily Telegraph*, 29 May, 2007

84. 'Beckham LA epic reveals England's weakened state', *The Daily Telegraph*, 29 May, 2007

85. *The Daily Telegraph*, 8 June, 2007

86. Russell Brand, *The Guardian*, 9 June, 2007

87. *The Sunday Tribune*, 7 July, 2007

of the All-Ireland hurling championship highlight the question of the redemption of sport. Image of darkness and light have often been employed to express both the need for redemption and transition to it, a theology that finds its classical treatment in the Gospel of John with its contrast of light and darkness leading to confession of Jesus Christ as the 'Light of the world' which 'the darkness could not overcome'. The need for redemption is rooted in and results from the recognition that there is a wound or hurt, gap or hole at the heart of human experience and the re-alisation that humanity itself cannot heal or fill this need within history. This search for wholeness and fulfilment is both vari-ously and vicariously spoken of and symbolised in different cultural forms and facets of restlessness and alienation. The real-isation that redemption is not within the reach of human achievement but available as grace was originally and classically formulated by St Paul. The line of songwriter and singer Leonard Cohen – 'the crack that lets the light in' – lyrically lays the ground for a soteriology which, in Christian terms, sees the possibility of release in the entry of God to history. In the words of Thomas Marsh, the human need and hope for redemption have an inbuilt 'intimation of incarnation'.[88]

Traditionally Christian theology related redemption to the events and effects of the passion, crucifixion and death of Jesus Christ. While this approach accentuates the reality of human evil/sinfulness and the need for its elimination, it runs the risk of reducing the value of the incarnation and the vision of the es-chaton. Emphasis on the darkness carries the danger of exclud-ing or eliminating entirely the possibility of enlightenment. A re-newed theology of God's mercy and justice in relation to history integrates the human dimensions of darkness and light, the need for liberation and the call to salvation into the process of the paschal mystery as the passion and passage of the world to God through the Christ-event. Gerald O'Collins states this syn-thetic soteriology succinctly: 'Nowadays it is more usual and convincing to acknowledge that the redemption of human be-ings and their world was, is and will be brought about through the entire Christ-story: by the incarnation, life, suffering, death

---

88. 'Saviour of the World', *The Furrow*, 43 (April 1992), 201

and resurrection, the sending of the Holy Spirit, and the transformation to come at the end of history.'[89] This redemptive vision
retains room both for the need for liberation of human existence
in its different historical dimensions and the partial experience
of 'righteousness, peace and joy in the Holy Spirit' (Rom 14:17).
At the same time it holds out the prospect for salvation as the
eternal sharing of humanity in the holiness of God, without
denying the possibility that earthly life will be taken over and
transformed fully after the end of the world.

Redeeming Sport
The redemptive potentiality of sport has often been referred to
by journalists, as for example, the statement by Tim Rich that
'one of sport's greatest qualities is the opportunities it offers for
redemption' which appeared in a piece entitled 'Italy play game
of redemption' the day after their victory over France following
a penalty shoot-out in the 2006 soccer World Cup final.[90] On the
same day Chris McGrath comments on the changed fortunes of
trainer Henry Cecil, who returned to the Classic winners enclos-
ure after seven years when his second horse Light Shift won the
2007 Vodafone Oaks: 'If the capricious nature of his vocation
seemed to destroy Henry Cecil, yesterday it proved his salvation
… After an 18-month battle against cancer, the exotic, faded genius
of the legendary trainer Henry Cecil flickered back to life at
Epsom. One of the most cherished figures in Turf history had
made a poignant comeback after seven years in the wilderness
… Light Shift was considered a mere understudy to Passage of
Time, who had been hailed as Cecil's redeemer and started
favourite.'[91] Notwithstanding the confusion of categories and
theomorphism in treating a race horse as a redeemer, the names
'Light Shift' and 'Passage of Time' assume a certain poetic ap-
propriateness in the context of celebrating Cecil's return to
Classic form.

Writing on the 2007 Champions League Final between AC
Milan and Liverpool, Henry Winter remarks that 'The joy of
sport is its opportunity for redemption, a chance to right

---

89. *Jesus Our Redeemer*, v.
90. *The Daily Telegraph*, 10 July, 2006
91. *The Independent*, 2 June, 2007

wrongs, whether perceived or real.'[92] This sentence follows the statement that 'if AC Milan had their revenge in Athens, Liverpool had their regrets'. The Italian team squandered a 3-0 lead against the same opponents in 2005 and subsequently lost a penalty shoot-out in what has been described as 'The Miracle of Istanbul'. (Melodrama rather than the miraculous would be a more fitting description of that admittedly memorable match, at least for Liverpool supporters.) Winter's words invite theological reflection for what they reveal about the relation between sport and redemption. Firstly, the relegation of the enjoyment of sport to an opportunity for reversal of fortune is both a fact and feeling that many fans might want to contest. Sport is at least equally about engagement and entertainment as about success. Secondly, redemption in its theological meaning cannot be merely reduced to moral categories and the contest of good versus evil, right versus wrong. It is difficult to describe defeat in sport in terms of wrongdoing, except in cases where a game or match is obviously thrown through cheating or lack of commitment. Thirdly, the reality of redemption does not result from human effort(s). Accompanying Winter's article there is a photograph taken after the final whistle depicting Liverpool striker Dirk Kuyt lying on the ground with his hands over his head while the AC Milan player Kaka is shown on his knees with eyes closed wearing an undershirt with the words 'I belong to Jesus'. As an expression of belief in redemption the scene of the brilliant Brazilian international here suggests reverence and thanksgiving rather than the taking of revenge. The rematch of the 2005 final opponents generated the proverbial forest of newsprint analysis and anticipation. Features on the Liverpool goalkeeper Pepe Reina – 'Keeper of the family faith'[93] – focus on the fact that he was following the footsteps of his father Miguel who had kept goal for Athletico Madrid in their 2-0 defeat by Bayern Munich in the 1974 European Cup final. The line that 'for one Spanish family, Athens 2007 is an opportunity for redemption'[94] highlights the link made by the media between sport and salv-

---

92. *The Daily Telegraph*, 25 May, 2007
93. *The Daily Telegraph*, 3 May, 2007
94. 'Athens is a family affair for Reinas', *The Irish Times*, 3 May, 007

ation which, however, in such terms is not only without risk but also ultimately dependent on the result at the close of play.

Winter refers to the theme of righting wrong(s) in a cleverly worked piece which weaved together the penalty kick misses of former England international soccer player Stuart Pearce and that of Reading player Leroy Lita in the country's under-21 side under Pearce's management: 'Pearce was understandably sympathetic towards Lita, having himself endured heartache against West Germany at Italia 90. Maybe the Reading striker can follow him and find redemption with a later successful kick. "We don't blame Leroy", Pearce said. "Players are people, not machines".'[95] If redemption is reduced to the rectifying of wrongs and failures that are non-moral in nature, such as missed scoring opportunities in sport or errors that cannot be evaluated ethically, the concept is theologically blasphemous and aesthetically banal. Ironically this may serve to restore the meaning of redemption to the trans-ethical experience of reconciliation where its true religious meaning may be applied and available to persons who stand in need of forgiveness in furtherance of the divine process of the earthly liberation and eschatological salvation of humanity and its history.

Winter explicitly links sport and salvation with religion in his profile of Burnley football club and community: 'Burnley using "new religion" to save local community'.[96] Describing the demise of a traditional way of life in which work and worship, community and sport were woven together, Winter refers to the generation of young people who have remained whose lives are governed by a complex of 'low esteem, low horizons and low wages'. The role of football in the town is likened to the power and influence that the church and religion played up to recent decades in promoting identity and integration. Quoting community and club figures to the effect that 'football is like a new religion, like the church was 20-30 years ago' and 'to call a football club like Burnley the new church is a great analogy', Winter warms to the theme that sport, and soccer in particular, could play a prominent role in addressing issues like racism and root-

---

95. 'England rue Lita lapse', *The Daily Telegraph*, 12 June, 2007. England played a 0-0 draw against the Czech Republic.
96. *The Daily Telegraph*, 28 April, 2007

lessness. While Winter's concern for the community in question is commendable and their liberation from economic difficulty and emotional distress is constitutive of the Christian mission for justice in the world, collapsing the concept of salvation only contributes to the community's (and humanity's) impoverishment in the long run.

How the ethical and evangelical dimensions of 'close-knit communities where everybody knew everybody in the street, people looked out for each other, and everyone congregated in church on the Sunday' and the moral-theological dimensions of redemption they embodied, are to be expressed and effected in the secular church of sport is evidently beyond the comprehension or concern of commentators like Winter. Moreover, such short term recourse by the sporting media to Christian tradition and theology is achieved without any accompanying reflection on how long and to what extent this ransacking of religious belief and the language of redemption the churches can continue.

'Even God won't save you today'

This banner at the England versus Ireland rugby international at Croke Park in 2007 recalls the faithful imagination which furnished 'God bless the Sacred Heart' for the nearby North Circular Road during the 1932 Eucharistic Congress. While on a surface level this sporting slogan seems innocuous, a bit of Irish fun at the expense of the English, interpretations of it might mean that there is no connection at all between sport and spirituality or that there is a divine preferential option for one side over the other. At a surface level, the latter option is dismissed by description of the fickleness of the sporting gods depriving Ireland at the same venue two weeks previously when France grabbed a last minute try against the so-called run of play to rob the host nation of the possibility of a greatly coveted Grand Slam. At a deeper level, the question of the relation between sport and redemption raises issues about the identity and interpretation of both.

On occasion players, coaches and columnists refer to sport as redemption in qualified, limited terms: Michael 'Babs' Keating mentions a 'form of redemption'; in his report on the 2006 World Cup final George Caulkin calls Italy's victory after a penalty shoot-out 'redemption of differing sorts';[97] Olympic walker Jamie Costin is profiled in 'A redemption of sorts'[98] while Laois footballer Beano McDonald complained 'to an extent we have redeemed ourselves but not as we'd like'[99] (ironically the profile piece was penned 'Full of Beans'); Henry Winter salutes Newcastle United's Joey Barton's return to the football pitch from prison in 'Barton enjoys spot of redemption'.[100] The Christian doctrine of redemption does not admit of qualification or limitation. Ultimately it is a condition of all or nothing, in eschatological terms eternal election or condemnation, heaven or hell. Redemption refers to the absolute outcome or end of human life, articulating a theological anthropology that sets the whole person in the contours of earthly and eternal existence. (The theory of *Apocatatstatis* – literally, the universal restoration – anticipates the eventuality that in eternity all people will be saved.) 'An attitude of redemption' (Pope John Paul II) is absolute and does not admit of degrees in God's dealing with humanity, for God's involvement in Christ is total. Christian theology is founded on the conviction and claim that, in Christ's paschal mystery, the Son of God has overcome limitation in all its dimensions, viz. suffering, sinfulness and death. If redemption is to be related to sport, the question of its limitation is linked to the nature of sport, that is, to the meaning of sport as activity and the measure of its achievement or lack thereof.

Reference to ratios of redemption in sport raises the issue of the relation between success and salvation. Former flat champion jockey Gordon Richards claims that the key to success was 'The Will to Win', while a sportswear company advertises their gear with the marketing motto 'Impossible is nothing'. Considering

---

97. 'Having been outplayed by France for most of an intriguing night, Italy dispatched all five of their penalties. They had taken their leave from three of the past four competitions by that hated method, including by France in 1998.' *The Times*, 10 July, 2006

98. *Sunday Tribune*, 21 December, 2008

99. *The Sunday Times*, 30 July, 2007

100. *The Daily Telegraph*, 29 October, 2008. 'Football moves in strange ways, or Strangeways in Joey Barton's case, and the controversial midfielder celebrated his first start since leaving jail in Manchester by converting the penalty that set Newcastle United on their way to a hugely important victory.'

the final round of games in the Spanish 2006-7, season Glenn Moore comments that 'Beckham has always been driven by the desire for redemption' and that should he manage to assist Real Madrid in winning *La Liga* in his last game for the club it would be 'the ultimate redemption for a footballer obsessed with proving he did not come to Madrid to sell shirts'.[101] Redemption is equated with success in each of these quotes and if success were simply substituted for redemption they would have the same meaning. The drive to achievement and attainment is a basic human instinct that is incarnated in a multitude of arenas and activities. As a positive force for growth and development of individuals and groups it is capable of both generating and contributing to the common good of the human race. Columnist Nicky Campbell considers the dialectic of desire for success and doubt, an inner competition in the minds of competitors, the zone where the zenith could only be stated as a sense of the sacred and transcendent: 'Sportsmen and women strive for it, yearn for it and revere it like medieval peasants catching a whiff of incense from the holy sacrament. It is an illusive promise of something beyond, something transcendent – but this is not some Never Neverland'.[102] The confusion of categories – psychological and spiritual, of senses – smell and sight, to say nothing of the contradiction between 'illusive' and 'Neverland' – casts into relief the cost of considering success in sport as salvation or redemption. His 'devilish paradox' – 'if you want to win, you must stop thinking about winning' is delivered as a Zen-like punchline. His quote from sports psychologist Pete Cohen that 'sportsmen put so much meaning into what they do and into the consequences of victory and defeat but it is literally self-defeating' logically leads to the question that if such is the case why they bother to compete in the first place. In the human journey from birth to death, achievement and attainment need to be set alongside frustration and failure, for success does not represent the whole story. England cricket coach Duncan Fletcher introduces a note of realism into the discussion of sporting success by

101. *The Irish Examiner,* 16 June, 2007
102. 'The shadow of a doubt breaks the sweet spell of success', *The Guardian,* 24 May, 2007

quoting a modern day saint: 'Mother Teresa said that when you are successful you win some unfaithful friends and some genuine enemies. I am quite philosophical about it.'[103] Mark Reason's piece on the possibility of Greg Norman winning the Masters at the age of 54 probes the meaning of sporting 'redemption': 'in '96 he was set for redemption. He took a six-shot lead into the final round ... In perhaps the most famous implosion in golfing history Norman was hunted down by [Nick] Faldo and torn apart. Norman took it like a man and the public loved him for it. Norman said last week: "I was elevated in the public eye by losing, not by winning. That changed my life. No matter where I walked, somebody would make a comment about how it changed their life toward their son or daughter by the way I handled it. So I won in a lot of ways, but I didn't win the green jacket".'[104] As the former Irish international rugby player and Lion great Willie John McBride once remarked, 'It matters a great deal who is going to win, but not at all who won.'

The danger of describing sporting success in terms of salvation or redemption is twofold, theological and anthropological. Redemption is not reducible to the result of a cosmic contest conceived in Manichean dualistic terms, the final score in the game of good versus evil. God is not involved in competition match with humanity, for given the fact of creation from the outset that would mean a mismatch. Redemption is not the result of or even reconciliation of metaphysical rivalries. It is the revelation, the reaching out of God to humanity, a movement commenced in creation, communicated in incarnation and carried to completion in resurrection and eschaton. Redemption is the realisation or restoration of relationship between God and people. As a call and not a contest, redemption is a gift to be accepted rather than a goal to be attained. Redemption is neither a Promethean grabbing of the Olympian fire or a Pelagian pursuit of self-perfection. To see sporting success as salvation, and reckoning redemption in terms of the right result, sets forth both a

---

103. 'Revealed: how Ice Man and Mother Teresa saved English cricket', *The Guardian*, 13 February, 2007
104. '*Shark* back in the hunt for Masters', *The Sunday Telegraph*, 11 January, 2009

false image of God and a faulty interpretation of human existence and ethics. Redemption refers to the transformation of the
whole human reality where good and evil, success and failure
are not dialectically resolved but recapitulated and reconciled
through the paschal mystery of Christ. The problem of perceiving success, in sport as in other areas of life, as redemption is the
risk of (mis)representing God as vindictive, who values only the
victorious. In such a perspective redemption leaves no room for
opponents, either on earth or in eternity. In his analysis of the
movie *Star Wars*, Robert Jewett refers to two gospels, rival versions of redemption: 'For *Star Wars*, it consists of the restoration
of a hierarchical order ... For Paul, [redemption] consists in the
restoration of an egalitarian order including male and female,
slave and free, Greek and Jew, educated and uneducated. It is
based on a new relationship that all persons may have with God,
based on faith rather than inheritance or merit. It involves freedom from unrighteousness, sin and death, which afflict everyone. There are no passive spectators and no incorrigible enemies
in the new age established by Paul's gospel.'[105] For God success
is the society of his sons and daughters gained through Christ
and gathered in the Spirit into the Kingdom of heaven.

'A matter of life and death'
Former Liverpool manager Bill Shankly's line that 'some people
think football is a matter of life and death. I don't like that attitude, I can assure them it is much more serious than that'[106] has
ironically assumed almost immortal status in the history of
sports quotes. While the terrible loss of his arch-rival Matt
Busby's 'Babes' in the Munich air disaster (as the young
Manchester United team was on the brink of a breakthrough in
the European Cup in the late 1950s) has tended over the decades
to capture the imagination and compassion of sportspeople
throughout the world, the tragic loss of its fans at both the
Hillsborough and Heysel stadia in the 1980s has literally taken
its toll on the club Shankly loved and devoted his life to.

---

105. *Saint Paul at the Movies: The Apostle's Dialogue with American
Culture*, Westminster, KY: John Knox Press, 1993, 22-23
106. Quoted in *Cassell's Sports Quotations*, 321

Generally considered to have concluded his managerial career too early, before Liverpool scaled the heights of European cup success, Shankly had plenty of time to ruefully realise that the expectations he engendered through his passionate commitment to the game as player and coach ended in failure to deliver what columnist Keith Duggan described as 'clubs and fans want[ing] managers to be leaders and faith healers, they want them to deliver salvation'.[107]

Others have been more realistic and rational in their reflection on sport and its place in the scale of life and death issues. Writing days after a bus crash which cost the lives of five young schoolgirls on their way home from school in Navan, former Meath footballer and television pundit Colm O'Rourke disagrees with Shankly's assessment: 'When we talk of football then, it is in the context of sport, nothing more. I have often remarked that what Bill Shankly said was a humorous throwaway remark, taken seriously by some who don't understand that it is still only a game. Of course it must be passionate and a man must give everything in pursuit of victory; he must also be able to accept bitter disappointments as they are the inevitable consequences of striving for the top. But there is no tragedy or disaster in a football game. And even if those terms are used, it is not with the same meaning as the struggle for life – and should never be intended as such.'[108] On the same day *The Observer* notes on its front page that the resignation of Glasgow Celtic manager Martin O'Neill (who had restored the fortunes of the club) in order to take time to look after his wife Geraldine who was ill with cancer, 'reminded fans, many of who do indeed see the beautiful game as a matter of life and death, how utterly trivial it can be'.[109] Shortly before these two statements, Michael Johnson critically weighed the effects of Hurricane Katrina against the outcome of the New Orleans Saints home game against the New York Giants which had to be transferred to that

---

107. *The Irish Times*, 3 December, 2005
108. 'Tragic events remind us that football is still only a game', *The Sunday Independent*, 29 May, 2005. In the same vein or vision Martin Breheny's piece 'Perspective please – sport is not a matter of life and death', *The Irish Independent*, 4 April, 2007
109. 'O'Neill's last hurrah', 29 May, 2005

city: 'I commend the NFL and those players who donated money to the victims, but for those same victims' loss and tragic experience to be trivialised by stating that a football game would ease their pain was absolutely ridiculous.'[110] Roy Collins states that for Italian striker, Alessandro Del Piero, the venue for the 2006 World Cup final 'Berlin's Olympic stadium will represent a kind of sanctuary, a place where all the madness associated with the world's biggest sporting occasion will seem normal and familiar compared to the problems to which his mind must return when the final whistle blows'.[111] The death of Pakistan coach Bob Woolmer after the country's shock defeat by newcomers Ireland at the 2007 World Cup in the West Indies created consternation among the cricket confraternity and beyond with claims even of murder. At his memorial service in South Africa, Woolmer's home for many years, Professor Tim Noakes, co-author of the Englishman's forthcoming training manual, reminded the audience that ' Bob's favourite maxim for those confronting a cricketing failure was "Gentlemen, always remember that it is only a game".'[112]

Adverting to issues of life and death in the context of sporting activity means asking about its meaning and purpose. Notwithstanding O'Rourke's opinion that Shankly's statement was somewhat tongue in cheek – though one can imagine the fiery Scotsman fiercely contesting that claim as if it were a cup match – sport is seen by some commentators as symbolic of the crucible of life and the human condition that has its earthly conclusion in death. The element of contingency has been expressed in terms of the so-called 'bounce of a ball', that is, as being the difference between victory and defeat. Former England cricket captain Mike Atherton adopts a more matter of fact, existential assessment: 'Indeed, surely the whole point of sport is to act as a necessary counterpoint to the grim realities of life. We know that death is a part of life because we see it, in one form or another, every day. And sport, like drugs and alcohol, provides a neces-

---

110. 'NFL trivialised pain of New Orleans', *The Daily Telegraph*, 20 May, 2005
111. 'A matter of life and death and a lot more besides', *The Sunday Independent*, 9 July, 2006
112. *The Times*, 5 April, 2007

sary escape from the absurdity of everyday existence – and thankfully, most of the time, without any of the side effects. It gives us the chance to experience the best that life has to offer, usually without serious consequences. We win, we lose, and we go home and get on with life.'[113] Tom Humphreys' comment that sport 'begins in hope and ends in despair, it's finite'[114] touches the topic of transcendence and sport. Is sport the perusal of, in Humphreys' previous phrase, 'eternal mysteries' or, to borrow the words of Patrick Kavanagh, to 'snatch out of time the passionate transitory'?[115]

In her article on 'Redemption' in *The Blackwell Companion to Modern Theology*, Esther Reed states that 'The unfamiliar language of "redemption" in everyday discourse (except for the redemption of gift certificates against the cost of a book, or financial bonds from a stock-exchange) creates for us, perhaps, inhibitions as regards interpretation for the present day.'[116] In response one might wonder what magazines and newspapers she has been reading with their multiple references to redemption. While theologians might exhibit inhibitions (thankfully a professional trademark) in interpreting and applying talk of redemption today, such reservation is not a quality readily recognised in some journalists and others associated with sport as their many allusions to salvation and redemption attest. The reasons for this fascination or fixation with the language of faith and theology and the possibility of redeeming it require analysis and reflection in the context of the dialogue between church and society, faith and culture.

113. 'Glorious futility of sport balances the grim reality', *The Sunday Telegraph*, 25 March, 2007
114. *The Irish Times*, 10 May, 2003
115. 'The Hospital', *Collected Poems*, London : Martin Brian & O'Keefe 1972, 153.
116. Gareth Jones,ed, Oxford: Blackwell Publishing, 2007, 227

CHAPTER EIGHT

Sport, Faith and Culture

'Fragments of biblical quotation continue to litter the transactions of contemporary life: half-remembered parables and scriptural figures shadow dance in our shared but near amnesiac cultural consciousness. Language deemed sacred is rarely contained by the narrow spaces of organised belief.'[1]

'Culture is concerned with value and meaning expressed in material realities – in words and sounds and shapes and images. The wonder is that they can bear and communicate such profundities. Religion is concerned with transcendent, spiritual truths which must be expressed in limited and inadequate words and rituals.'[2]

Faith seeking culture
The relationship of faith to culture is crucial for Christian self-understanding, that is, theology. The original Christian movement emerged from the matrix of Judaism in the years counted and called after the birth of its founder, Jesus of Nazareth. Making its way into the countries and cultures of the Mediterranean the Christian gospel encountered the legacy of Greece and the world of the Roman Empire. The proclamation of the good news, the incarnation of God in Jesus Christ through the paschal mystery of his life, death and resurrection which empowered the experience of salvation in the Holy Spirit, the church(es) occurred among people with, in Shakespeare's

---

1. Andrew Tate, 'Postmodernism' in John F. A. Sawyer, ed, *The Blackwell Companion to the Bible and Culture*, Oxford: Blackwell Publishing, 2006, 515-532 at 517
2. Donal Murray, 'Faith and Culture: A Complex Relationship', in Eoin G. Cassidy, ed, *Faith and Culture in the Irish Context*, Dublin: Veritas, 1996, 16-34 at 25

phrase, 'a local habitation and a name'. This process of evangelisation embraced elements of the expressions and ethos of Homer
and Horace, Aristotle and Augustus, Greek philosophy and
Roman law. Indeed the doctrines of Christian faith concerning
Christ (christology) and his relationship to God (Trinity) developed out of this process of involvement with the Greco-Roman
worldview through its philosophy and language. Conscious of
its universal calling to 'make disciples of all nations' (Mt 28:19)
Christianity down through the centuries has become immersed
in – and on occasion even identified with – the particularity of
human living in history that is heuristically interpreted as culture. This process of inculturation retains an inevitable though
indispensable tension for Christian faith and its universal meaning in relation to the particularity of culture(s).

Calling culture 'a shorthand for living' Eileen Kane describes
it in the following categories: 'The common, learned way of life
shared by members of a society; not only the society's art and
sciences, but also its law, political organisation, patterns of child
raising, methods of making and using tools, ways of resolving
dispute, in short all its shared patterns and content of ideas, values and behaviour.'[3] However, the indexical relationship between culture and society is no longer a given fact and feature.
Most societies today, especially in the Western world, are no
longer monocultural. 'Multiculturalism' has become the measure, if not indeed the mantra, of most European societies. In
September 2007 a survey showed that more than one-fifth of primary school pupils in England come from ethnic minority backgrounds while one-in-ten of students in both primary and secondary schools there do not have English as a mother tongue.[4]
The presence of a common and shared 'way of life' in particular
societies is increasingly a goal to be pursued rather than a reality
to be presumed. Evidence of alienation from the so-called majority culture and its expression in attendant violence, particularly
by youths, has been displayed in abundance in recent years in
several European societies. Issues of immigration and integra-

---

3. *Window on the World – An Essay on Culture*, Baile Átha Cliath:
Clódhanna Teoranta 1983, 2
4. 'Schools show the new make-up of Britain', *The Times*, 28 September,
2007

tion are increasingly political issues within the countries that constitute the European Union.

Acknowledging that 'cultures are changeable, and, in fact, are constantly changing', Kane gives the quaint example of the ironically entitled 'Holy Hour' in Dublin pub culture: 'One of [its] original functions was to deal with the problem of getting men out of pubs to go home to their dinners; now, however, fewer men go home to dinner and those who do certainly would not be doing it from 2.30 to 3.30.'[5] Notwithstanding the gender qualification, the 'Holy Hour' has long since given way to the 'Happy Hour' and the increasing problem, especially in towns and cities at weekends, is to get people to go home or to their hotels between 2.30 and 3.30 am rather than pm. The changing face and form of cultures can be described in terms of their de-traditionalisation, whereby a shared sense, symbolically and literally, of meaning and morality makes, or more likely gives, way to modes of a more individual 'pick and choose' mentality and manner of living. Comprised of its component categories of consciousness, communication and consumption, culture has become a fluctuating currency whose value is in a state of constant change where standards of calculation and comparison are conspicuously difficult to see, let alone to set.

In St Anselm's classic definition, theology is *fides quaerens intellectum*, faith seeking understanding. This intelligence of faith is integral, involving heart, mind and imagination in its investigation of God and humanity and their intersection in history and hope. 'In reality it is only in the mystery of the Word made flesh that the mystery of humanity truly becomes clear ... Christ the Lord, the new Adam, in the very revelation of the mystery of the Father and of his love, fully reveals humanity to itself and brings to light its most high calling.'[6] The threefold reference to 'mystery' in this brief passage – to God the Father, Jesus Christ and humanity – turns on the fact and faith that it is Christ who both bears and bridges divinity and humanity thereby disclosing their truth. Theology and anthropology, the mystery of God and the meaning of humanity, are inextricably linked in 'the Word

---

5. *Window on the World*, 15
6. *Church in the Modern World*, par 22, in Flannery, ed, *Documents of Vatican II*

made flesh'. The history of Jesus of Nazareth is the unique 'place' where the universal outreach of God to humanity is both represented and realised. The hinge of Christian faith is thus the incarnation, the personal identification of the Son of God with humanity, 'the Word became flesh and lived among us' (Jn 1:14). This 'absolute involvement of God with humanity' is the foundation of theology. To employ a housing metaphor, the floors built on this belief represent the veracity and variety symbolised by the term 'faith and culture(s).'

The Second Vatican Council (1962-5) articulated, in its closing document, *Church in the Modern World*, the rationale for the relation of Christian faith and the human reality that is the world: 'The joy and hope, the grief and anguish of the people of our time, especially of those who are poor or afflicted in any way, are the joy and hope, the grief and anguish of the followers of Christ as well.'[7] Stating that it 'longs to set forth the way it understands the presence and function of the church in the world of today' the Council seeks to connect this understanding with the universalist agenda coming from modernity, especially in relation to the promotion of solidarity, the perception of human dignity and the pursuit of justice and peace. Seeing and stating a sense of continuity between the orders of creation and redemption, nature and grace, the pastoral Council emphasises an engagement of faith and culture in expressions that are both existential and evangelical. Stressing that the revelation of God in Christ reached out to 'the whole of humanity' the church aimed to both address and answer 'the most fundamental of all questions: "What is humanity? What is the meaning of suffering, evil, death which has not been eliminated by all this progress? What is the purpose of these achievements, purchased at so high a price? What can man contribute to society? What can he expect from it? What happens after this earthly life is ended?"'[8] In the Council's view the relationship between church and world offers the possibility of collaboration and dialogue between them. The adaptation of the gospel message to different audiences throughout history is a corollary of the process of evangelisation

---

7. *Church in the Modern World*, par 1
8. *Church in the Modern World*, par 10

which, while listening to 'the many voices of our times' seeks to discern and 'interpret them in the light of the divine Word, in order that the revealed truth may be more deeply penetrated, better understood, and more suitably presented.'[9]

Chapter 2 of the document is devoted to the theme of faith and culture in its many dimensions. The contribution of culture(s) towards the greater humanisation of the world is acknowledged and accepted as both a foundation for and a fruit of the church's own mission in the world. In a prescient passage the process of globalisation and its implications for culture are spelled out: 'There are nowadays many opportunities favourable to the development of a universal culture, thanks especially to the boom in book publication and new techniques of cultural and social communication.' The same paragraph sees the possibility that sport can not only promote but 'create harmony of feeling even on the level of the community as well as fostering friendly relations between men of all classes, countries and races.'[10] The criterion for a human and Christian consideration of culture consists in 'a deeply thought evaluation of [its] meaning and knowledge of the human person'. (However, Tracey Rowland is critical of the treatment here of culture and its connection to faith.[11]) While hanging onto the principle that whatever is authentically human is not alien to the truth of Christianity and the task of its mission in and for the world, the Council holds that 'faith throws a new light on all things and makes known the full ideal which God has set for humanity, thus guiding the mind towards solutions that are fully human'.[12]

There is a strong note of Christian realism in the Council's reflections on the world and culture(s). Human activity in the

---

9. *Church in the Modern World* , par 44
10. *Church in the Modern World,* par 61
11. 'Although the authors of *Gaudium et spes* [*Church in the Modern World*] acknowledged that the concept of "culture" is multifaceted, they nonetheless failed to identify precisely what they meant with each usage of the term. The definition that appears in the document is in paragraph 53 … is extremely broad in coverage, but shallow in analysis, and not explicitly related to the grace-nature problematic as one would expect in a theological document.' *Culture and the Thomist Tradition,* London: Rouledge, 2007, 20
12. *Church in the Modern World,* par 11

world is recognised as being engaged in a conflict with the powers of evil throughout the course of the history of the human race which involves a constant struggle for integrity and moral identity. While acknowledging the (relative) autonomy of earthly realities, the Council is aware of the biblical notion of 'world' which brings to the fore the frustration, falling short and failure which so often characterise and compromise the human condition and its cultures. Situations that fail both the service of God and human solidarity are properly portrayed as sinful and in need of purification and perfection. A close reading of the Council documents, and in particular *Church in the Modern World*, corrects any impression of a naïve and false optimism in the face of human and historical realities. Written less than twenty years after the end of the Second World War, in an era of increasing tension between Cold War superpowers, the Council Fathers felt the tension between human joy/hope and grief/anguish and the tragedy traced between them. The paschal mystery of Christ's life, death and resurrection is the Council's – and church's – response to the 'signs of the times'. This realistic theology reaffirms that while the consummation of the course of human history intends a completion which involves a correction, that is, a process both of perfection and purification, Christian faith seeks incarnation in the form of loving activity in and for the world through involvement with human culture(s). This faith in and love for cultures creates a climate of hope though which 'we will find them once again, cleansed this time from the stain of sin, illuminated and transfigured, when Christ presents to his Father an eternal and universal kingdom of truth and life, a kingdom of holiness and grace, a kingdom of justice, love and peace'.[13]

Cultures seeking faith

At its root the issue of 'faith and culture' interprets the relation between transcendence and immanence. Theologically this traces the dovetailing of nature and grace, the dialogue between the created order and the offer of God's communication in Christ and the Holy Spirit. Thus 'faith and culture' corresponds

---

13. *Church in the Modern World*, par 39

to the search for a theological anthropology which takes human experience as the arena for evangelisation and God's entry into its history. The relation of faith and culture can be considered in terms of four models: correlation, condemnation, conflation and call/challenge. The correlation model corresponds to an analysis of 'faith in culture' while that of condemnation is convertible to 'faith above or against culture'. The conflation model eschews this counter-cultural polemic and removes the relation by effectively reducing religious faith to culture. Ironically this interpretation may reflect an earlier version which collapsed the relation in the opposite direction, effectively equating culture with an epiphenomenon of faith. The call/challenge model considers the cultural context as a given, though this is conceived as the ground where the seed of the Word can be sown. This approach places the central Christian category of conversion at the core of the church's message and mission.

Correlation is the correspondence between faith and culture which considers the questions of the human mind and desires of the human heart as effectively answered in the address or response of revelation. This method of dialogue means a dovetailing between evangelisation and experience. This involves a reading of the 'signs of the times' and a recognition of human civilisation. Conversation constitutes the economy of this exchange which envisages a concordance or harmony between church and culture, heaven and history. Theological warrant and witness for this are found in the wisdom of sayings such as 'grace presupposes and perfects nature' and *nihil humanum a me alienum* (nothing that is human is foreign to me), where the truly human stands at the threshold of transcendence. However, critics of this perspective consider the teaching of the Second Vatican Council, especially *Church in the Modern World*, to be overly optimistic in its assessment of human nature and history and its allowance of an earthly autonomy that has alienated itself from the Absolute.

Condemnation (not surprisingly) considers the dis-continuity between Word and world. 'Culture' is considered to be an ambivalent concept, a compromise of high standards at the cost of the transcendental qualities of truth, goodness and beauty. In contrast to a historically 'high culture', popular and mass culture have created an environment where even religious symbols are 'easily vulgarised, stripped of depth, and reduced to decorative functions, or to patterns of entertainment and lifestyle enhancement' ... This tendency is evident, for example, when the crucifix and rosary beads become a fashion accessory for celebrities from Madonna to David Beckham or when mass-produced statues of the Buddha feature as prominently in garden centres as wood chips and super-phosphate.'[14] The price of this compromise is precisely the point proponents of this view emphasise, as patterns of consumption and commodification become the criteria for constituting and continuing personal and cultural identity. This is captured in the words of Mary Grey – *tesco, ergo sum* – where its connotations of purchase and possession provide the logic of this cultural *zeitgeist*.[15] However, critics of this 'faith above/against culture' approach accuse it of escape rather than engagement. They assert that the gospel is not a ghetto, a home for the pure and uncontaminated and that while the Areopagus of contemporary culture is not a comfortable place, it remains the venue and perhaps even the vehicle of proclamation and prophetic practice. Recognising the ambiguity of 'culture', they do not condemn it absolutely.

In the conflation model there is an accommodation of faith to culture, where *fides* is transmuted into *mores*. Whether this transition is due to the dilution of faith and its denial or to the prevailing and persuasive power of culture, this acculturation of faith means its alienation and ultimate abandonment. The three 'R's of Christian teaching and theology – revelation, resurrection and redemption – are reduced to, at best and most, ciphers of a religious quest for meaning. Traditional Christian symbols and doctrines, the language and logic of faith seeking understanding that underpins hope, are fair game for cultural creators, commentators and consumers. Revelation is reified and reduced to spirituality, which is seen and stated solely 'from below', that is, as the human quest for direction and purpose. This undermines

---

14. Richard Lennan, 'Looking into the Sun: Faith, Culture, and the Task of Theology in the Contemporary Church', *The Australasian Catholic Record*, 84 (October 2007), 460-1

15. See Jim Corkery, 'Technology and transcendence', *The Furrow*, 55 (February 2004), 98

the traditional Christian interpretation of spirituality as response to the God who, 'from above', reaches out to and redeems humanity in Christ. Richard Lennan characterises this collapse in cogent terms: 'At issue is not the fact that contemporary spirituality tends to be insufficiently traditional, but that it tends to be insufficiently spiritual, that it avoids engagement with transcendence.'[16] A state of affairs that is saturated with what Michael Paul Gallagher expresses as the 'enoughness' of the here-and-now[17] has little time for eternity. However, the removal of the essential 'eschatological reserve' of Christian faith renders this accomodationist approach not only intellectually incoherent but also spiritually shortsighted and practically pointless from the viewpoint of theology. Tracey Rowland has given the *coup de grace* to the conflation of culture and faith with her comment that 'no public relations campaign driven by spin-doctors is able to substitute for the witness of saints'.[18]

The call/challenge model distinguishes but does not separate faith and culture. While the gospel always contains a call for the conversion of culture (considered in the three-fold sense of T. S. Eliot as the culture of the individual, of the group/institution and of society as a whole[19]), this carries an element of judgement and correction without necessarily concluding in condemnation. If the gospel is to serve as leaven and light for the life of the world it must become involved with that world and its many ways. With this recognition of inculturation comes a realisation of a reciprocal challenge and questioning from and by culture(s) with a corresponding acceptance of pluralism and diversity. Thus the universal mission of the church is authentically advanced and the lie given to false forms of globalisation. This dialectic of call and challenge aims to show how 'the relationship to God, especially when lived within the Christian community, offers an enriching alternative to the promotion of a one-dimensional secularity ... [and] demonstrates that, in the felicitous

---

16. 'Looking into the Sun: Faith, Culture, and the Task of Theology in the Contemporary Church', 465
17. 'From Social to Cultural Secularisation', *Louvain Studies*, 24 (1999), 105
18. *Culture and the Thomist Tradition*, 32
19. *Culture and the Thomist Tradition*, 2-21

phrase of Michael Paul Gallagher, Christian faith offers a "poetry and praxis" that are a viable alternative to contemporary "prisons of dullness".[20] The current crisis for the church(es) consists in the manner it can conceive this call and challenge of faith in a culture characterised as 'postmodern'. Tina Beattie describes the postmodern culture of (western) Europe in the following terms: 'The term "postmodernism" refers to a loosely-knit movement of ideas which extends from popular culture, art and architecture across the academic spectrum of the arts and humanities, including theology and philosophy. It is a worldview which asserts that there is no worldview, paradoxically laying claim to the universal truth that there is no universal truth ... The ostensible diversity which proliferates under the banner of postmodernism is a banal and barren sameness, masked by a surface gloss of corporate images, brand names, fashions and lifestyles.'[21] Ironically, the iconoclasm identified with postmodernity has spawned an immensity of cultural icons ranging from entertainment to fashion and media to sport. Paradoxically, postmodernism's cultural disenchantment with rationality does not demand a dilution of Christianity's intended dovetailing of faith and reason but an engagement with what Lennan describes as 'every dimension of being human, since being Christian engages imagination and emotion, energy and passion, not as "extra" to belief but as integral, central to it.'[22]

Aidan Nichols states that Christianity has 'a claim, in divine revelation, to a fulcrum independent of the world's fashions'.[23] Rather than positing an independent fulcrum, perhaps a better image for Christian faith in relation to postmodern culture might be borrowed from T. S. Eliot, 'the still point of the turning world'.[24] While indicating a point of reference this also intimates

20. Lennan, 'Looking into the Sun', 468
21. *The New Atheists*, London: DLT, pp 132-3. Kevin J. Vanhoozer has cleverly considered postmodernism with the question 'Concept, Culture, or Condition'? cf his 'Theology and the condition of postmodernity: a report on knowledge (of God)' in Kevin J. Vanhoozer, ed, *The Cambridge Companion to Postmodern Theology*, Cambridge: University Press, 2003, 3-25
22. Lennan, p 468
23. Ibid., p xi
24. 'Four Quartets' in *Collected Poems*, London: Faber, 1963

a place of repose and, more importantly, invites people to find a home for their restless hearts. There is a need for, in the words of Australian theologian John Thornhill, 'a wholesome theology' that can serve as in the postmodern wasteland. This search for spiritual wisdom in the midst of a society saturated by speech, sound and symbol can find both encouragement and example in the classical statement of Augustine who 'sees the spiritual journey as something that takes place within the context of a *cor inquietum* longing to become a *cor quietum*'.[25] The contemporary Cardinal Martini contemplates what both the challenge of the church might demand and the call of culture draw forth: 'Christianity has an opportunity to show better its character of challenge, of objectivity, of realism, of the exercise of true freedom, of a religion linked to the life of the body and not only to the mind. In a world such as we live in today, the mystery of an unavailable and always surprising God acquires greater beauty; faith understood as risk becomes more attractive; a tragic view of existence is strengthened with happy consequences in contrast to a purely evolutionary vision. Christianity appears more beautiful, closer to people, and yet more true.'[26]

A Level Playing Ground?
The survey and study of religion in Western societies in recent decades has largely been conducted through the theory of 'secularisation'. However, as Grace Davie notes, the terms and conditions of this theory often vary depending on the discipline doing the research and reflection.[27] Her survey of sociological approaches and analyses includes the view of Jose Casanova that 'what usually passes for a single theory of secularisation is actually made up of three very different, uneven and unintegrated

---

25. David Kelly, 'From the *Cor Inquietum* to the *Sabbatum Cordis*', *Milltown Studies*, 59-60 (2007), 1-20, at 4. ('Augustine's journey is one of restlessness and inner struggle, leading to a discovery of the real reasons for his restlessness (*cor inquietum*): a quest that continues in the light of faith, until faith yields to vision and the *inquies* becomes the final *quies* or *pacem sabbati*. This latter state of repose and peace Augustine describes elsewhere as *sabbatum cordis*', 3)
26. 'Teaching the Faith in a Postmodern World', *America*, 12 May 2008, p 18
27. *The Sociology of Religion*, London: Sage, 2007, p 49

propositions: secularisation as differentiation of the secular spheres from religious institutions and norms, as decline of religious beliefs and practices, and as marginalisation of religion to a privatised sphere'.[28] Thus, for example, in the view of demographer David Voas, in terms of the conventional indicators of affiliation, belief and conduct, 'Britain is ceasing to be a Christian country in anything but a residual sense'.[29] Debates about the presence and progress of secularisation or not may be illustrated in the image of 'the sacred canopy'.[30] First associated with the prominent American sociologist Peter Berger, the 'sacred canopy' symbolises the construction and communication of a system in human consciousness which supplies and sustains belief both in human existence and its experience of 'ultimate concern' (a phrase associated with the American theologian Paul Tillich).

The 'sacred canopy' represents a religious reading of reality and response to the fundamental questions of human existence in society and history, such as those referred to above in the document of the Second Vatican Council. The image of canopy raises a series of interesting and interrelated questions. Is this religious reading to be understood in the specific Christian sense, that is, as a response (conversion and communion) to God's self-communication in creation, Christ and church? If so, under what conditions could this social and cultural canopy unravel or ultimately give way? Could other religions compete with and replace this traditional Judaeo-Christian covering? Or is the canopy to be conceived more loosely, in terms of a tapestry of transcendence that corresponds to a general sense of religiosity and the typology of *homo religiosus*? How can the church(es) and other religious bodies respond to the cultural challenge that conceives the canopy as a comfort blanket, serving as a (temporary) transitional object in the development from infancy to indepen-

---

28. Ibid., p 51

29. Ibid., p 58. The columnist Polly Toynbee noted that while a third of all schools were faith based only 7% of families were churchgoers where 'most parents at these schools pretend to religion'. *The Guardian*, 6 November, 2007

30. The image of a canopy is found in the prophet Isaiah: 'Indeed over all the glory there will be a canopy. It will serve as a pavilion, a shade by day from the heat, and a refuge and a shelter from the storm and rain'. (4:5-6)

dence, from a situation of being supported to standing on one's own feet? Expanding the image of the canopy as a conveyor of meaning in society embraces the possibility of envisaging other forms of cultural covering and consciousness. Could alternatives, for example, consumerism and communications (the media circus), coalesce and perhaps conspire to undermine and ultimately replace the sense of the sacred in society? If such surrogate or substitute canopies arise, could they adopt or adapt religious symbolism and language to further ideological and commercial interests? Are art, music and sport, possible candidates for such alternative (and competing) cultural canopies? Berger's own views on secularisation have undergone a significant shift. Originally associated with the theory as an account and analysis of the demise of religious faith in the democratic societies of the West, Berger has reconsidered the thesis and its terms, particularly in the light of data deriving from America and the so-called developing world.[31] Following him, Davie declares that 'secularisation should no longer be the assumed position for theorists in the sociology of religion; it becomes instead a theory with relatively limited application, particularly suited to the European case'.[32] In this context the interrelation of Christian faith and culture and the challenge it involves is starkly stated by Volker Kuster: 'Exposed to multicultural societies that are characterised by the interaction between the hyperculture of global consumer capitalism and hybrid subcultures [Christianity] has to demonstrate its capability to inculturate itself anew.'[33] However, in this perspective, the task of building a bridge between faith and cultures, between 'hyper' and 'hybrid', looms large.

In his study of religion in contemporary Europe, Lieven Boeve begins by explaining and evaluating the standard secularisation thesis that posits a direct relationship between the process of modernisation and the disappearance of religious be-

---

31. This trend is evident in his *A Rumour of Angels – Modern Society and the Rediscovery of the Supernatural*, Middlesex: Penguin Books, 1970
32. *The Sociology of Religion*, p 64
33. 'Speaking of God in Memory of September 11th, An Aesthetic Approach', *Exchange*, 36 (2007), 243

lief, belonging and behaviour.[34] Central to this thesis is the so-called 'zero sum theory', that sees an inverse relationship between the increase of modernisation and the decrease of religious identity. This thesis states that the more modernity emerged (in Europe) the more religion would be evacuated from the make-up of the lives of individuals and society. However, both sociologists of religion and theologians have come to acknowledge the fact that history does not fit this hypothesis of a religion-free zone, a secular Ground Zero witnessing to the collapse of religious – in particular Christian – involvement in and influence on institutional realities and individual identities. Among the reasons cited by Boeve for this socio-theological reservation regarding a European secular vista are the rise of interest in spirituality, the emergence of new religious movements both inside and outside the churches, residual adherence to classical expressions of Christian conviction, celebration and conduct and 'the reference to, or appearance of, classical religious symbols, narratives and rituals in contemporary (popular) culture'.[35] Nevertheless, the impact of Christianity on the cultural consciousness of Europe has undergone considerable change throughout the course of the last century and in the case of some countries this process has been particularly rapid and remarkable in recent decades. Two examples indicate this changed situation. The first involves the debate about the proposed constitution of the European Union and the decision to delete any reference to God and the Judaeo-Christian tradition in its preamble. The second is illustrated in two issues of *Newsweek* with their respective covers and captions – 'Is God Dead? In Western Europe, It Sure Can Look That Way' and 'Good God! Why Europe is turning churches into gyms, pizzerias and bars'.[36]

Boeve describes this transformation of Europe as the transition from society with a dominant Christian involvement and

---

34. *God Interrupts History – Theology in a Time of Upheaval*, London: Continuum, 2007. See also his 'Religion after Detraditionalisation: Christian Faith in a Post-Secular Europe', *The Irish Theological Quarterly*, 70/2 (2005): 99-122

35. Ibid., 15

36. 12 July 1999 and 12 February, 2007

input at the institutional level to one where individual identity is formed as a matter of personal and autonomous meaning in which religiosity and spirituality may play a part rather than predominate. He suggests that the term 'detraditionalisation' – rather than the classical secularisation thesis – is more suitable to situate and state the decline of institutional Christianity in Europe and the implications for the demise of individual identity formation: 'Detraditionalisation as a term hints at the socio-cultural interruption of traditions (religious as well as class, gender) which are no longer able to pass themselves from one generation to the next. The latter definitely applies to the Christian tradition in which the transmission process has been seriously hampered. Christianity no longer is the given and unquestioned horizon for individual and social identity ... Detraditionalisation is understood as a descriptive category, indicating the socio-cultural developments that have influenced Europe in modern times. In this regard, [it] is not only a feature of post-Christians, but affects all religious and ideological affiliations. All of them in one way or another have to deal with this changed socio-cultural reality'[37] The consequence and cost, including a political one, for Christianity is that it can no longer assume an automatic and unquestioned role in public and personal life. He illustrates this process of detraditionalisation in the case of Catholic Belgium by indicating the titles of three books detailing the results of the European Values Study in that country – *The Silent Turn* (1984), *The Accelerated Turn* (1992) and *Lost Certainty* (2000). The nexus between Christianity and culture has been cut, creating individuals who choose rather than receive their religious affiliation, if any. This changed cultural context in Europe is also composed of a range of religious and spiritual positions and perspectives that Boeve characterises as 'pluralisation'. Pluralisation proceeds from a significant reduction in the religious monopoly traditionally enjoyed by Christianity as well as out of the emergence of a general sense of religiosity which corresponds to personal preferences and practices which witness to the prevalence of *homo* remaining *religiosus*. The effect of these twin developments is not the extinction of religion from Europe

---

37. 'Religion after Detraditionalisation', 104-5

but rather the emergence of a multiplicity of spiritual stalls, services and symbols. In summary Boeve states that 'Christianity has not been replaced by a secular culture, but by a plurality of life options and religions – among which the secularist (atheist) position, in all its variants, is only one – that have moved in to occupy the vacuum left behind as a result of its diminishing impact'.[38] Linked to detraditionalisation and pluralisation is the privatisation of religion. Joan Estruch identifies 'the fundamental characteristics of this social, modern and privatised form of religion [as] institutional de-specialisation of religion, de-monopolisation of the production and diffusion of worldviews, and immediate accessibility (through the communication media) to a whole repertoire of collective representations referring to transcendent realities'.[39] Thus questions remain about the fate of Christianity, either as a relic of the past or as a reservoir for the present generation of stories, symbols and sayings supplying a pastiche of increasingly *á-la-carte* spiritual identities. However, an advance, perhaps accelerated, of cultural amnesia raises the question about how long into the future the Christian memory can remain a resource for such images, ideas and icons.

Interpreting Ireland
The country and culture that created the 'Happy Hour' offers an interesting and even intriguing example of the changing conditions and contours of the relationship between faith and culture. In a homily given in January 2008, Diarmuid Martin, the Archbishop of Dublin, stated that when he arrived in Rome for his *ad limina* visit the previous year, armed with statistics about every aspect of the local church, he was surprised when Pope Benedict asked him about 'the points of contact between the church in Ireland and those places where the future of Irish culture is being determined?'[40] Archbishop Martin went on to underline the importance of this issue, stating that 'the dialogue between the church and Irish culture is one of the most import-

---

38. Ibid., p 27
39. 'A Conversation with Thomas Luckmann', *Social Compasss*, 55/4 (2008), 532-540 at 539
40. Milltown Institute Jubilee Mass, 14 January 2008. Available at http://www.dublindiocese.ie. [Accessed 21 January 2009]

ant questions that the church in Ireland, in all its components, should be asking and perhaps it is not doing so adequately'.[41] Several years previously Enda McDonagh stressed this impera- tive of the interaction of faith and culture when he wrote that 'the real challenges to the Irish church are in the areas of faith and theology as they face a powerful social and cultural interrog- ation'.[42]

Tom Inglis begins his analysis of the relationship between church and culture in contemporary Ireland by indicating the importance of issues of identity and institutional involvement: 'Catholic Ireland is not what it used to be. The church was once the backbone of strong, cohesive family networks and commu- nity structures that created a sense of identity and belonging ... The church was a spiritual and moral colossus. It stretched out over the country like a giant sacred canopy. Its teachings perme- ated the hearts and minds of every Catholic man, woman and child. It was central to the way they understood themselves and the world in which they lived ... The church was also a major in- stitutional player. In many important social fields such as family, education, health and social welfare, it rivalled the state.'[43] As such a 'player' in Irish society, the role of the Catholic Church in the field of sport, particularly in relation to Gaelic Games, is a valuable index of its social, cultural and even political identity and involvement. A picture of a large group of seminarians gathered around High Field in Maynooth during the 1950s pro- vides a striking contrast with the small number of students and sportsmen there fifty years later. The drop off of involvement and interest by clergy in sport in the past two decades has had its own impact not only on local playing fields throughout the country but also in the parishes of which such fields traditionally formed an integral part. De Valera's vision of material sufficiency making space for, *inter alia*, 'the contests of athletic youths' was delivered on St Patrick's Day 1943, just over two months before Vincent O'Brien trained his first winner at Limerick Junction

---

41. Idem
42. *The Furrow*, 55 (June 2004), 354
43. 'Individualisation and Secularisation in Catholic Ireland', in *Contemporary Ireland – A Sociological Map*, Sara O'Sullivan, ed, Dublin: University College Dublin Press, 2007, 67

(now Tipperary) racecourse. Six and a half decades later the huge commercial and communications complex committed to horseracing testifies to the changed vision and values of contests, both athletic and animal, in the country.

Inglis presents the decline of the traditional social and spiritual cachet of the church as a change of *habitus* whereby its control in the areas of consciousness and conduct has ceded significant ground to both 'the market and the media who, with their messages of self-fulfilment, narcissism and hedonism have come to dominate the hearts and minds of Irish Catholics'.[44] While Voas' reference to Britain as being only a residual Christian country does not accurately describe contemporary Ireland, the traditional simile of its Catholic identity as 'a fish swimming in water' is no longer suitable. The streams of water have become much wider, the fish population more varied and no longer moving in the same direction simultaneously. Inglis' interpretation of the loss of the church's monopoly involves the processes of religious individualisation and secularisation. Individuals no longer rely wholeheartedly on the institutional church for their moral and spiritual identities. The dichotomy of 'believing without belonging', previously a feature of Protestantism in Britain and Europe, is one option for describing developments in Ireland south of the border. A variation of this socio-theological viewpoint may be the socio-cultural version of 'belonging without really believing' which Inglis identifies in the following terms: 'In other words, it may well be that for an increasing number of people, being Catholic in Ireland may have more to do with belonging to an inherited social identity. Participating in rituals may reaffirm that collective consciousness but have less to do with any rigorous pursuit of salvation.'[45] An example of this trend may be the commercialisation of sacramental celebrations, especially (first) communion and confirmation. Anecdotal evidence in this area includes the story of a young girl telling her classmates that she went straight from the hairdresser to the hotel because there was not time to go to the church to receive her first (holy) communion.

---

44. Ibid., 68
45. Ibid., 74

Rugby on Gaelic Ground

Ireland's rugby internationals against both France and England in the 2007 Six Nations Championship, which were played at Croke Park, provide a fascinating framework for articulating and analysing cultural and religious change and the relation between them in contemporary Ireland. Against the background of the 'Peace Process', with the prospect of establishing a cross-community power-sharing executive in Northern Ireland, and in terms of relations between Britain and Ireland as a whole, the venue itself was a vector of meaning at many levels. The games received massive media coverage at home and abroad. Radio, television and the print media devoted considerable commentary and columns to the themes of remembrance and reconciliation in the context of recreation and the readiness of the Gaelic Athletic Association to open the gates of its headquarters to 'foreign games', which had once been placed out of bounds to members of the association. Where once it had seemed (ironically in Kipling's phrase) 'ne'er the twain shall meet', the *rapprochement* between the Irish Rugby Football Union (also soccer's Football Association of Ireland) and the Gaelic Athletic Association represented a triumph of economy and emotion over traditional enmity. While being handsomely remunerated, the generosity of the GAA in opening its flagship stadium to both rugby and soccer for the duration of the development of Landsdowne Road on the south side of Dublin was generally lauded. Both the development of the magnificent new sports ground that is Croke Park and the proposed refurbishment of the Lansdowne location owed a lot to the country's socio-economic boom, the so-called 'Celtic Tiger'.

The decision of the GAA, after much internal discussion which included a degree of dissension, to allow the increasingly popular game of rugby to parade and play in Croke Park was magnanimous and merited a fitting response, which both the players and administrators of the other All-Ireland game graciously gave in a spirit of gratitude. Perhaps this mutual respect was rooted in part in the sense of communal pride that Ireland could take its place among the sporting nations of the world, where Croke Park could stand its ground alongside such great sporting venues as the Bernabeu in Madrid and Johannesburg's

Ellis Park, London's Twickenham and Paris' Stade or any Olympic arena of recent memory. The spectacle and success of the Special Olympics there in 2003 was also fresh in many people's minds.[46] The opening two matches served up moments of sporting joy and success, despair and defeat when, in the first game, Ireland succumbed in the closing minutes to a final French foray into their half of the pitch and succeeded in the second in sending a powerful message to the rugby world in their passionate, professional outplaying of the 'old enemy'. Despite the disappointment of defeat by France and the despondency over the loss of a coveted Grand Slam, a shared sense of respect between the different sporting codes and their respective constituencies was seen as the overall winner, a prize perhaps more important in the long term than sporting success.

In the run-up to the rugby internationals and to the game against England in particular, much space and statement was devoted to the historic significance of Croke Park hosting the event(s). Sporting greats and celebrities from all codes were interviewed on Irish and British television. The BBC presented both rugby's Keith Wood and soccer's Kevin Moran (who had enjoyed All-Ireland senior Gaelic football success there with Dublin in the 1970s) who both reminisced and looked forward while, on match day, RTÉ paraded present-day hurling stars to hail the occasion. The history of the ground was recounted, with reference to the rubble of the General Post Office after the 1916 Easter Rising providing the material for the appropriately named 'Hill 16'. The events of 'Bloody Sunday' in November 1921 were recalled, when a Black and Tan death squad shot dead fourteen players and spectators at a Dublin versus Tipperary football match in supposed retaliation for the assassination that morning of a group of spies by members of Michael

---

46. In their pastoral letter marking both the European Year of People with Disabilities and the Special Olympics World Summer Games, the Irish Catholic Bishops' Conference commented that 'the games are a magnificent symbol of what may be achieved when we focus on the abilities and skills of people rather than on their disabilities. The athletes will teach us much about motivation and determination and will bring enormous enjoyment to a worldwide audience [and] there could be no better advertisement for the power of inclusion and participation'. *Life in all its fullness*, Dublin: Veritas, 2003

Collins' dubiously named hit-squad 'The Twelve Apostles'. Debates developed over the playing of the respective national anthems with their various martial associations, which on the day(s) were recited and received respectfully. The English (and former Irish) coach Brian Ashton arranged for former Irish international and RFU staff member Conor O'Shea (whose father had won several All-Ireland medals with Kerry) to brief the squad on the significance and symbolism of the event. The sight of a protestor sporting a Glasgow Celtic jersey was not without its share of irony.

The intense emotions and passions engendered in and around the England/Ireland game both enabled and expressed a form of catharsis, a clearing and cleansing of relations on a range of levels, sporting as well as cultural and political. While the event did not have the resonance of the 1995 Rugby World Cup final in Johannesburg, where the recently elected democratic President of South Africa Nelson Mandela donned a Springbok jersey to present the Webb Ellis trophy to his fellow number six, the victorious captain Francois Pienaar, there was a palpable sense of relief. This relief partly reflected the general sense that things had gone well both on and of the field, particularly that there had been no repeat of the violent scenes surrounding the 'Love Ulster' march in Dublin the previous year. A dimension of reconciliation could also be discerned in particular scenes such as the pathos of the playing of the national anthems and the respective silence(s) that greeted them, while the skill of Ireland's fourth try through the kick and catch of Ronan O'Gara and Shane Horgan would have graced an All-Ireland Gaelic Football final there. For those fortunate to be present and the huge television audiences around the world such moments made deep and lasting impressions. As both a contribution to human solidarity and a catharsis for the healing of history, the Ireland versus England game played no small part. Both in its build-up and on the day itself the match carried moral and spiritual symbolism and significance as well as sporting success. Rugby correspondent Mick Cleary declared: 'A victory for a nation as much as for a team. The Queen respected, England decimated. A past was buried with dignity and a future promised with panache. Ireland won on all fronts.'[47]

47. *The Daily Telegraph*, 26 February, 2007

'Hallowed Be Thy Ground'

Three years previously priest and writer Brendan Hoban described the venue 'a triumph of modern engineering with a capacity of almost 80,000 people, and a part answer to a modern need ... a new cathedral for a new faith'.[48] Both in the build-up to and aftermath of the rugby games at Croke Park there was an abundance of religious references to the stadium itself. On the day after the first floodlit (installed for the soccer and rugby games) football game there between Dublin and Tyrone, Mark Souster headlined his report, 'Croke Park prepares for historic conversion to new sporting creed' in which he states that it was 'more than a sporting citadel, a shrine'.[49] Perhaps there is a suggestion, if not a sub-text, of enlightenment here. Several writers spoke of the stadium's 'sacred turf', including Ireland correspondent of *The Independent*, David McKittrick, who declares that 'the phrase "hallowed turf" may be a cliché but if one stadium merits the description it is Dublin's Croke Park, as not just the home of Gaelic games but also, to many, a central respository of the spirit of Ireland ... historically consecrated territory'.[50] Described variously as a 'cathedral', a 'sacred ground' and a 'temple to amateurism', the theme of pilgrimage is also present in some presentations. On the day of the French game, Malachy Clerkin wrote about 'the first day of the rest of the GAA's life' and referred to the fact that Terenure College, a traditional rugby playing school, had recently won a primary school GAA competition, stating that sport was 'a church big enough for miracles of all sizes'.[51] This sequence of spiritual and sacred references to the stadium reached a pinnacle in a piece penned by Irish religious affairs commentator David Quinn: 'Rugby at the GAA's *sanctum sanctorum*'. Hailing Croke Park as the 'Holy of Holies', Quinn likens the attitude of the GAA in preserving its 'hallowed turf' till the recent past for the Association's codes of hurling and football to a process of reservation in order to retain its reverence: 'The GAA treated Croke Park as a sort of inner

48. 'Is Sport the New Religion?', *Spirituality*, 10 (September/October 2004) p 259
49. *The Times*, 8 February, 2007
50. 8 February, 2007
51. *The Sunday Tribune*, 11 February, 2007

sanctum, and as anyone with the least familiarity with religion knows, the way to keep an inner sanctum special, or holy, is to attach very strict conditions to entry into it, and to guard those conditions zealously and fiercely.'[52] However, he notes that the effect of extending entry to other castes and codes is the cost of sacrificing the stadium's special status or holiness.

The equation of Croke Park with religious spaces and symbols such as shrines, cathedrals and other holy places is highly suggestive, especially in a country with places of pilgrimage such as Knock, Lough Derg and Croagh Patrick attracting large numbers of people from both home and abroad. In her biography of Patrick Kavanagh, Antoinette Quinn notes his journalistic preference for pilgrimage locations where company and consumption were primary considerations: 'Good-humoured crowds dressed in their Sunday best; tea and sandwiches in the open air; hawkers and stallholders plying their wares; such easy commerce between the secular and the sacred, piety and gaiety, met with his approval.'[53] The abandonment of traditional forms and features of pilgrimage and the statement of such desire draws closer to the description of a GAA match in mid-summer, though in the case of corporate Croke Park the fare has probably been converted to something closer to strong beverages and prawn sandwiches. David Quinn's description of the 'Holy of Holies' both draws on and depends on the Old Testament with its point of departure in God's disclosure to Moses in the so-called 'Burning Bush' (Exodus 3:2). Both the superlative 'Holy of Holies' and the injunction to Moses – 'Remove the sandals from your feet, for the place on which you are standing is holy ground' (Exodus 3:5) – serve to show and shore up the sense of *mysterium tremendum et fascinans* experienced in encounter with the divine self-revelation of God to Israel and in the incarnation (Hebrews 9:3-5). Dependence on traditional biblical and theological imagery and metaphors to describe sporting venues and events runs the risk of debasing and dumbing down what is disclosed in divine revelation rather than supporting distinction

---

52. *The Irish Catholic*, 1 March, 2007
53. *Patrick Kavanagh*, Revised and Expanded Edition, Dublin: Gill & MacMillan, 2003, 193

between the realms of the sacred and the profane, the eternal and the ephemeral.

In his description of the new Wembley stadium, Jonathan Glancey states that, despite the history of the venue and the major soccer events hosted on the site, what the construction firm Multiplex 'has delivered is definitely not a cultural centre, there are no artworks on display, no plaques, nor cups, nor even signed and framed photographs (as yet); there is absolutely nothing to get in the way of the building's primary purpose, that of watching games in what is surely one of the world's finest arenas'.[54] Croke Park with its proud museum and place in the history of the country assured in perpetuity is now also one of the world's finest sporting arenas. However, the conjunction of sport and Christian sacramentality in its case is more than a confusion of categories. This is a new cultural phenomenon that calls for theological analysis. In an article on the GAA for its centenary, Liam Ryan cleverly adopted the line of a current television advertisement 'Part of What We Are'.[55] Tracing the links between nationalism, religion and the association he asserts as one of its greatest achievements was 'that it provided a suitable medium through which Irish people could give expression to their collective identity'. Historically this expression was closely identified with the Catholic Church such that the hymn 'Faith of our Fathers' was sung at All-Ireland football finals in conjunction with the National Anthem while the Archbishop of Cashel, patron of the GAA, threw in the *sliotar* at the start of the hurling final.[56] It is interesting, if not ironic, that both practices ceased in 1979, the year that Pope John Paul II visited the country. As historical homogeneity in both cultural and religious dimensions decreases, an article assessing the Association today might adopt the line used in the advertisement of a daily newspaper, 'Keeping up with the changing times'.

In his account of the changes effected and reflected by the playing of international rugby at Croke Park, Fintan O'Toole

54. *The Guardian*, 9 March, 2007
55. 'The GAA – "Part of What We Are" – A Centenary Assessment', *The Furrow*, 35 (December 1984), 752-764
56. See Louise Fuller, *Irish Catholicism since 1950 – The Undoing of a Culture*, Dublin: Gill & MacMillan, 2002, 9-10

comments that 'big forces – media globalisation, the death of the old rural Ireland, the transcending of nationalism, the waning of religion as a marker of religious identity in the Republic – have all changed the nature of the game'.[57] 'The Holy Ground' is an allegorical reference to Ireland itself. In this context it is critical to clarify the nature of the ground on which we are standing: the naming of venues and games is of secondary concern. The recent rugby internationals at Croke Park represented a spectacle of sport and realised some solidarity between communities and countries which have been separated historically. However, to hail the venue as holy ground does not do justice to either sporting culture or Christian spirituality. Lazily or loosely identifying the island of saints and scholars with the Ireland of sporting stadia and stars is historically dishonest and does not ultimately help to understand the relationship between faith and culture in this context.

Sport as the New Religion

In his comment on Ireland's victory over England at Croke Park, Keith Wood remarked that 'Saturday was better than good and bigger than sport' and the collective hangover in post-match Dublin was 'quite simply a hangover from heaven'.[58] Notwithstanding the proverbial *craic*, the consumption of copious quantities of alcohol at and after sporting events raises questions about the sponsorship of national and international competitions by drink companies and the accompanying advertising The mixture of both mantra and cliché in 'post-Catholic Ireland' that 'sport is the new religion' hit the headlines a year after the Croke Park internationals. The Irish Catholic Bishops Conference criticised the prevalence of sports practice and playing games on Sunday mornings. A headline in the *Irish Independent* highlighted the dilemma, particularly for young people, of playing or praying: 'Make Sunday a day to pray, not play, our bishops plead.'[59] Recalling that Sundays in Ireland have been regarded as a sacred time with a vital link between liturgy and leisure, the bishops stated that 'one of the essential ways by which this balance

---

57. 'The Croker conversion', *The Irish Times,* 10 February, 2007
58. *The Daily Telegraph,* 26 February, 2007
59. 12 March, 2008

was maintained was the tradition whereby sporting and leisure activities for young people on Sundays did not begin until early afternoon'.[60] The bishops note that a change in policy on the part of sporting organisations has created a conflict of interest, particularly for young people: 'Dedicated young sports people can be afraid to miss a training session or a game for fear they will lose their place on the team. When practice sessions or competitions occur repeatedly on Sunday mornings then a young participant can lose the habit of going to Sunday Mass.' Reminding parents of their responsibility for themselves and their families in relation to their Sunday obligation, the bishops appeal 'to all people of goodwill, to respect the spiritual needs of children and adolescents, particularly as these relate to family life and religious practice on Sundays, and to refrain from organising events that clash with Sunday morning religious services.' Their statement also asks employers to allow time for attendance at church to young people who work part-time work at weekends and referred to the number of children who do not take part in any physical activities or pastimes. Both concerns reflect significant changes in the economy and ethos of the country. However, the response of both the GAA and the IRFU to the request reiterated the difficulty and impracticality of ceasing practice and play on Sunday mornings, while the FAI did not reply. Not surprisingly, if somewhat unimaginatively, the bishops were even described by some as spoilsports.

Michael Moynihan mimics a Sunday sermon on the subject: 'Dearly beloved, we are gathered here together to cast light again where once there was only darkness. I'm glad to see so many young people here in church today. I know that you would all prefer to be out on the playing fields of Ireland this morning – or, if truth be told, nursing your hangovers at home, ho ho ho. Seriously, however, how gratifying it is to know that even now, in these godless times, that a fine smack of the crozier can still bring the masses to heel.'[61] The reasonableness of the bishops' argument and appeal stands in complete contrast with

---

60. 'Keep Sunday as a sacred time', Press Release from the Irish Catholic Bishops' Conference, 11 March, 2008. Available at http://www.irish-catholicbishopsconference.ie [Accessed 21 January, 2009]
61. *Irish Examiner*, 14 March, 2008

this *reductio ad absurdum*, with its range of clichés and *non se-quiturs* more reminiscent of Father Ted and company than a priest at the pulpit at a regular parish Mass. Indeed the *ad hominem* tone, from reference to a belt of the episcopal crozier to the naming of certain former bishops, McQuaid and Lucey, underscores a crude and sometimes inane anti-clericalism that has become a feature of elements of the media in Ireland. A little research would have reminded him of the refusal of soccer supporters to heed the instruction of Archbishop McQuaid to boycott an international game against Yugoslavia in October 1955.[62] While reference to 'hangovers' recalls Wood's comment about Dublin after the England versus Ireland game, a far more serious and worrying resonance is the issue of under-age and binge drinking throughout the country. If the measured tone of the bishops' appeal can only be met by 'a storm of laughter and disbelief' the prospect of dialogue between faith and culture, of which sport is a considerable component in contemporary Ireland, seems to be poor. Indeed Moynihan's reference to 'godless times' in a column entitled 'Talking Sport' only serves to indicate and intensify the impression that the sporting commentariat, with their huge Sunday coverage of sport in newspapers, television and radio programmes, is a substitute for the clergy and their church services.

Katie Liston contends that sport is a crucial area in Irish culture and a central theme for sociological enquiry, highlighting the levels of people's emotional attachment in Ireland to sport.[63] This is expressed, for example, in the enthusiastic following of Munster in the European Rugby Cup and the wave of nostalgia for the Republic of Ireland's efforts at the 1988 European Championships and World Cup in Italy two years later. While measuring such attachments at local, provincial and national levels is a task for social psychology, their meaning calls for a deeper interrogation and discernment. Emotional attachments to events on the fields of play may mirror or mask expectations in other areas of people's lives, for example, issues of belonging

---

62. See Diarmaid Ferriter, *The Transformation of Ireland 1900-2000*, London: Profile Books, 2004, 519
63. 'A Question of Sport', in *Contemporary Ireland*, Chapter 9

or even believing. In an increasingly individualised society the fact of being a fan and following a particular club or county in sport may function as a form of bonding, where other forms of social engagement are extremely limited. (However, being part of a crowd at a game or match may still be a lonely experience, particularly if the individual or team being followed loses.) At a societal level issues of meaning and happiness are increasingly being mentioned, if not actually measured. The ninth Céifin conference considered the effect of economic success on and in Irish society. Conference organiser, Father Harry Bohan, speaks of people being culturally poor in a society that 'has been overwhelmed by the rise of a consumerist culture where values of communal concern or of individual self-denial seem to be very remote'.[64] In a lecture entitled 'The best of times, the worst of times', author and economist, Finola Kennedy, identifies a malaise in Irish society, telling the conference 'that this sickness in society persisted despite triumphs such as Irish victories in the Cheltenham Gold Cup, the Grand National and the Triple Crown'.[65] The inability of success in sport to alleviate a sense of social *anomie* is an issue that needs to be interpreted in terms of cultural identity. Focus on the case of the newly appointed Republic's soccer manager, Giovanni Trapattoni, could provide a fascinating study of the relation of faith and sport in the context of contemporary Irish culture. A devout Catholic, the former successful player and club manager has been deified in sections of the Irish media and described as a redeemer to restore the glory days enjoyed in the era of Jack Charlton in the late 1980s and early 1990s. Analysis of both attachment and achievement around the aesthetically inclined (he encourages his players to listen to Bach and Mozart) Italian could afford a valuable avenue into interpreting Irish sporting culture. More generally, the prevalence of sport is a phenomenon of present day mass popular culture, a phenomenon that theology is increasingly attending to.[66] The parallelism of religion and sport has been particularly identified in relation to the so-called 'Generation Y':

---

64. *The Sunday Times*, 12 November, 2008
65. Idem
66. See Gordon Lynch, *Understanding Theology and Popular Culture*, Oxford: Blackwell, 2005

'The classic example of popular culture as religion pertains to sport "as religion" – for example football in Britain or baseball in the United States. In this respect, sport offers the potential for personal transformation, such as transcending the normal limitations of the body. Sport also provides a basis for community, identity and history. Sports can be said to have their own liturgy with rituals and ceremonies for devotion in the form of top sportsmen and women.'[67] In the context of the rejection of meta-narratives of meaning by postmodernism, the irony and implications of social commentator Brian Appleyard's assertion that 'football is no longer a mere game, it is the great popular narrative of our time'[68] invite cultural investigation and theological interpretation.

A culture concentrating on, consumed by and communicating (partly through its connection with advertising) on athletic competition in a variety of codes offers society the opportunity to accord sport the status of an alternative, albeit secular, religion.[69] The paradox and parameters of this perspective are well presented by David Goldblatt: 'Were [a] historian to search for our era's understanding of itself, he would find few clear or coherent voices. Some of those voices would sound bemused, claiming that despite the immensity of its reach, sport is an ephemeral pastime. Others would cast sport as a religion without a god, its rituals a late modern liturgy, its champions touched by divinity.'[70] During the 2008 European soccer Championship, co-hosted by Austria and Switzerland, the museuem at Vienna's Catholic cathedral of St Stephen sported an exhibition entitled *Helden, Heiligige, Himmelssturmer – Heroes, Saints and Heaven Stormers* aimed, in the words of director Bernhard Bohler, at showing that 'there are many parallels between the cult of football and the rituals of the Christian

---

67. Sara Savage, Sylvia Collins-Mayo, Bob Mayo with Graham Cray, *Making Sense of Generation Y – The worldview of 15-25 year olds*, London: Church House Publishing, 2006, 25

68. Quoted in Hoban, 'Is Sport the New Religion?', 260

69. See Karl-Josef Kuschel, 'Aesthetic Culture as a Secular Religion?', *Concilium* (1999/1), 114-120

70. 'Taking sport seriously', Prospect, December 2007, 34

Church'.[71] A piece by Greg Watts and Emma Clancy in the English weekly Catholic paper *The Universe* about the Catholic Church's attempt to employ Euro 2008 in evangelisation proclaimed the following parallels: 'English fans have spent over 40 years in the wilderness since Sir Alf Ramsey led them to glory when they defeated the West Germans at the nation's temple to football, Wembley Stadium. Many false messiahs have come and gone since then, each failing to deliver the promises they made to the fans when they arrived. These disappointments have tested the faith of many followers ... The kind of passion and devotion some football fans show to their club has strong echoes of religious fervour. For some, football is more of a religion than a sport. Both football stadia and churches use ritual and also provide an outlet for communal singing ... What really binds Christianity and football is that they are both messianic belief systems with the idea of saviour at their core. While Christians wait for Jesus to return, football fans await the manager or player who will be the one to lead them to the promised land of a league title or cup. Like a church, a football club provides you with a focus for worship, a community with shared beliefs and a history and a way of defining who you are. It can lead you to the heaven of winning a trophy or, in the case of England, to Euro 2008 hell.'[72] This plethora of biblical images and theological ideas, presented in a Catholic newspaper, serves as both summary and in support of the thesis of this work, that is, how sport is seen and stated in the spiritual, sacramental and soteriological categories and concepts of Christian faith. An alternative version might view sport as a new opium of the people, as Kevin Garside suggests in his commentary on the 2008 Ryder Cup: 'Had Karl Marx been observing 21st-century mores, sport not religion might have been his opium for the masses.'[73] Here sport (and soccer in particular) with its saturation in the popular media, is seen as a combination of both entertainment

71.See Catalogue of the exhibition, *Helden – Heilige – Himmelsstürmer. Fussball und Religion*, Frankfurt am Main: Ikonen Museum der Stadt Frankfurt am Main, 2006
72. 'Church's goal is to use Euro 2008 as evangelisation tool', 15 June 2008
73. *The Daily Telegraph*, 10 September, 2008

and exploitation, promising an earthly rather than a heavenly pie, promoted by the relentless pursuit of profit by the capital-ism-communications complex. Whether as a form of adoration or alienation, consumption or communion, sport needs to be sit-uated more centrally in the context and concern of cultural stud-ies. Commenting on the view that 'sport is the religion of the people', Maurice Roche points out that 'it provides apparently secular, but (from a sociological perspective) quasi-religious ex-periences such as those of sacredness and transcendence, com-munal ritual and symbolism, collective drama and emotionality' and that as 'an important sector of popular culture in modern societies' sport is both 'a quasi-religious institution and also an industry'.[74] Increasingly study of sport and its relation(s) with economics, politics and religion will require reflection on both the process and perspective of globalisation.[75]

Transcending Sport
There are different responses to the meaning and value of sport. Following critical comments by rugby players about the national coach, Brian Ashton, former England cricket captain turned com-mentator Michael Atherton remarks that 'grown men should be allowed [to say] what they think, especially about something as inconsequential as sport'.[76] Disagreeing with this perspective, while demurring from the (in)famous view of Liverpool manag-er Bill Shankly, soccer pundit and author Eamon Dunphy pro-fesses that 'It's not life or death, but [for] those of us who love sport, it's passion.'[77] Lionel Shriver's delightful description of one particular game gives the lie to labelling sport as superficial and of little or no human significance: 'Grace, cunning, astonish-ing feats of fine motor co-ordination, high drama … Personalities galore, which both perk up the game and help to determine its results. Snooker, boring? Come, now. Who could ask for more

---

74. 'Mega-Events and Media Culture: Sport and the Olympics' in *Sport, Culture and the Media*, Berkshire: Open University Press, 2004, 165-181 at 169

75. See my 'Global Games', *Doctrine & Life*, 58 (July/August 2008), 12-17

76. *The Daily Telegraph*, 6 November, 2007

77. *The Sunday Tribune*, 25 May, 2008

from any sport?'[78] The prevalence and popularity of sport in countries that are not in the grip of war or famine are proof that people are entertained through this medium of mass culture, even if they cannot all enjoy the taste and fruit of victory. The many cultural variations of sporting engagement and entertainment are evidence of a universal search for something beyond the mundane and monotonous. However, questions remain about the meaning of sport and its location, both literal and metaphorical, in life. Are the venues of sport vehicles for lifting both participants and spectators above, in Philip Larkin's lines, 'the thought of high windows/The sun-comprehending glass/ And beyond it, the deep blue air, that shows/Nothing, and is nowhere, and is endless'?[79] Is sport, in the transposition of Henry James' saying about life, only 'capable of nothing but splendid waste'?[80] A dissenting voice from the definition of sport as redundant activity is that of Mark Dowd. In defence of football he describes it as 'undoubtedly offer[ing] a sense of communion and transcendence which the human psyche craves', declaring that 'I sincerely hold that the game's highs offer us a glimpse, a window if you will, into the kingdom of God: that parallel world where rampant individualism is trumped, where the body of humanity will be united and connected by being held by the source of life that underpins all of creation.'[81]

The Christian interpretation of transcendence sees it as an invitation to humanity, the truth of the human condition and not a threat that undermines its history. The closing line of the frequently quoted paragraph 22 of *Church in the Modern World* speaks of 'the nature and the greatness of the mystery of humanity as enlightened ... by the Christian revelation'.[82] In the words of Francis Oborji, 'A secularised world finds this message of transcendence hard to grasp, but the church's message is that

78. *The Observer Sports Monthly*, May 2007
79. 'High Windows', *Collected Poems*, London: Faber and Faber, 1990, 165
80. Quoted in George Dennis O'Brien, *Finding the Voice of the Church*, Notre Dame: University Press, 2007, 46
81. 'For the love of the game', *The Tablet*, 29 January, 2005
82. Flannery, ed, *Documents of Vatican II*

our commitment to that transcendence is an aid, not an impediment, to concern for the world's problems.'[83] The assertion of sport as a 'secular religion' and the attribution of the symbols of Christian faith to its activities are often articulated in terms analogous to art. However, this needs to address the challenge of Thomas Mann when he stated that 'an aesthetic worldview is simply incapable of dealing with the problems which we are obliged to resolve.'[84] Ultimately redemption, as a remainder concept, refers to the problems that humanity is unable to resolve by and for itself and within its history. Sport may not be redundant human activity in the sense of being useless or without value but it cannot be considered redemptive in the theological sense. There is a need to posit a *via media* between the extremes, on the one hand, of trivialising sport and throwing out its earthly enjoyment(s) and, on the other hand, of sport substituting for a sense of transcendence and the mystery of God. In language reminiscent of the opening lines of *Church in the Modern World*, Cardinal Joseph Ratzinger spoke, on the eve of the 1978 soccer World Cup, of football as 'a global event which unites people the world over in their hopes, fears, passions and joys, [which] shows that it must appeal to something primordially human and the question is what is this powerful attraction based on'.[85] His analysis is fascinating, with a focus on games that 'symbolise life itself' while also representing 'an attempt to return to Paradise, to get away from the enslaving seriousness of everyday life and enjoy what does not have to be and is therefore wonderful'. This eschews seeing sport as either an escape from the world and its problems or a replacement for redemption. In this perspective sport finds its rightful place as the human experience and expression of a longing that finds its end in eternity.

---

83. *Concepts of Mission*, Maryknoll: Orbis Books, 2006, 149
84. Quoted in Kuschel, 120
85. Quoted in *The Tablet*, 7 June, 2008

CHAPTER NINE

Sport and Journalism

'A Brazilian journalist once said that the one-twos between Pelé and Tostão offered convincing proof of the
existence of God.'[1]

'After the press collect their pound's worth of quotable
words from the players, leaning into the crestfallen and
broken losing players like priests hearing confession, they
retreat back upstairs to the working room.'[2]

Quis custodiet ipsos custodes?
The Roman satirist Juvenal once famously asked, 'Who will
guard the guardians?' Transposed to the context of communications and media in the twenty-first century, the terms of the
question become 'Who will judge the journalists?' Readers of
this book will recognise that the journalists referred to here are
those who cover and comment on sport, mostly in the print
media but also on radio and television. The focus of this inquiry
is well illustrated in the colour photo advertisement, against the
backdrop of Croke Park, for the 'Championship Team' of sports
journalists in *The Irish News* under the banner 'WORSHIP – The
Game.'[3] In similar vein, the blurb at the back of *The Daily
Telegraph* journalist Jim White's recent book on Manchester
United asks about about the club as 'a point of secular worship'.[4]
While the issue of judging the use and understanding of faith
symbols and theological language in sports reportage is at issue,
it cannot be completely separated from media coverage of religious affairs in general. Columnist and academic Colum Kenny
delineates the domain of mainstream religious journalists and

1. John Carlin, *White Angels*, 13
2. Keith Duggan, *The Lifelong Season*, 56
3. *Sunday Tribune*, 27 July, 2008
4. *Manchester United : The Biography*, London: Sphere, 2008

the ten divisions of their work.[5] He states that 'at the heart of the media's reporting of religion there is frequently a sort of "clash of civilisations".'[6] This suggests a state of (potential) conflict between religious institutions and the fourth estate, a situation reminiscent of Kipling's scenario where 'East and West' do not meet, whatever about 'before God's great Judgement seat'. Kenny states that the decision of editors/journalists to 'go' or not with a particular religious story depends on a number of factors, including public interest, their own ideological background and/or bias and social trends. Among the 'barriers to the better reporting of religion' he notes from the side of religious institutions and leaders 'a failure to sustain dialogue with key media journalists and the use of arcane or archaic forms of language', and on the side of the media 'prejudice on the part of some journalists and editors in respect to religion generally' and, *inter alia,* lack of respect for journalism, cliché and indifference to religious belief/practice in society.[7]

The amount of coverage devoted to sport in the media is massive. One need only consider, if not actually count, the number of so-called column inches involved in the reporting of games and accompanying features of sports men and women. Many newspapers have separate sections dedicated solely to sport, with weekly and monthly supplements for special events extending from a range of World Cup competitions involving cricket, rugby and soccer to intercontinental contests such as the Ryder Cup and Compromise Rules. The many hours of coverage on radio and television add up, in the opinion of some commentators, to saturation, in the course of which there is a need to spice up commentary with a raft of references which are considered to be both easily discernible and digestible. If, as an Irish

---

5. 'The journalist who is involved in reporting or writing about religion may work on a newsdesk or as a feature-writer, columnist, programme reporter or presenter. He or she will not always be a designated religious affairs correspondent or even be a person who considers him or herself to be religious.' 'Reporting Religion', in *Contemporary Catholicism in Ireland : A Critical Appraisal*, John Littleton and Eamon Maher, eds, Dublin: The Columba Press, 2008, 111-42 at 111-2
6. Ibid, 112
7. Ibid. 114

Catholic bishop anecdotally exhorted his priests to 'horse things up' in advance of a canonisation ceremony, perhaps it is not too surprising that a degree of religious exaggeration, even rhetoric, is availed of by sports journalists in anticipation of their audiences, in what Kenny calls 'our hyper, multi-cut, sound-bite culture'.[8] The extent of such practices and their evaluation need to be explored from both ethical and theological angles.

Theologian Donal Harrington states that 'Journalism seems to me to be, not so much a univocal term, as something of an umbrella term that covers different, contrasting and even contradictory realities.'[9] In his review of a book of interviews with prominent Irish journalists, former editor of *The Irish Times*, Conor Brady, wonders whether 'idealistic, searching for something, restless, looking for a buzz' were the terms that characterised them, leading him to worry about the lack of self-doubt in the profession of the pen: 'Not many are moved to reflect on the immense power and influence we wield. There is a disturbing assurance about what we do and the way we do it. We are not disposed to too much critical self-examination. It may not be what Roger Greene wanted to highlight in this exercise. But like Sherlock Holmes' dog – that did not bark in the night – it is significant.'[10] (Reference to 'a disturbing assurance' may be code for arrogance, an attitude that journalists may be all too often ready to attribute to other professions.) This lack of self-examination is evident at the first ever conference on sports writing to be held in Ireland. While celebrated *Sunday Times* writer David Walsh warns about the lack of investigative journalism in the field, the irony of the opening lines of the *Irish Examiner*'s sports editor in relation to journalists themselves is striking: 'It was Earl Warren, the late US Chief Justice, who summed up the appeal of sports writing in a nutshell. "I always turn to the sports section first [for] the sports page records people's accomplishment; the front page has nothing but man's failures".'[11] 'The ap-

---

8. Ibid. 127
9. 'Moral discourse and journalism', in *Contemporary Irish Moral Discourse*, Amelia Fleming,ed, Dublin: The Columba Press, 2007, 66-75
10. Review of Roger Greene, *Under the Spotlight, Village*, 1-7 December, 2005, 27
11. 'Words of Wonder', in *The Art of Sportswriting, Irish Examiner –Arena*, 9 November, 2005

peal of sports writing' as an article of journalistic faith needs further analysis.

Scrutinising the Sportswriters

Like all journalists, sportswriters adopt and articulate a stance in which to situate their reporting of games, matches and other forms of competition in their specialised field. These stances express different ways of writing about and perhaps even of watching sport through which they seek to express its meaning for their readers or audiences. The stances of these sporting scribes may be broadly seen in terms of two different models of media, as either critical or celebratory, whereby and wherein sporting events are reported in terms which are either evaluative or expressive. Thus *The Times* Chief Sport correspondent Simon Barnes contrasts his own stance with that of one of his predecessors, David Miller: 'David was and is very serious about sport, believing in the importance of sport as a social and moral force. I don't share this view. For me, sport is a monstrous triviality that produces stories that people want to hear, that I want to tell. For me, sport is not moral. Truth is in the performer, in the performance. Truth is in what sport reveals about the person who does it. Compared to that, the idea of sport as a moral force seems rather small.'[12] The model of sports writing as evaluation consciously adopts an ethical stance both in its way of looking at and writing about sport. The parameters of sport are seen and stated morally, involving both the performance of the players themselves and the particular rules on the pitch that govern their engagement as competitors. In this perspective sport is not viewed and valued as a series of isolated events where the involvement of spectators and scribes is purely passive. The impact of sport on society is here subjected to scrutiny, with its cultural and commercial implications interpreted and investigated.

The entertainment model of sports writing embraces both elements of the sporting encounter and the emotional engagement of the commentator expressing excitement and exasperation. By extension these communications may be conveyed as if

---

12. *The Meaning of Sport*, London: Short Books, 2006, 14

they were part of the competition itself, the commentary thereby contributing as a means to the end of mass enjoyment. The nostalgic comment of the late *Daily Mail* columnist Ian Woolridge captures this model: 'I longed to see a gymnasium in Russia where somebody laughed. I longed to see schoolboys skylarking and fat girls doing something hopelessly badly. I longed to see somebody dropping in after school for an hour's enjoyment.'[13] Coverage of Roy Keane's departure as manager of Sunderland by columnists such as Tom Humphries and Keith Duggan employ the imagery and language of entertainment media: 'He's gone, but he'll be back – he's box office';[14] 'Premier League circus loses a compelling act.'[15]

Barnes envisages the sportswriter as a teller of tales that are 'not [only] of bodies but of hearts and minds and souls'.[16] While possessing an artistic temperament and performing artistic antics 'without producing art' he asserts that those who point the sporting pen 'are artists in the sense that we start with nothing and end up with something, creation *ab nihilo*: a definition of both an artist and God'.[17] His concern as a writer is the communication of greatness, both on the pitch and on paper. The enjoyment of sport can be hierarchically ordered from partisanship through drama to greatness. While admitting that such greatness does not amount to an amelioration of the world or approach artistic or spiritual heights, he asserts that it represents a genuine 'level of human achievement that goes beyond anything done before [which] cannot fail to be vivid and meaningful and inspiring'.[18] Barnes observes sport from the optic of enjoyment and opines that it is all about fun. In a piece entitled 'The ten commandments remind us that sport was always meant to be fun', he states that its function is entertainment and enjoyment: 'We all know that we watch sport for fun. It is not supposed to be serious. In newspapers we put sport at the back, to set it apart from the war, pestilence, politics and the four horse-

13. Quoted by Robert Philip in *The Daily Telegraph*, March 8 2007
14. *The Irish Times*, 5 December, 2008
15. *The Irish Times*, 6 December, 2008
16. *The Meaning of Sport*, 12
17. *The Meaning of Sport*, 33
18.'True greatness is a cause for celebration', *The Times*, 25 August 2008

men.' He considers the final commandment of commending an exchange of respect between competitors at the end of a contest as constituting the meaning of sport: 'That nobody died. That it was all play. That life goes on. That sport is not war, nor even anything remotely like war. That sport is fun.'[19] In support of Barnes' thesis about sport as theatre rather than tragedy is the letter sent to *Tribune* magazine by E. S. Fayers in response to the statement of George Orwell that sport 'is war without words': 'These crowds, if he got among them, are not great ignorant crowds of sadistic morons. They are a pretty good mixture of just ordinary men. A little puzzled, a little anxious, steady, sceptical, humorous, knowledgeable, having a little fun, hoping for a bit of excitement. I'm sorry for George. He's missed a lot of fun in life.'[20]

On the subject of comparing sport and religion Barnes refers to the 'many semi-facetious terms that acknowledge this [which] began as jokes, at least, but by degrees have become accepted terms, from which most of the humour and irony has been removed'.[21] Among the examples given are cathedral, messiah and the faithful as symbols, if not indeed synonyms, for stadium, new manager and fans respectively. While acknowledging that he writes in and for a 'largely godless society', he is not adverse to borrowing from the language of faith and theology. In an article analysing change in sport he begins with Cardinal Newman's immortal lines addressed to God, 'who changest not'.[22] He uses the language of redemption in relation to the fortunes of David Beckham. Sent off in the 1998 World Cup and subsequently suffering as a 'national hate-object', it seemed he would have to wait another four years for redemption. Nevertheless, 'there was redemption to be found as soon as the following year' in performing 'one of the great self-rescuing acts in the history of sport' when he 'inspired Manchester United to their immortal

19. *The Times*, 11 January, 2008
20. Quoted by E. Sweeney in 'Hold the Back Page', *Sunday Independent*, 10 August, 2008
21. *The Meaning of Sport*, 173-4
22. 'Cricket facing ultimate test: to preserve the five-day game', *The Times*, 28 September, 2007

treble of the 1998-99 season'.[23] However, he himself writes in this vein without a vestige of awareness of the ironic reductionism involved in relegating redemption to such forms of self-rescue. In the context of such sports writing, cliché might be the correct term to translate the entertaining of readers through references to religion. Indeed, a comment of his on the employment of cliché might *a fortiori* be applied to the over exposure and evacuation of religious and theological language in its equation with sport: 'Did I invent the cliché, or was I just on the leading edge of the clichés wave? It's impossible to say. These things happen by a curious and elusive process ... The cliché reached general acceptance because we needed a word to cover a genuine phenomenon but, of course, once it gained currency, it lost some of its original meaning and went fuzzy at the edges.'[24] A presumption that theology and religious faith also represent such a 'genuine phenomenon' would help to level the proverbial playing pitch.

Under the headline *That's Entertainment* Paul Wilson profiles the final days of the summer transfer period in the Premiership. Quoting from W. B. Yeats about anarchy being 'loosed upon the world', he contrasts the enjoyment of England's national sport with the experience of events at the Bejing Olympics, considering that 'truly, to be tired of football at the minute is to be tired of life'.[25] From the face of Manchester United manager Alex Ferguson at the prospect of Dimitar Berbatov joining his City rivals through the declining fortunes of Newcastle United to the advent of foreign owners as the new stars of the soccer scene, Wilson wittingly writes about the drama beyond the pitch and in the boardrooms. His advice for any future owner of Newcastle, cast in explicitly christological terms, 'not to welcome [Kevin] Keegan as the returning messiah then appoint a team of London-based suits to crucify him', seems to send up his claim that 'it is as well to remember we are talking about a small corner of the entertainment industry, not life and death'.[26] His reference to the fate of Keegan and fellow (former West Ham

23. The Meaning of Sport, 64
24. 'On to glory with Rooney ... or out', *The Times*, 24 June, 2006
25. *The Observer*, 7 September, 2008
26. *The Observer*, 7 September, 2008

United) manager Alan Curbishley draws attention to implications for individuals and their families in the corporate games
conducted far from the field of play. Further examples of his entertainment journalism are expressed in captions for his weekly
column, 'From top to bottom, England is the home of entertainment' and 'Curtain falling with a thud on [Manchester] City's
January slapstick.'[27]

In contrast the stance of columnist Sue Mott is evaluative.
She casts a critical, though not cold, eye on the spectrum of
sporting activity and its many associations. Displaying a measure of courage in the face of managers, ministers and media she
discusses and discerns the moral implications of the massive
economic and entertainment industry involved in the sports
'circus'. Analysing the link between the prize of victory on the
pitch and the profits to be made off it, she comments that while
sport claims to occupy a space in society free of corruption and
'corporate stitch-ups' 'it has never been more profitable, and
perhaps we can extrapolate from that the notion that it has
never been more corrupt either' with 'the result that we have become corrupted watchers'.[28] Considering the connection between cheating and gambling, she cites the tragic case of Hansie
Cronjie who 'twisted a game of his beloved cricket despite being
captain of South Africa' and quotes the warning of Uefa president Michel Platini about the dangers involved in the association of games and gambling 'for football and for all sport in the
future'.[29] There is a refreshing honesty in her lack of sycophancy
towards individuals and institutions in the sporting world and
its ideological surroundings.

While decrying the 'brattish self-indulgence' of Manchester
United's Rio Ferdinand in blasting a ball into the crowd and hit-
ting a woman spectator, she also takes aim at the efforts of administrators to control the type of language commensurate with
fair comment and criticism of players and their performances:
'It is really reaching a dangerous pass when playing badly and

27. *The Observer*, 30 November, 2008 and 25 January, 2009
28. 'How corrupt is sport? Let me count the ways', *The Daily Telegraph*,
13 November, 2007
29. 'Cancer of cheating lurks in football's links to gambling', *The Daily
Telegraph*, 4 December, 2007

managing badly are blamed on the messengers ... Heaven knows how many clauses in the contract with ITV and Setanta forbid sarcastic phrases. What about irony? Will that also be banned, by the thought police of the FA, when the BBC relinquish the deal. What about comedic detachment?'[30] Her targeting of the intemperate language of former Chelsea boss Jose Mourinho directed against referee Mike Riley is particularly apt in the aftermath of the allegation he aimed at Swede Anders Frisk after a European Champions League match against Barcelona. Her analysis of thuggery on and off the pitch of play and questioning of the causal thread between them reveals a fearlessness in the face of both football managers and fans alike.[31] Commenting on the first television soccer match commentary by a female she concludes that 'having invited women to become full members of society, sport could not be sequestered forever'.[32] While listing and lamenting many of the temptations and moral failures that sport is prey to, Mott also looks to the idealism it can involve and incarnate. Writing in the aftermath of both London's triumph of the 2012 Olympics and the tragedy of the bombing of the city's transports system, she states that 'at a time when one maniacal faction of man is trying to assassinate random innocents for its shadowy cause, it is useful to see man's other, better, decent side'.[33] Seeing sport as the means towards the end of 'togetherness' whereby 'humanity in all its shapes, sizes, colours, creeds and faiths can find a way to tolerate, but celebrate, each other', Mott also invokes the Olympic ideal as an antidote to the nexus of obesity and obsession and 'lure [children] away from their burbling pieces of technology, their orgiastic button-pressing and their perception of legs as a means of stumbling to the nearest vehicle'.[34]

Mott's evaluative and ethical stance employs religious com-

---

30. 'Petulant Ferdinand proves football needs to grow up', *The Daily Telegraph*, 3 April, 2007

31. 'Mourinho insult should not have gone unpunished', *The Daily Telegraph*, 13 March, 2007

32. 'First the vote, now soccer commentary...', *The Daily Telegraph*, 20 April, 2007

33. 'London must unite around sporting ideal', *The Daily Telegraph*, 9 July, 2005

34. 'London must unite ...'

parisons and concepts. Stating that 'sport, despite being trivial, is often biblical in its themes' she speaks of the failure to find perfection with the concomitant necessity of humility while at the same time hailing the life and kicking legs of rugby player Jonny Wilkinson 'as practically a saint'.[35] Criticising the 'vested interest' of Frank Lampard in showing his vest (with sponsor's logo) proclaiming his century of goals for Chelsea, she states that 'Moses did not broadcast the Ten Commandments by vest' while, at the same time, stating that Brazilian star Kaka should keep his footballing skills and religious fervour separate: 'Kaka's vest says "I belong to Jesus". Fine, but tell him not us.'[36] However, her penchant for irony itself pays the price when she concludes a piece entitled 'Leeds pay devilishly heavy price for sins of the past' with the statement that 'there is nothing supernatural about the story of Leeds United'.[37] Commentator and columnist John Inverdale draws on Shakespearean and literary language rather than scriptural and theological imagery to evaluate sport and its effects on society. Though not referring to 'the state of Denmark' in his contrast of the certain ending of *Hamlet* with the uncertainty of sporting competition (without cheating), he links lines from the play, 'To thine own self be true', with Macbeth, 'Out damn spot, fixing', to make the point that 'sport can no longer afford to be conciliatory and offer forgive-and-forget platitudes to individuals and their coaches who blatantly flout the rules with no regard for the integrity of their profession'.[38] At the same time he argues for the integrity of people involved in media for their insight into and interpretation of sport so that spectators and readers can have 'faith in the individuals who voice the opinions [which] is not the same as agreeing with them, it's about accepting their credibility and the motives behind them'.[39]

35. 'By falling short, Beckham shows he is still one of us', *The Daily Telegraph*, 5 February, 2008

36. 'Nauseating sentiments of getting shirty', *The Daily Telegraph*, 19 February, 2008

37. *The Daily Telegraph*, 19 February, 2008

38. 'Something is rotten in sport when cheats return', *The Daily Telegraph*, 28 March, 2007

39. 'Sporting bodies cannot be allowed to censor media', *The Daily Telegraph*, 4 April, 2007

An interesting example of evaluation by the sporting media is expressed in coverage of the on-off saga of Brazilian and AC Milan star player Kaka's transfer to Manchester City in the January 2009 transfer window for a reported fee of £100 million. In the midst of a global economic recession and national depression the view that a footballer could change hands for such a sum seems ludicrous to many involved in the game. Referring to the 'phone-in fulminators' who considered City's bid 'obscene in the current economic climate', Paul Hayward's remark is apposite, 'as if it would have passed the morality test back in the boom days when it was raining jobs and mortgages'.[40] However, a week later Hayward's colleague Will Buckley criticises the connection of football and morality. Considering that 'Kaka's individual rights were being blithely overridden by the sportswriters' need to show that the sport they cover is "better" than it actually is', he added that 'this is a common misperception' and that 'if you're dim-witted enough to consider football a religion it is only consistent to believe that it is imbued with a particular moral quality'.[41] The Achilles' heel of Buckley's analysis lies not in his association of morality and religious belief as 'dim-witted' but in the absence of a basis for his assertion of the Brazilian's rights. More tongue in cheek Sam Wallace, beneath the caption 'Cross Purposes', wonders whether Kaka's belonging to Jesus 'mean[s] that Manchester City have to pay him an agent's commission as well?'[42]

Sporting Evangelism

Tom Humphreys writes passionately about sport. He regularly portrays the passion and pain, the price and pride of people who put themselves literally on the line in playing on pitches and performing in all kinds of athletic arenas. He pours forth a stream of sporting consciousness which captures the spirit and sweat, solidarity and sacrifice of the men and women for whom gender is an appendage to the word 'sports'. Fellow writer Paul Kimmage sees himself as Salieri to Humphreys' Mozart, while

---

40. *The Observer*, 18 January, 2009
41. 'The Kaká saga conclusion? Kick morals out of football', *The Observer*, 25 January, 2009
42. *The Independent*, 19 January, 2009

RTÉ presenter and media professional Bill O'Herlihy pronounces him 'the greatest sportswriter of his generation'.[43] If soccer is called the 'beautiful game', on occasion his humorous, laconic and throwaway style rises to take writing about sport to the level of the beautiful genre. Writing under the byline of *Locker room,* Humphries displays a popular but never pedantic form of prose which presents a passion for people and places where sport is played. In a few sentences he manages to express both the effect of the weather and the essence of Kilkenny's All-Ireland 2008 Grand Slam in attaining achievement mastery at minor, intermediate, under-21 and senior levels: 'A summer of unrelenting stripeyness. Sunsets of amber and black. The year of the cat.'[44] An excellent example of his oeuvre and craft is his piece on Cork's resurgent second half performance to rob runaway Galway of a place in the 2008 All-Ireland hurling quarter-finals.[45] A reference to 'hurling's homely cathedral' sets the scene for an account that imitates his description of Cork's intensity, 'all heart but a leavening of brain'. The proverbial 'clash of the ash' is almost palpable in his penmanship. Despite a mixed metaphor – 'Galway brought just one sharpened blade to the gunfight' – he manages to depict the respective fall and rise of fortunes on the field of play in Thurles dubbed 'the greatest drama of the GAA summer, the best of many summers'. He sees the battle and bonding of (team) sport as transcending, at least temporarily 'all those trespasses of the real world, money, worries, sick children, bereavements, illnesses'. For Humphreys, the struggles and success of such sporting greats represent, in a reference to Dylan Thomas, a 'rage [once more] against the dying of the light'. This piece represents sports writing at its most persuasive and moves readers to pathos. In his profile of this blood and bandage Band of Brothers he is light years from the 'pickled Gods and archetypes', a prior reference to the remark of Marshall McLuhan about those 'on the sports desk [who were]

---

43. Tom Humphries, *Booked: Selected Writings,* Dublin: Town House, 2004

44. 'Kilkenny complete the clean sweep', *The Irish Times,* 15 September, 2008

45. 'Cork find spark in cooling embers to catch fire', *The Irish Times,* 21 July, 2008

perpetually busy about the business of retailing'.[46] Humphreys' writing and worldview are inspired by and in turn illustrate what he once called 'the core humanity of sports'.[47]

His turns of phrase throw up a sacramental, biblical and spiritual stock of knowledge. A line about 'the childhood penance of the Railway Cup on Paddy's Day'[48] recalls childhood for many readers reared in the era when the inter-provincial hurling and football finals were the main focus of Ireland's national celebration before the advent of prosperity and parades. Wexford's winning ways in the All-Ireland football championship are wound into a reference to both the scriptural witness and the wet summer: 'Repent your sins just in case the apocalypse is nigh. Sunday's biblical floods may just have been the start of Wexford's subversion of world order'. (The caption managed to connect both Greek mythology and the Bible.)[49] In a piece on Bobby Locke he depicts the South African golfing legend at the Masters course in Augusta 'entering the old cathedral without so much as the genuflection of a practice round',[50] while his reference to 'the Meek and Contemplative Order of Dublin Footballers inherit[ing] the earth'[51] could be taken with the proverbial pinch of salt, though preferably not of a biblical kind. The GAA rulebook is referred to as 'Holy Writ' while, surprisingly in the light of the church's contribution to the history and development of the Association, he comments that 'Catholic Church plc has mightily betrayed its stockholders'[52] in the context of a debate about drink sponsorship.

Humphries' references to God reveal a literary conceit, if not a (theo)logical contradiction. In a piece on boxer Evander Holyfield he writes: 'We wait for the God Is My Pal Act. Am sick to death of sporting Christians. Plan to yell to Evander: There Is No Bloody God.'[53] The emotive, almost expletive, 'bloody' is

46. Humphries, *Booked*, 69
47. *Booked*, 239
48. *Booked*, 238
49. 'Jason's quest takes on biblical character', *The Irish Times*, 24 August, 2008
50. *Booked*, 283
51. *Booked*, 73
52. *Booked*, 415
53. *Booked*, 231

ironic, at least in the context of boxing. In a profile of (then) Irish soccer manager Humphries hails him in explicitly divine terms: 'This column subscribes to the view that Jack Charlton is God. An Old Testament version of God who doth smite the unworthy and drink stout and catch fish, but God nonetheless. God is always on the record. We sports journalists are the handmaidens of the Lord.'[54] While this evocation of the man affectionately admired by the Irish public as 'Big Jack' may seem to have more to do with fun rather than faith, Humphries' penchant for profanity is particularly associated with images of divine retribution and the club Charlton played for: 'This column does its purgatory on earth by being a Leeds fan. The last Leeds revolution was built on vanities and venialities. It was punished by the gods eventually, the deities displaying some very Old Testament wrath as they smited Davo's [O'Leary] babies and Ridsdale's credibility.'[55] However, the reference to credibility raises questions about truth in the course of referring to divinity and doctrine.

Humphries' colleague, Keith Duggan, presents a perceptive and probing commentary on sporting matters in his column *Sideline Cut*. His style is less immediate, leaving words and phrases which linger in the memory, particularly in his pieces about the GAA. Recalling the original 'Corinthian drive among counties', he refers to the temptation of local pride and the 'transcendent feeling of having achieved something rare and immortal'.[56] Relying on a religious register he describes how 'Na Déise reached the promised land on a transcendent afternoon at Croke Park', when Waterford defeated Tipperary to reach the 2008 hurling final.[57] His ability to analyse sport in a wider context is evidenced by his reference to the rise of the GAA in a country where 'the old pillars of religious and political infallibility came crashing down' alongside the challenge of continuing to count on a spirit of sacrifice whereby county players had 'something

54. *Booked*, 60
55. 'The appeal of some old-fashioned values', *The Irish Times*, 19 February, 2007
56. 'Silent summer doesn't bear thinking of', *The Irish Times*, 10 November, 2007
57. 'Nobody said there'd be *Déise* like this', *The Irish Times*, 18 August, 2008

of the monastic spirit, living lives of self-denial, living for Sundays'. Analysing the Cork versus Galway hurling qualifier, he refers to Cork's 'almost spiritual response' in the second half which negated the 'miracle point after miracle point' piled on by Galway player Joe Canning.[58] An earlier reference to the city's famed mid-summer race meeting combines the comments about 'Galway folks observe Race Week the way Muslims observe Ramadan' and visitors to the city viewing the hurling on television while waiting to receive pints of stout 'with the rapturous anticipation of the devout at the Vatican'. However, this admixture of fasting and faith is unlikely to advance interreligious understanding and dialogue. Writing about the detail of Diego Maradona's paranoia which drove him to discharge a shotgun at people outside his mansion, he notes humorously the comment of former Tipperary hurler and occasional fellow columnist Nicky English that 'they weren't real people, only journalists'.[59]

Although Frank McNally does not write in the sports pages of *The Irish Times*, a number of his contributions to *An Irishman's Diary* often piece together both reference to sport and religion and reflection on the relation between them. A column on Liverpool, looking ostensibly at the city's Anglican and Catholic cathedrals and its Premiership soccer clubs Everton and Liverpool, contains both sociological information and cultural interpretation. Referring to the fact that by the time the Catholic 'Paddy's Wigwam' was opened in the mid-sixties both religious faith and the city's economic fortunes were in decline, he remarks that even though 'it was probably already a cliché then that soccer had become the new religion, it may not have been a coincidence that the period of Merseyside's worst decline coincided with an era of unrivalled football supremacy, as Liverpudlians turned from Hope Street to Anfield Road in search of consolation'.[60] He remarks that rivalry between the clubs has been reduced to the field of play and their respective

---

58. 'Galway conundrum continues to mystify', *The Irish Times*, 26 July, 2008
59. 'Maradona's story might still inspire', *The Irish Times*, 31 March, 2007
60. *The Irish Times*, 16 May, 2007

fortunes at English and European levels, thus representing a very different picture to relations between, for example, Glasgow Celtic and Rangers: 'Today, older fans recall a time when nuns collected for charity outside Goodison Park, while the Salvation Army looked after Anfield. But having briefly flourished, the sectarian identities have long since withered. The Liverpool-Everton rivalry has become unusual among the genre for having no geographic, political, social, or religious *raison d'être*'.[61] The final paragraph of this piece picks up a previous reference to local musical legend the Beatles and their line about being 'more popular than Jesus': 'Among John Lennon's permanent memorials now is the city's airport. Not only is it named after him, it also takes a line from one of his songs as its motto. Christians and nervous flyers may not be reassured by the thought. But everywhere you look in the airport these days, from the duty free shop to the roof of the terminal building, you see the message: "Above us only sky"'.[62] Reminiscent of Philip Larkin's lines about 'the deep blue air, that shows / Nothing, and is nowhere, and is endless',[63] Lennon's Liverpool is an insightful image of both the loss of Christian vision and the 'pie in the sky' view ultimately offered from venues such as Anfield and Goodison Park.

McNally displays a delight in mixing ideas and imagery drawn from both spiritual and secular spheres. Welcoming the Vatican's 'Ten Commandments for Drivers' he wondered if the church could utilise underused facilities on motorways: 'The next logical step now, surely, is the drive-thru confession. We have the necessary infrastructure already, in the form of the toll-booths currently multiplying on roads. The church could simply rent some of these at weekends or other off-peak teams [times] and put up the necessary signs. Then it could install priests who – not unlike the regular occupants – would demand change from drivers.'[64] Notwithstanding his reduction of the sacrament of divine mercy to a roadside transaction, the identification of

61. *The Irish Times*, 16 May, 2007
62. *The Irish Times*, 16 May, 2007
63. 'High Windows', *Collected Poems*, (London: Faber and Faber, 1990), 165
64. *The Irish Times*, 21 June, 2007

moral conversion with mere coinage is inane, as is the idea that 'God knows, it is easier for a camel to pass through the eye of a needle than for a driver to get out of Dublin on a Friday.'[65] In a column on the Cheltenham racing festival he mixes theological and sporting metaphors: 'The aptly named Lough Derg was among the runners in yesterday's big race. It was a 50-1 chance and short of its owners renaming it 'Lourdes', it could hardly win. But it didn't need to win to make it another purgatorial day for the pilgrims circling the course here in search of redemption. When the race's hot favourite Black Jack Ketchum fell at the first, punters must have wondered what they'd done to so offend heaven, apart from taking up betting.'[66] The author of these imagined witticisms would do well to reflect on the opening line of his own piece inspired by football player Cristiano Ronaldo: 'English must be the Zimbabwean dollar of European languages, so devalued have many of its words become in popular usage'.[67]

In the wake of Ireland's poor performance(s) in the 2007 Rugby World Cup he plays on the Genesis report into events both before and during the competition. Referring to the 'Book of Genesis report into the catastrophic events in the Garden of Eden', McNally makes literal references to the biblical narrative, including Adam and Eve, the Tree of Knowledge of Good and Evil, the Flood, the Tower of Babel, Destruction of Sodom and Gomorrah, the Children of Israel in Egypt, Abraham and Isaac in his imagined interpretation of the unfolding events both on and off the field of play. His 'Overall Conclusion' is a conflation of theological categories and corporate terminology which collapses the language of revelation to the level of rugby (mis)management: 'While no blame whatsoever should be attached to God, who should be allowed to see out his already-agreed contract for the remaining period (all eternity), the consultants note his extremely heavy workload during the events in question, especially during the initial seven days. The consultants recom-

---

65. *The Irish Times*, 21 June, 2007
66. 'Another purgatorial day for punters at Prestbury', *The Irish Times*, 16 March, 2007
67. *The Irish Times*, 3 April, 2008

mend that, without diluting his authority in any way, God should henceforth be divided into a three-person Committee. We believe that this would be the best way to meet the challenges facing us as we move forward into the New Testament.'[68] In similar vein sports journalist Ciaran Cronin, commenting on criticism of the findings in the Genesis report, considers 'the reason the company chose to call themselves after that particular part of the Bible and not another is because they would have been done under the trade descriptions act had they called themselves "Revelation"'[69] might seem unduly harsh on the Scottish consultancy firm. The same company were called in by the English FA to evaluate the national team's failure to progress beyond the quarter-final stage of recent major international competitions. Playing on its name, Jasper Gerard wonders whether the headline 'Genesis called in to save English football' refers to the seventies rock band or scripture and somewhat cynically surmises that, since everything else having been tried and trusted, 'why not divine intervention'.[70] Commenting that 'Genesis preaches a more modish religion, still full of hockum pockum, but chargeable at several hundred quid an hour' his view of their 'Vision' is that it 'mixes impenetrable jargon, the bleeding obvious and blithe assumption' and asks 'is there anything in this report' that couldn't be arrived at over a few beers?[71] This assessment holds out little hope for either the future of faith or football in the country.

His reference 'Vatican-approved crusade to save professional soccer's soul',[72] and its symbolic launching of 'Progetto Soccer' by presenting a number 16 jersey of third division club AC Ancona to Pope Benedict, gives McNally the licence to look at how Catholic concepts have been introduced into sports. Linking the project of promoting morality in soccer to the 'prophetic' figure of Roy Keane, formerly the fiery wearer of the same number as the present successor of Saint Peter, McNally

68. *The Irish Times*, 3 April, 2008
69. *Sunday Tribune*, 23 December, 2007
70. 'Genesis' vision of England – not exactly the Book of Revelation', *The Daily Telegraph*, 8 May, 2008
71. 'genesis' vision of England…'
72. *The Irish Times*, 12 October, 2007

comments: 'Admittedly, for most of his playing career, Keane's sense of justice leant perhaps a little too heavily on the Old Testament. "I will render vengeance to mine enemies, and will reward them that hate me" (Deuteronomy 32:41), was his cry. For more than a decade, his eye-for-an-eye, cruciate-for-a-cruciate approach was a cause of concern to opposing midfielders and liberal Christians alike. Since becoming a manager, however, he has mellowed. Great is his righteousness, still, but the message has been refined for a broader audience. His recent encyclical on materialism – and specifically on the dangers of excessive shopping by footballers' wives – was a masterpiece of moral clarity. I expect him to issue an epistle on the subject of gamesmanship soon.'[73] In relation to rugby McNally mentions the role of the referee as being analogous to that of priests in giving advice to players to avoid temptation and in cases of the need for atonement remitting them to the temporary 'sin-bin' from 'which they emerge cleansed and vowing never to do anything bad again, until the next time'.[74] Widening his analysis, he wonders whether the Vatican initiative might indicate a degree of self-interest involving 'a Trojan horse for the old religion, the start of a reverse take-over' given that 'it has become almost a truism that football is the new religion and that the great stadiums are to modern cities what gothic cathedrals were in medieval times.'[75] The range of McNally's reduction of biblical images and theological language to sporting references is testimony to this truism, at least in media terms.

Fellow columnist John Waters considers the relation between religious faith and sport in the context of the Irish Catholic bishops' concern about the scheduling of training and competitive fixtures on Sunday mornings and the resultant non-attendance at Mass by players and their parent(s) or guardian(s). He states that 'the implication of the bishops' complaint, put simply, is that our society has allowed sport to become more important than God' and surmises that 'indeed, if they had put it this way, we might have been able to mount a far more interesting discussion, for then we might come to consider why this has occurred

73. *The Irish Times*, 12 October, 2007
74. *The Irish Times*, 12 October, 2007
75. *The Irish Times*, 12 October, 2007

– if indeed it has'.[76] Seeking a *via media* between the distortion of the human religious impulse by either ecclesiastical moralism or the economic market, Waters identifies the key problem as pertaining to the presentation of the Christian message, particularly in the form of communication found in church services and concludes that there is really no contest between 'what happens on Sunday morning sports field[s]' and 'what doesn't happen at Sunday Mass'.[77]

Playing at Prayer

In his book *Foul Play*, Joe Humphreys casts a critical eye on sport. Subtitled 'What's Wrong with Sport', he describes his growing disillusionment in reverse religious terms: 'Ask anyone whose faith in God has been shaken, when exactly they started having doubts and they'd be hard pressed to answer. The same goes for my faith in sport. I cannot say when I started doubting myself. Nor can I speak of a Road-to-Damascus-like conversion.'[78] Events involving the fascist salute of West Ham United player Paolo Di Canio, the playing up in the media of two former Manchester United players, the departure of Roy Keane and the death of George Best, contributed to his adoption of athlete Roger Bannister's advice, adapted from Plato, that 'the unexamined sporting life is not worth living'. Referring to the replacement of faith and its practice by the time and energy expended by fans of sport, he remarks on the fact that 'sport is increasingly appropriating the language of religion'.[79] A chapter entitled *Headers and Headcases* explores the connection between sport and stupidity on the part of players and fans, managers and media. Quoting a piece in *The Times* headed 'How Zidane's Belief Brought Him Down', which referred to the French player's 'moment of madness' in headbutting an opponent the 2006 World Cup final against Italy, Humphreys comments that 'as a representation of sports analysis today, it is perhaps the best argument you could come up with to scrap such commentary

---

76. 'Sunday morning blues – Has society allowed sport to become more important than God?', *The Irish Catholic*, 17 April, 2008
77. *The Irish Catholic*, 17 April, 2008
78. Cambridge, UK: Icon Books, 2008, 6
79. *Foul Play*, 8

from newspapers, or at least move it into the same page as the horoscopes and the funnies'.[80] Analysing sport from a moral angle, he complains about the lack of ethics in those who play, administer and follow it, cataloguing a culture of cheating and a climate of hatred in some corners. However, he appears inconsistent in his insistence that the comparison of sports fandom with religious belief involves the wrong sort of such belief while interpreting the display of Christian faith by some professional golfers as irritating and by some professional footballers as incongruous.

Turning to sports journalism, he connects its excesses and endless search for entertainment with the malaise common to all media as expressed by a former editor of *The Independent on Sunday*: 'Today a spectre haunts the editorial floor – the spectre of the reader's boredom, the viewer's lassitude. If customers are to stay with the product, they need, or are thought to need, a diet of surprise, pace, cuts-to-the-chase, playfulness, provocation, drama.'[81] Commenting on the notorious sensitivity of sporting organisations to any form of criticism, he resorts to what amounts to a cheap shot that would not be out of place in some of the media circles he allegedly attacks: 'Dare to identify wrongdoing in the church of soccer, athletics or swimming and you can expect a cover-up and a closing of ranks of which the Vatican would be proud.'[82] Among the 'meta-lies' of sports he lists its competitive and entertainment values, its atmospheric quality and sentimentality, its capacity for creating and maintaining happiness among the hordes of fans. Quoting a social theorist about the retarding effect of sport on society, Humphreys derides obsession with sport as an opting out of critical exploration of and engagement with issues in the real world. Citing himself as an example, he confesses, 'Ask me about August 1998 and I can tell you that West Ham were then enjoying a rich vein of form in the Premiership [though] I had to look up the fact that it was also the month the Congolese war started in earnest.'[83] Summing up his observations on obsession

80. Ibid. 38
81. Ibid. 148
82. Ibid. 150
83. Ibid. 178-179

with sport as the symptom of a closed society, he contrasts its following with the fate of Christian faith: 'Today, sport is our primary form of communion. Few people under 40 will be able to name traditional religious holidays outside of Christmas and Easter. But many would be able to rattle off at least approximate dates for important fixtures on the sporting calendar ... As for the feast day commemorating Jesus' crucifixion, it's the occasion these days of more than a couple of Premier League fixtures. It's surely only a matter of time before Christmas Day is used as a relief date for games over the festive season.'[84]

Aiming to debunk the myth that sport supports the move-ment for and towards a better world based on justice and peace, Humphreys claims that, on the contrary, it contributes to the re-inforcement of racism and poverty. Citing the example of South African rugby, he sees little evidence of transformation twelve years after its first World Cup victory. In a devastating judge-ment he describes as 'probably the three industries with which [sport] has closest ties (after gambling) are drinking, smoking and prostitution'.[85] In summary he sees sport as a refuge and not a release for serious social evils and attitudes. His conclusion reprises the comparison of sport and religion, since the most re-cent figures from FIFA show that more people follow football than either Christianity or Islam. Resuming his Holy See simile, he focuses on the organisation's president Sepp Blatter, stating that 'if I have occasionally been overly harsh on sport, it's only because there is a distinct lack of self-criticism within the church of Cardinal Blatter who, by 2011, will have held office for longer than many a Pope has lasted in the Vatican'.[86] While this confuses the role of cardinals and office of the papacy in the Catholic Church, his succeeding statement is trenchant and true: 'Sport today appears to occupy a special place in society – above censure. In the western world especially, you can satirise religion, you can poke fun at Jesus, you can write like Richard Dawkins does. But dare to label sports fans as delusional and you'll be met with a wall of intolerance bordering on hatred.'[87]

---

84. Ibid. 184-185
85. *Foul Play*, 216
86. *Foul Play*, 231-2
87. *Foul Play*, 232

Ironically, given the fact that he sees sport in general and soccer in particular as having replaced religion, in his remedy to cure the ills and right the wrongs of sport he relies on a precedent within the history of Christianity, the Reformation: 'It's perhaps a little fanciful, but one could argue that sport – as today's dominant religion-of-sorts is at a juncture in its history similar to that faced by Christianity close to 500 years ago … The then Pope sold his followers 'indulgences' – tickets to salvation – to fund pet projects. Today, Sepp Blatter flogs executive boxes and prawn cocktail buffets for a dream no less lofty than St Peter's Basilica.'[88] Seeing himself in the guise of a latter day Martin Luther, he nails his treatise to the door of FIFA headquarters. Drawing on Martin Luther King's famous speech at the Washington Mall, Humphreys dreams of a world where sport sheds the language of tragedy after loss and defeat, when 'sports fans will take the Special Olympics as seriously as they take the Olympic Games and that neither is taken too seriously', with less televised events and football analysts finding useful work in society, where 'men and women, religious believers and secularists, Arsenal supporters and regular people' join hands and sing together 'Free at last! Thank God Almighty, we are free at last.'[89] Humphreys' principled approach (though occasionally moralistic in tone) presents a systematic attempt to articulate a stance towards sport, its supporters and the media which is evaluative without denying its entertainment value. While his diagnosis of the problems of sport may be perceived as prescriptive and presented as prophetic, his proposed remedy is trite and contrived. Reducing religion to the status of sport, he renders faith and theology redundant in society. While avoiding use of the language of redemption in relation to sport, his comparison of sport and Christianity is a caricature of revelation. Falling into the same trap that he criticises others for, he is cavalier in his characterisation of the Reformation. This rupture in the Latin Church led to a legacy of bloodshed, bitterness and brokenness which only serves to show the real need for redemption as divine deliverance and not a journalistic device. This book con-

---

88. *Foul Play*, 234
89. *Foul Play*, 237

tributes well to what he himself considers 'the proliferation of what Umberto Eco calls "sports chatter".'[90] The put-down by fellow journalist Malachy Clerkin, in his review of *Foul Play*, preserves the authenticity of religious faith and the autonomy of sport: 'Not to come over all Billy Bible-Thump about it, but does it not make the teeth grate when people straightfacedly compare sport and religion? Even those of us who make our living from following it know better than to do that – or should know better at the very least. Of course people have been saying it forever but in a tongue-in-cheek way, no? A kind of knowing wit, a look-what-helpless-fools-we-are-to-be-stuck-with-this curse deal. Joe Humphreys has taken this premise a step further. In setting out to tackle "the sports delusion" as he puts it, he confers upon sport the quasi-religious characteristics that he goes on to try to skewer. That he does so eloquently and entertainingly just about makes up in the end for the fact that the premise doesn't quite stand up.'[91]

Hyping It Up
A tendency to exaggeration is an evident feature of much contemporary media commentary and communication. Writing on the return of European Commissioner Peter Mandelson to the British cabinet for the third time, Andrew Rawnsley asks about the difference between him and Jesus Christ and answers 'Christ rose from the dead just the once.'[92] While political disbelief might describe the reaction of political commentators and columnists to the recall of Mandelson from Brussels to London by Prime Minister Gordon Brown, his similarity to and even supplanting of Jesus Christ is over the theological top. Comparison with the fate of former Newcastle United manager Kevin Keegan seems more appropriate, though his own series of returns to the club have been characterised as 'Second/Third Comings'.

Irish Times columnist Fintan O'Toole defines the inflation of language as 'the hyping-up of the ordinary into the extraordi-

---

90. 'Worshipping at a new altar', *The Irish Times*, 29 March, 2008
91. *Sunday Tribune – Mad About Sport*, May 2008, 60
92. *The Observer*, 5 October, 2008

nary, the mundane into the epic' and describes it as out-strip-ping 'even that of money in modern culture'.[93] Claiming that it has crept into every corner of culture he considers the comment of FIFA president Sepp Blatter as constituting a new high. Referring to the dispute in the summer of 2008 over the possible transfer of Cristiano Ronaldo from Manchester United to Real Madrid, Blatter referred to slavery in the selling and buying of players. Taking issue with this insensitive interpretation of the historical horror of slavery and its contemporary forms in the fate of sexual trafficking and sweatshop workers, O'Toole states that the implication of Blatter's blather is the denial of 'modern slavery' and its downgrading to that of 'an empty linguistic ves-tige of a dead world'.[94] (This tendency in sports writing may be described as the 'garryowen' approach to grammar!) Identifying the word 'iconic' as indicative of this linguistic inflation and the involvement of journalism in it, O'Toole opines that 'this relent-less hyperbole is corrosive and eats at the sense of proportion that is crucial to any set of values'. Ironically, he may be over-stating the case against by asserting that it is 'horrific, cata-clysmic, disastrous and apocalyptic'.[95] Similarly Guy Keleny criticises a report which diagnoses West Ham United fans as suffering from paranoia since the fact that their club was at the foot of the Premiership table was a fact and not a delusion. At the same time he comments that '*iconic* continues its disrep-utable career as this year's most fashionable meaningless word'.[96] The conjunction of 'fashionable' and 'meaningless' creates an interesting conundrum.

Headlines regularly record the recourse of sports journalists to hyperbole. In this regard it is illustrative to compare different versions of the same headline bearing the same byline. The waning fortunes (literally) and wearied fans of Newcastle United continue to provide raw material for a regular soap opera, if not indeed at times a homegrown 'Toon' tragedy. A re-

---

93. 'Language of hyperbole has floated free of reality', *The Irish Times*, 15 July, 2008
94. Idem
95. Idem
96. 'West Ham fans need a win, not psychiatric help', *The Guardian*, 10 March, 2007

port by Rob Stewart reveals two different headings for Newcastle's 1-0 defeat by neighbours Middlesborough, the original 'Yakubu uses head to cause a Tyne revolt'[97] and the copy 'Shepherd loses flock as Toon crisis grows'[98] which refers to relations between the club's chairman and fans. Angus Fraser's report on the English cricket captain's efforts to make his team competitive in one-day internationals during their tour of Australia carries the original caption 'Vaughan in search for strategy to salvage tour'[99] whereas the copy claims that 'Vaughan seeks a salvation strategy',[100] despite repeating the admission that a win was unlikely. The changes in both copies contain references to biblical symbols and theological terminology and are made in the same newspaper.

The sporting summer of 2008 revealed further examples of 'hyping it up' and reliance on the language of Christian revelation and redemption. A season of second-half resurgence(s) by Cork in both football and hurling codes culminated in the result of drawing their All-Ireland semi-final against Kerry which was greeted with the gospel reference 'Like Lazarus, Cork rise from the dead', while Sean Moran refers to the scorer of Cork's equalising goal from the penalty spot as 'an unlikely saviour given his low profile for the preceding 70 minutes'.[101] A reference to the 'borderline miraculous' fact that Cork ended the first half a point in arrears appears superfluous in the context of the overall result. Both headline and half-time assessment may have inspired the exchanges on RTÉ 2 a week later between anchor and experts during the half-time analysis of the replay, with Michael Lyster asserting that 'every time you say the last prayers for Cork they sit up in the coffin again' and Joe Brolly advocating that Cork 'need more than God, nothing short of a miracle is needed here'. Journalist Mary Hannigan reports these exchanges which range from references to the television show *Father Ted* through the Third Secret of Fatima to Lourdes, adding

97. *The Daily Telegraph*, 23 October, 2006
98. *Irish Independent*, 23 October, 2006
99. *The Independent*, 11 January, 2007
100. *Irish Independent*, 11 January, 2007
101. *The Irish Times*, 25 August 2008

her own allusion to 'yet another resurrection' and answering the question posed in The Kingdom headline two years previously whether God was a Kerryman with the affirmation that Kerry's god 'need it be said, was – and remains – Gooch Cooper'. A comment on Cooper's contribution to 'saving certain people back in the studio from punditry damnation' provides the supposed rationale for the headline stopping 'Gooch Almighty stops Brolly making a holy show of himself.'[102]

At the beginning of 2008 Brian Viner's answers to his Christmas sports quiz appeared under the headline of 'Eden, Easter and reincarnation, with revelations in full.'[103] Question three 'Easter' refers to the remark of the previous year's Masters' winner Zach Johnson that his Lord and Saviour Jesus Christ had walked with him on the course while the following question furnishes the answer that Pádraig Harrington had, in the same year, stolen Fred Daly's unique claim to fame by becoming the second Irishman to win the British Open. Harrington's remarkable second shot to the 17th hole in the course of his repeat of this feat in 2008 is graphically analysed under the caption of 'A Five Wood from Heaven'.[104] His conquest of a third Major title a few weeks later is captured in the headline 'Harrington enters new universe' while Kilkenny's defeat of Cork in the All-Ireland semi-final on the same day only merits 'Kilkenny are on a different planet'.[105] A mere earthly example of exaggeration by Henry Winter sees Manchester United's Cristiano Ronaldo elevated to 'Himalayan heights',[106] though his earlier account of Theo Walcott's hat-trick for England against Croatia attempts an analogy with the work of physicists at the Cern laboratory to simulate the origin of the universe: 'The end of the world, let alone the World Cup, was far from nigh last night. The collision of English and foreign particles here at the Maksimir Stadium produced only oblivion for the Croatians, who were sent spinning by the comet-like Theo Walcott.'[107] While he admits that calling the

102. The Irish Times, 1 September, 2008
103. The Independent, 12 January, 2008
104. Sunday Tribune, 27 July, 2008
105. The Irish Times, 11 August, 2008
106. The Daily Telegraph, 22 September, 2008
107. The Daily Telegraph, 11 September, 2008

annual *Wisden Cricketers' Almanack* a Bible has become something of a cliché, Michael Henderson considers it 'fairer, and, I trust, not blasphemous, to find parallels with the *Book of Common Prayer*, with Collects and Epistles for every occasion'.[108] Newly appointed editor of *Wisden*, Scyld Berry hearkens back to the scriptural simile, hailing 'nothing quite like it in cricket, sport or literature' and holding it up to 'become the conscience of the worldwide sport' with its 'reputation for impartiality and infallibility'.[109] However, a reference to the decline of spin in the field of play may be more than compensated for by these excessive ethical and evangelical expressions. Terence Blacker's reference to 'the shark-pool occupied by sports columnists'[110] resonates with the reaction of Richard Gillis in his 'Cricket Column' which pours opprobrium on the role of the media in promoting the view that Pakistan coach Bob Woolmer was murdered at the 2007 World Cup: 'The absence of facts and the pressure of the 24-hour news cycle led to rumour, gossip and innuendo running on front and back pages ... Most of the stories we have read over the past 12 weeks have been figments of journalists' imaginations.'[111]

The headline 'Ireland saves Ireland' hailed the last-minute goal scored by Manchester City player Stephen Ireland in the Republic of Ireland's 2-1 victory over lowly ranked San Marino.[112] However, he quickly turned from a hero to being hounded after his lie about a dying grandparent as his reason for leaving the Irish camp and cause. A year later speculation intensified about the player's intention and involvement in the campaign to qualify for the 2010 World Cup. Beneath the headline 'Redemption realistic for exiled Ireland, but only on Trap's terms', James Lawton writes 'that if the player did have second thoughts, if he displayed some inclination to climb out of the appalling hole he dug for himself when his brief international career ended so ig-

108. *The Daily Telegraph*, 10 April, 2008
109. *The Sunday Telegraph*, 6 April, 2008
110. *The Independent*, 20 April 2007
111. 'Media played major part in myth of Wolmer "murder",' *The Irish Times*, 5 June, 2007
112. *Irish Examiner*, 8 February, 2007

nominiously, well, redemption might be available'.[113] However, the headline is far from realistic, as the reason for Ireland's exile is self-imposed, a refusal to represent his country. In the absence of acknowledging this reality such a reference to redemption is illusory, at home equally in hysteria as in hyperbole.

If Colum Kenny can quote with approval the advice of John Horgan that 'we journalists should be the last to believe our own press notices, our big by-lines',[114] the case for *caveat lector* – let the reader beware – is considerable.

Issues of honesty versus 'hyping it up' and holding back the truth are matters of professional integrity and ethics. In his 'Comment' column, carried beneath a caustic headline 'Weasel Words A Cancer At The Heart Of Sport', Kevin Mitchell complains that 'there has never been more acreage devoted to sport than is spread across our national newspapers – and never, surely, has there been more barefaced twisting of the truth, more cosmetic surgery applied to the facts'.[115] The immediate target of his ire is the role played by former Number Ten Downing Street spinmeister Alistair Campbell in the 2005 Lions rugby tour of New Zealand and the breaking of the bonds of trust between players, media and the public. His diagnosis of 'the disease that lies in the core of modern sport as entertainment is hypocrisy', a damning indictment that makes Sue Mott's paean to 'quiet understatement' inviting: 'O Lord, we had forgotten what it sounds like, inaudible as it is over the babble of lachrymose sentimentality and comical hyperbole that attaches itself to most sporting matters.'[116]

What's in a Game?

The 2008 All-Ireland Senior Football final between Kerry and Tyrone was an eagerly awaited and anticipated contest between two teams who had arrived via the proverbial 'back door', having been beaten in their respective provincial championships. Both teams were seeking the 'three in a row', with Kerry looking

---

113. *Irish Independent*, 10 October, 2008
114. 'Reporting Religion', 135
115. *The Observer*, 16 October, 2005
116. 'Give a quiet cheer for our understated overachievers', *The Daily Telegraph*, 10 April, 2007

for the blue riband status of three successive championships while Tyrone were aiming to achieve a third victory in six years over them. Sub-plots included the return of Tyrone's Stephen O'Neill from retirement and the re-appearance of the Kerry captain Paul Galvin after his summer long suspension for striking referee Paddy Russell's notebook to the ground in their opening match in Munster. Team selection and styles of play, managerial strategies and use of substitutes were the feverish talk of fans on both sides and none, fuelled by the informed and intuitive opinions of journalists and pundits at both local and national levels. Billed as the battle of the decade bearing the prize of bragging rights, Colm Keys states that 'not only are they the most successful teams of the decade, they are also the busiest production line for managers and trainers – the Kingdom and Red Hand gospels are spread far and wide across Gaelic football's version'.[117] However, on the eve of the game, news of the death of the father of Tyrone goalkeeper John Devine appeared as the latest chapter in the connection between the team and tragedy, recalling once again the memory of its young footballers who had died suddenly in previous years. On these occasions Bill Shankly's words about football being more important than life and death definitely did not apply to the Gaelic version.

After one of the most open games in recent years, Tyrone's team ethic and determination prevailed over their rivals' individual flashes of inspiration. Journalists turned to the Bible and Christian doctrine to support their accounts and assessments in the aftermath of a match that restored confidence for many in the quality of the All-Ireland Championship. Vincent Hogan calls on the Exodus in his effusive opening lines: 'Clarity came late, but with irrevocable force in the end. The great sea parted as if by a divine hand and Tyrone fell over the line into a white thicket of arms'.[118] (On the same day he extols the value of sport in a piece entitled 'Sport Heaven-Sent In Days Of Hell On Earth'.) Calling it the 'day of Tyrone's Ascension', Keith Duggan comments that in the course of the team manager's post-match press conference the unanswered call on his mobile phone may

---

117. 'Spreading the Gospel', *Irish Independent*, 18 September, 2008
118. *Irish Independent*, 22 September, 2008

'have been God himself trying to get through – be that Peter Canavan or the Man Above'.[119] He considers that Tyrone alone 'have mastered the trick of remaining immune to the power of [Kerry's] iconic jersey'.[120] The fusion of football, fate and faith finds expression in some journalistic memories of the match and its meaning. Under the headline 'Hands of History', Michael Foley includes among the images of the week 'the Sam Maguire Cup sitting on a church altar in Ballygawley [with] John Devine's jersey cradled in its belly as he buried his father'[121] while Duggan declares that 'for sure, spirituality has played a strong role in this Tyrone story', seeing 'the extraordinary series of genuine tragedies that have afflicted the Tyrone squad and their families in the last 10 years' as also shaping 'this latest rising'.[122] His reference to Tyrone's triumph in terms of 'this latest perceived Lazarus act'[123] is more blasé than blasphemous, serving only to belittle the county's achievement.

Recalling the belief of former Kerry chairman Sean Walsh, in the wake of the defeat by Tyrone in the 2003 semi-final encounter, that 'the Kingdom needed a new creed', Philip Lanigan remarks that this refers to 'a county where football is its own religion'.[124] Beneath a picture of Paul Galvin with his raised hands opened wide, Ewan MacKenna presents the erstwhile captain as 'Resurrection man' and perceives his tenacity in training perceived as 'perhaps the end of the God-says-turn-the-other cheek but-God-never-played-football attitude'.[125] Denis Walsh wonders 'why should his appearance in Croke Park today be seen as some kind of glorious redemption' while, in the same paper, he profiles the replacement captain Tomás Ó Sé under the caption 'Don't doubt Tomás'.[126] On the day before the game Billy Keane, invoking the spirit and scenery of his native county, intercedes

119. *The Irish Times*, 22 September 2008
120. *The Irish Times*, 27 September, 2008
121. *The Sunday Times*, 28 September, 2008
122. *The Irish Times*, 22 September, 2008
123. *The Irish Times*, 27 September 2008
124. *Irish Mail On Sunday*, 28 September, 2008
125. *Sunday Tribune*, 21 September, 2008
126. *The Sunday Times*, 21 September 2008

for success: 'Candles are being lit from the vastness of the cathedral in Killarney to the little oratory on the fastness of the Skellig ... This All-Ireland final will pick the next pantheon of the immortals. God be with you Kerry.'[127] Writing post match, Keane interprets the divine intervention in favour of the victors when 'the Tyrone guardian angels minded their net yesterday'.[128] Despite seeing Tyrone manager Mickey Harte as being a good advertisement for spirituality – which includes his expression of gratitude to God after the game – Eugene McGee expresses the view that the team 'don't depend on spirituality'.[129] Martial metaphors are also employed in the assessment of the match, with Joe Brolly likening the Tyrone torrent 'pouring through the Kerry defences in the manner of the Zulu hordes at Isandlwana',[130] while Dara Ó Cinnéide looks at the team's success in terms of the serenity and surety seen in the ancient Chinese military text *The Art of War*.[131] However, the preference for and preponderance of the symbols language of Christian faith in the newspaper coverage surveyed here is of a piece with the 'theological' trend of sports journalism in general.

'The theological tenets of the press'[132]
A year earlier Ó Cinnéide quoted lines from T. S. Eliot about the challenge confronting Kerry footballers which concluded: 'For us, there is only the trying/The rest is not our business' and comments that 'The *rest* is the business of the media and every year the media role from the players' and managers' perspective becomes more and more distorted.'[133] However, as his own role as columnist and television pundit testifies, sport cannot be confined to the confines of playing pitches and arenas and the attention of spectators alone. Media involvement in sport raises questions of perception and presentation, interpretation and in-

127. 'God be with you Kerry – the candles have all been lit', *Irish Independent*, 20 September, 2008
128. *Irish Independent*, 22 September, 2008
129. *Irish Independent*, 22 September, 2008
130. *Irish Mail On Sunday*, 28 September, 2008
131. *Irish Examiner*, 27 September, 2008
132. Patrick Kavanagh, 'Living In The Country', *Collected Poems*, 166
133.*Championship – Irish Examiner*, 12 September, 2007

terests. This raises the issue of distortion and whether this is due to deliberate misrepresentation and manipulation for ideological reasons or simply down to laziness and a lackadaisical attitude. Where Paul the Apostle once used the language of athletic activity to understand and underpin the meaning of the Christian life, journalists and commentators today increasingly take the symbols and doctrines of that same faith to talk and write about sport and its successes or lack of them.

At the start of the 2008 Six Nations Rugby Championship radio presenter and rugby commentator George Hook, in his column called 'The Big Opinion', analysed Ireland's prospects in a piece entitled 'Absolution without penance for an unchanged Eddie' under the banner 'Search for Redemption'.[134] An analogy between the confession of an adulterous affair by Carmella, the wife of Mafia boss Tony in the very successful American television series *The Sopranos* and the Irish coach Eddie O'Sullivan sees Hook refer to the spiritual, sacramental and soteriological connotations connected with the conscience of Catholics and priesthood, absolution and purpose of amendment. In a spirit of ecumenical sensitivity he cleverly implicates O'Sullivan's bosses, the Irish Rugby Football Union: 'As a strongly non-sectarian organisation [it] was hardly likely to quote Catholic doctrine and upset some of its Ulster members after the Rugby World Cup debacle, but the sturdy Calvinists, Methodists and Presbyterians would have understood the concept of individual responsibility.'[135] While Cathleen Kaveny writes about 'Salvation and the Sopranos' and wonders what 'redemption, if any, awaits, [whether] Tony's vision is one of heaven, or of hell',[136] Hook reduces the Christian faith in redemption and the sacrament of reconciliation to the state and fate of Irish rugby. Reporting on Ireland's first game against Italy, Rupert Bates states that 'such has been the talk all week you expected *Redemption Song* rather than *Fields of Athenry* to roll down from the stands of Croke Park', though he summarises that a 'scrappy victory is not enough to earn Irish World Cup redemption'.[137]

134. *The Sunday Independent*, 27 January, 2008
135.*The Sunday Independent*, 27 January, 2008
136. *Commonweal* CXXXIV(9 February 2007), 10-14 at 14
137. *The Sunday Telegraph*, 3 February, 2008

Recourse to redemption and other biblical, spiritual and theological allusions relies on a reserve of religious knowledge which is rapidly running out of social and cultural capital. Reduction of the sacred canopy of Christian faith to cover the commitment of sports men and women and the coverage of journalists requires a reflection on the meaning of sport and its relation to transcendence. If veteran columnist and vaunted 'Voice of Sport' Hugh McIlvanney can claim that the lines of a minor Scottish poet – 'Throughout the sensual world proclaim/One crowded hour of glorious life/Is worth an age without a name' – capture the ethos of the Cheltenham Festival and commend that 'the glorious Gold Cup duel between Kauto Star and Denman should be watched with reverence',[138] perhaps the equine origin of the term 'tacky' denoting 'an inferior horse, of unknown origin'[139] reveals the 'theological tenets' of the sporting press. Transposing the terms of the tribute paid to the late psychiatrist and radio/television presenter Anthony Clare – 'religious prophet speaking in a secular language'[140] – sports journalists run the risk of being secular prophets who speak in a religious language. The redemption of sport as a segment of the human condition and culture calls for a number of ethical and theological investigations, including the register of language used to represent it, the need for sport to be saved from ideological interests who manipulate it in the media/market and for sport to be interpreted as a symbol of the restless transience of what the Second Vatican Council terms 'the things of the world'. If sports journalists cannot resist the temptation, in Patrick Kavanagh's words, 'to take over the functions of a god in a new fashion', who will 'smelt in passion the commonplaces of life',[141] especially those exchanged and encountered in sporting events?

'Keep the rumour of redemption alive'[142]

Sports journalists do not always take refuge in redemption in

---

138. *The Sunday Times*, 9 March, 2008
139. *The Times English Dictionary*, Glasgow: Harper Collins, 2000, 1558
140. *The Guardian*, 31 October, 2007
141. 'After Forty Years Of Age', *Collected Poems*, 148
142. From a letter of Richard Harries, retired Church of England bishop and honorary professor of theology at King's College, London, *The Guardian*, 25 October, 2008

referring to players, clubs and results in matches, games or competitions. There is a wide range of other 'R' words which they have recourse to. A range of medical analogies include: 'Patient recovers in doing nicely', Sean Moran's report on the 2008 International Rules series between Australia and Ireland, wherein he states that it 'has survived its first *rehabilitative* steps';[143] 'Liverpool fall to Redknapp's *revival*',[144] while '*Revatilised* Wearsiders thump hapless West Brom'[145] is obviously a misprint; '*Rejuvenated* Derby man says he was best at St Andrew's since Trevor Francis'.[146] Architectural analogies add the following: 'Now that the bulldozer of Kevin Pietersen's ego has been stopped in its tracks, Andrew Strauss will want to view what he has inherited not as a pile of psychological rubble but as a building site with inviting potential for a rapid *reconstruction* project';[147] 'the principal reason the province held on to the most influential player of his generation was the Australian's [coach Michael Cheika] *redecoration* of the Leinster mindset';[148] 'considering the amount of *rebuilding* required over the coming season'.[149] Dara Ó Cinnéide prefers images from nature to a supernatural interpretation in indicating the challenge facing Kerry after their failure in the 2008 All-Ireland final: 'The laboratory conditions of next season's National Football League should provide the opportunity for *recovery*, *rehabilitation* and *regrowth*.'[150] In similar vein Brendan Gallagher describes 2008 as 'a year of *rebirth*' for rugby.[151] Other references include: Brendan Fanning's report on the Ireland versus Italy game which is head-

143. *The Irish Times*, 1 November, 2008
144. Duncan Castles' caption for report on Tottenham Hotspur's 2-1 victory over Liverpool, *The Observer*, 2 November, 2008
145. *The Observer*, 14 December, 2008
146. Heading for piece on Derby County midfielder Robbie Savage prior to return to former club Birmingham City, *The Daily Telegraph*, 27 January, 2009
147. Hugh McIlvanney, *The Sunday Times*, 11 January, 2009
148. Johnny Watterson, 'Interview Brian O'Driscoll', *The Irish Times*, 17 January, 2009
149. Gavin Cummiskey, 'Interview Davy Fitzgerald', *The Irish Times*, 10 January, 2009
150. *Irish Examiner*, 27 September, 2008
151. The Daily Telegraph, 2 January, 2009

lined 'O'Gara's boot *reprieves* shaky Ireland';[152] the issue of golfer Ernie Els' return to form is referred to in 'Els targets Florida for *resurgence*'.[153] Racing columnist J. A. McGrath calls jockey Timmy Murphy's victory in the Grand National a 'Proud day for *reformed* rider Murphy',[154] while surveying the prospects of Tipperary hurling in 2008 Keith Duggan states that for the county 'winning Munster will not mark the kind of *reclamation* as informed Richie Stakelum's emotional words of 21 years ago, "The famine is over".'[155] The American basketball team's victory over Spain in the 2008 Olympic final is described as aiming to '*rectify* a poor, uncommitted performance in Athens', albeit beneath the banner 'Dream Team survive Spanish inquisition to achieve redemption'.[156] Writing about Everton manager David Moyes' willingness to recommit himself to the club in 'Ready to *rededicate* himself to the cause', Michael Walker states that 'one hopes for the club's sake that it brings a sense of *renewal*'.[157] In his assessment of Galway hurling after the departure of manager Ger Loughnane, Keith Duggan states that 'there was no revolution and he left Galway as much of a broken-down enigma as he had found it'.[158] 'To the rescue ... again'[159] highlights the invaluable contribution of Captain Steven Gerrard to the cause of Liverpool FC while 'rebirth' and 'renaissance' are also referred to in describing the return to form of players and teams. In relation to the use of religious and theological language, sports journalists would do well to attend to (and apply) the wisdom of Muiris Houston in his ironically inscribed piece 'Battling to lose the military health terms: George Orwell wrote about the powerful role of words. "Never use a foreign phrase, a scientific word or a jargon word if you can think of an everyday English

---

152. *The Observer*, 3 February, 2008. (A cover caption for the future of Ireland's rugby team offers the option 'Redemption or Reprieve?', *Village*, 135/March 2008.)
153. *The Irish Times*, 28 February, 2008
154. *The Daily Telegraph*, 7 April, 2008
155. *The Irish Times*, 12 July, 2008
156. *The Daily Telegraph*, 25 August, 2008
157. *The Irish Times*, 18 October, 2008
158. *The Irish Times*, 'Interview with Ger Loughnane', 20 December, 2009
159. *The Sunday Telegraph*, 14 December, 2008

equivalent", he said. His advice is especially apposite when it comes to the use of military jargon in healthcare.'[160]

In his study of *Spirituality and Popular Religion in Europe*, Hubert Knoblauch states that 'religious symbols and forms of religious communication that belonged predominantly or exclusively to the 'sacred' religious sphere have been disseminated into other cultural spheres and used in non-religious cultural contexts, most importantly in popular commercial media and leisure culture.'[161] The process and practice of this dissemination in media coverage of and commentary on sport is the concern of this book, a concern both generated and governed by the perspective of Christian faith and the profession of theology. Ó Cinnéide's 'distortion' is rather mild when compared to the words of Hugo Rahner, in the introduction to his classic *Man at Play*, when he describes 'the putrid corruption of an age in which our lives are largely governed by the ephemeral stimuli of journalistic caprice'.[162] The corruption of Christian spirituality, symbols and sacraments is clearly evident in media reporting of and 'reflection' on sport. The practice and process of taking what is transitory for transcendence, of exchanging the ephemeral for the eternal and converting human restlessness into heavenly revelation and divine redemption are a central challenge to Christian faith and the mission of the church(es). In the words of Robert Barron, 'the basic problem is the all-too-human tendency to substitute the less than unconditioned for the unconditioned – in biblical terms, to fashion idols'.[163] The need for theology to analyse and address this alienation of Christian life and language in the area of sporting accounts is urgent. Sport needs this intellectual interest and intervention to avoid lapsing into an absence of logic and absurdity. While the competing claims of sport seem to be captured in the comment that 'Clare are bent on redemption after the disappointment of their Munster final collapse, the Rebels [Cork], back to their defiant best, will raise themselves again', the theological Achilles'

160. *The Irish Times – Healthplus*, 13 January, 2009
161. *Social Compass* 55 (2008), 140-153 at 147
162. London: Burns & Oates, 1965, 4
163. *The Priority of Christ – Towards a Postliberal Catholicism*, Grand Rapids: Brazos Press, 2007, 29

heel of sport coverage and media commentary is articulated in the closing lines concerning Clare: 'Expect them to redeem themselves here. But to fall short nonetheless'.[164] 'Falling short' is where sport ends and redemption enters in.

Bruce Arnold's claim to realism is a call to responsibility from the media to recognise limits, not least in relation to language: 'We journalists write about what is there. In a simple yet profound statement, quoted not quite accurately in the *New Yorker* at the end of August, Bishop Joseph Butler, an 18th-century theologian, said: "Everything is what is and not another thing".'[165] Taking his call to heart, sports commentators and journalists need to have the humility to halt hailing sport as synonymous with Christian sacraments, salvation, spirituality and respect the tenets, even if they do not accept the truth, of religious devotion and doctrine. They could start with considering the words of Jim White when, comparing new signing Dimitar Berbatov to former Manchester United great Eric Cantona, he writes: 'While Cantona's religious leanings tend towards self-worship, Berbatov adheres to more traditional spiritual affiliation. "I take the Bible everywhere with me", he said earlier this week. "There are many good pieces of advice for those like me in the Bible." One of which appears to be do not make false football idols.'[166]

Sporting idols involve an image of God, including representations of the 'soccer-Christ',[167] for example, Eric Cantona (and some of his Manchester United team mates) transposed to Piero della Francesca's painting of the Resurrection (c. 1465) and bookmaker Paddy Power's portrayal of Cristiano Ronaldo as the Risen Lord.[168]

---

164. 'Brotherhood of Cork to scale the mountain', *Sunday Tribune*, 27 July, 2008
165. *Irish Independent*, 6 September, 2008
166. *The Daily Telegraph*, 13 September, 2008
167. Russell Brand, *The Guardian*, 9 June, 2007
168. 'Paddy Is Whacked – Power pulls "Ron as Christ" web ad', *The Irish Sun*, 7 April, 2007. 'Those good old boys from Paddy Power have entered into the spirit of Easter with some great specials. Their wonderfully-named Second Coming market focuses on how many Prem[iership] teams come from behind to win today … Top class, too, is Defending the cross, a market on which team will score the fastest Prem goal from a corner.'

Sporting images of God and the Son of God raise crucial issues of interpretation and central theological questions. How are God and Christ to be communicated, engaging in competition or existing in communion? Is redemption reckoned a successful result for the divine team or the realisation of the Trinity's desire to draw humanity into a heavenly relationship? The image of a sporting God can convey ideas of contest and conquest which clash with values of celebration and compassion. Moreover, there are moral and spiritual implications of such divine debasement and downplaying. These include individualism and partisanship, narcissism and the negation of transcendence. Paul's adoption of sporting activity as a metaphor for the Christian life and Pope John Paul's analysis of sport as aspects of genuine human culture offer an alternative theological vision of 'the world of sport', described by David Goldblatt as 'one in which most of us at different times and in different ways are participants, spectators or commentators; it is a world in which we can delight in contradiction, a social space that is dependent on the state and the market but knows how to hold them both at arm's length. This space, after all, is not merely where we play – it is where the good life must be lived.'[169]

---

169. David Goldblatt, 'Taking Sport Seriously', *Prospect*, December 2007, 39

APPENDIX A

References to REDEMPTION – ATONEMENT – SALVATION

(References in Italics to Cricket/Gaelic Games/Golf/Racing – Human, Motor & Horse/Rugby/Sailing and Soccer are mine)

'Saviour [Shane] Warne – Australia avoid the follow-on as rain disrupts Old Trafford Test'. (*The Sunday Times,* 14 August, 2005)

'South Africa get a shot at *redemption* – but they need to win the toss', *The Guardian,* 25 April, 2007 – Reference to semi-final match in Cricket World Cup which South Africa lost to Australia after winning the toss.)

'Harmison confident of rapid *redemption'.* (*The Times,* 20 October, 2006 – reference to England cricket player Stephen Harmison prior to one-day international against Australia.)

'Panesar still to convince in England *saviour* role'. (*The Daily Telegraph,* 9 December, 2006 – reference to England bowler Monty Panesar in preparation for 2006 Ashes series in Australia.)

'MCC to nurse US to cricket *salvation.'* (*The Daily Telegraph,* 8 June, 2007 – Reference to role of Marleybone Cricket Club to re-store the United States after expulsion by the International Cricket Council for its failure to furnish a coherent plan for the organisation and administration of the game in the country.)

'Strauss hits back in battle to *save* himself.' (*The Times,* June 18, 2007 – Reference to much needed boost given to career of England cricketer Andrew Strauss with innings of 72 against the West Indies.)

'England hold heads high after tour of *redemption.'* (*The Independent,* 24 December, 2008 – reference to English cricket team's series win over India.)

'Hail Mary's saving grace.' (*Sunday Independent,* 17 March, 2002 – reference to injury time equalising point for Roscommon versus Galway.)

'Armagh's journey to *salvation* – This weekend the All-Ireland football qualifiers offer their next chance of *redemption*, and few counties have more desire to grab it than Armagh'. (*The Irish Times*, 19 June, 2003)

'Contrite Kerry to take shot at *redemption*.' (*The Sunday Times*, 24 August, 2003)

'In dire need of *redemption*'. (*Sunday Independent*, 6 June, 2004 – reference to fortunes of Tipperary hurlers.)

'Sacking of the Kingdom is a perfect *redemption* for the Dubs.' (*Ireland on Sunday*, 8 August, 2004 – Kerry went on to win the All-Ireland Championship.)

'*Redeemer* seeking one more *miracle*.' (*The Irish Times*, 30 August, 2003 – Tom Humphries on how five decades of turning water into wine has made Donegal manager [and former player] Brian McEniff the pivotal figure in every one of the county's successes in the period.)

'Laois and Tyrone enjoyed a day of relief and *redemption* in Croke Park when victories in their respective All-Ireland championship games against Derry and Monaghan eased them through both to the quarter-finals'. (*The Sunday Times*, 7 August, 2005)

'Mortimer's road to Mayo *redemption*.' (*Irish Independent*, 17 July, 2006 – Reference to final score by Mayo's Conor Mortimer to defeat arch-rivals Galway in Connacht senior football championship semi-final.)

'*Redemption* is the theme of the weekend as Kerry, Galway and Offaly react to their provincial final defeats by restyling team line-ups.' (*The Irish Times*, 29 July, 2006 – reference to 'last-chance saloon' qualifiers in All-Ireland championship.)

'Wexford seek *redemption*.' (*The Sunday Times*, 23 July, 2000 – reference to Wexford's All-Ireland hurling quarter final match against Clare which they lost.)

'Ó hAilpín seeking final *redemption*.' (*Irish Independent*, 8 September, 2005 – reference to hopes of Cork captain in All-Ireland final against Galway.)

'An indispensable figure in their *redemption* was their captain.' (*Sunday Independent*, 20 November, 2005 – reference to Thurles Sarfields' captain Ger 'Redser' O' Grady.)

'I was hoping we would *redeem* ourselves. But, it was even worse.' (*Irish Examiner*, 1 March, 2006 – reference to Tipperary hurling manager Babs Keating's quest for a form of *redemption* in League match loss by nine points against Kilkenny.)

'A quest for *redemption*.' (*Sunday Tribune*, 18 June, 2006 – reference to Clare versus Limerick All-Ireland qualifier hurling match which joined "these neighbours in *temporary unholy matrimony*" in which the Bannermen ran out easy victors.)

'Hurling's system of *resurrection* through the back door.' (*The Irish Times*, 25 June, 2007 – reference by Tom Humphries to Tipperary's attempt to attain success through the qualifying system after their loss to Limerick in epic three-match encounter in the Munster semi-final.)

'Messrs Boylan and Cavanagh together with vice-captain Graham Canty, are removed from these travails and reflecting on a *redemptive* night's international football'. (*The Irish Times*, 25 October, 2008 – reference by Sean Moran to Ireland's victory in the first International Rules Test against Australia.)

'For Phil Mickelson, *redemption* has arrived early. Five months after his woeful Ryder Cup effort, he is the hottest golfer in the world'. (*The Observer*, 20 February, 2005)

'Mickelson finds *redemption*.' (*The Daily Telegraph*, 13 February, 2007 – reference to Phil Mickelson's 30th career victory in the AT&T Pebble Beach Pro-Am.)

'Swing guru Harmon enjoys *resurrection* with Mickelson'. (*The Guardian*, 12 June, 2007 – reference to former Tiger Woods coach Butch Harmon and his new charge Phil Mickelson.)

'Watching David Duval snaphook his drive into the stream that runs alongside the second hole of the TPC Sawgrass course, it was never more apparent that, in golf, *redemption* is a lot harder to find than par ... He might usefully have spent his downtime during yesterday's rain-interrupted play chatting to one man who knows exactly what it takes to find *redemption* in golf, England's Lee Westwood'. (*The Guardian*, 26 March, 2005)

'Last week's French Open end may have been darkly familiar for Jean van de Velde, but it brought a long-awaited *redemption*'. (*Sunday Tribune*, 3 May, 2005)

'Eager Els ready for *redemption.*' (*Irish Independent*, 13 July, 2005 – reference to 2004 runner-up in golf's British Open, before the 2005 event.)

'He [golfer Paul McGinley] had his overdue victory, his *redemption* and a temporary world ranking of 18.' (*Sunday Tribune*, 1 January, 2006)

'Thanksgiving brings Harrington *redemption.*' (*The Irish Times*, 1 December, 2003 – reference to Joey Harrington, quarter-back with Detroit Lions in NFL and cousin of Irish golfer Pádraig.)

'Broadhurst takes step to *redemption.*' (*The Daily Telegraph*, 2 June, 2007 – reference to second round score of English golfer Paul Broadhurst after his disastrous score in the PGA Championship final round the previous week saw him drop from first to twentieth place.)

'There was *redemption* a couple of years later at the British Open at Muirfield.' (*Sunday Tribune*, 10 June 2007 – reference to golfer Ernie Els.)

'This was to be Phil Mickelson's week of *redemption*, when he used that new swing and new philosophy to rid himself of the ghosts of Winged Foot, to show us where he's gone while we ruminate on where he was.' (*The Daily Telegraph*, June 14, 2007)

'*Redemption* for [Kieren] Fallon as Kris Kin powers to Derby victory.' (*Sunday Tribune*, 8 June, 2003)

'For a man seeking vindication, even a kind of *redemption*, Fallon's emphatic victory on Foostepsinthesand in the 2,000 Guineas seemed quite sufficient to be going on with.' (*The Times*, 2 May, 2005)

'Devastating Dubawi delivers *redemption.*' (*The Sunday Independent*, 22 May 2005 – reference to winner of Irish 2,000 Guineas.)

'Golden redemption.' (*Irish Independent*, 18 March, 2006 – reference to Michael 'Mouse' Morris, trainer of Cheltenham Gold Cup winner War of Attrition.)

'*Redemption* for peerless jockey after years of hurt.' (*The Independent*, 15 March, 2006 – reference to Tony McCoy's victory on Brave Inca in the Cheltenham Champion Hurdle.)

'Rail Link on track to *redeem* unlucky sire.' (*The Independent*, 21 July, 2006 – reference to Group One winner and his sire Dansili who failed to win at this level.)

'Radcliffe takes another big step on road to *redemption*.' (*The Daily Telegraph*, 18 April, 2005 – reference to Paula Radcliffe's victory in the women's London Marathon.)

'Radcliffe finds *redemption*.' (*The Irish Times*, 15 August, 2005 – reference to Radcliffe's victory in the women's marathon at the World Championship in Helsinki.)

'Road to *redemption*.' (*The Times*, 24 August, 206 – reference to American athlete Justin Gatlin's attempt to be reinstated in time to defend his Olympic 100 metres title in 2008 after failing a drugs test in 2006.)

'Can this man *save* F1?' (*The Observer Sport Monthly*, March 2005 – reference to driver Jenson Button and the future of Formula One.)

'ITV hails Sunday *saviour* – and his dad'. (*The Times*, June 12, 2007 – reference to rookie Formula One driver Lewis Hamilton after his victory in the Canadian Grand Prix, the rescue of Sunday television audiences and the role of his father Anthony in his development.)

'Latest red-letter day can be *divine*. So here it is then. *Redemption* day'. (*The Irish Times*, 1 February, 2003 – reference to Celtic League final Neath versus winners Munster.)

'Blower *saviour* for Christians.' (*Irish Independent*, 11 February, 2004 – reference to try scorer Gavin Blower in 5-0 victory for Cork's CBC over Ard Scoil Rís in Munster Schools Senior Cup competition)

'Nobody has been a more influential presence on the world rugby stage over the past 15 years. [Graham] Henry was coach of Auckland when they were quite the most formidable sub-international side in the game. He *redeemed* Wales and coached the Lions in the thrilling series of 2001'. (*The Observer*, 17 April, 2004)

'Wherever the head coach [Clive Woodward] finds enjoyment through the final week in Auckland, it shall not be in *redemption*. The All Blacks are too good, his team too ordinary.' (*The Sunday Times*, 3 July, 2005)

'From church mouse to *saviour*, [Gavin] Henson lets his feat do the talking.' (*The Independent*, 10 February, 2005)

'Shattered England squander chance to *save* themselves'. (*The Daily Telegraph*, 14 February, 2005 – England 17 France 18 in RBS Six Nations match.)

'He is hardly in the *messianic* category yet. The worrying part is that we need a *saviour* in the first place.' (*The Sunday Times*, 20 March, 2005 – reference to prospective international tighthead prop Tony Buckley of Shannon.)

'Shaw given *redemption* chance after O'Kelly injury'. (*The Times*, 3 June, 2005 – reference to call-up of English lock Simon Shaw to Lions tour.)

'Horne and Hull take road to *redemption*.' (*The Guardian*, 30 July, 2005 – reference to Hull player Richard Horne and his team's chance of 'collective redemption' in Rugby League Challenge Cup semi-final against St Helens.)

'Two teams, two coaches, two men battling for a break and vying for immediate *redemption*.' (*The Daily Telegraph*, 10 November, 2005 – reference to Cook Cup match between Australia and England.)

'Wallabies offer shot at *redemption*.' (*Irish Examiner*, 16 November, 2005 – Australia won the autumn rugby international at Lansdowne Road against Ireland.)

'Eddie O' Sullivan hopes his players will respond to his vote of confidence by seizing the chance to *redeem* themselves against France.' (*The Independent*, 8 February, 2006 – France defeated Ireland.)

'*Redemption* day for Staunton'. (*The Independent on Sunday*, 5 March, 2006 – reference to role of Jeremy Staunton who scored 17 points in Wasps 22-17 victory over Leicester in Powergen Cup semi-final.)

'Pumped-up Leinster find measure of *redemption.*' (*The Irish Times*, 7 October, 2006 – reference to Leinster's 27-20 victory over Munster in rugby's Celtic League.)

'England's road to *redemption* leads to Paris, an arduous route at the best of times'. (*The Daily Telegraph*, 27 February, 2006)

'Wales may find the road to *redemption* that much tougher.' (*The Daily Telegraph*, 21 February, 2006)

'England ready for *atonement.*' (*The Daily Telegraph*, 18 March, 2006 – reference to English rugby team prior to defeat by Ireland in final game of 2006 Six Nations tournament.)

'How to *save* English rugby.' (*The Guardian*, 21 April, 2006)

'Why I am ready to be *saviour* of England rugby'. (*The Guardian*, 25 April, 2006 – reference to Brian Ashton, Bath club coach.)

'Nothing Toulouse – Girvan goes in search of European *redemption.*' (*The Daily Mail*, 1 April, 2006 – reference to Leinster full-back Girvan Dempsey prior to Leinster's ERC quarter-final 41-35 victory over Toulouse.)

'Springboks waste shot at *redemption.*' (*The Daily Telegraph*, 7 August, 2006 – reference to SANZAR series 18-20 defeat for South Africa against Australia in Sydney.)

'England are desperately seeking Jonny and *salvation.*' (*The Irish Times*, 3 February, 2007 – reference to return of England player Jonny Wilkinson for 2007 Six Nations championship.)

'"Bloody marvel" steers Sweet Chariot on road to *redemption.*' (*Irish Independent*, 5 February, 2007 – reference to Wilkinson's role in scoring 27 points in 42-20 defeat of Scotland.)

'Another step to *redemption.*' (*Irish Examiner*, 15 December, 2006 – reference to Munster and international flank forward Alan Quinlan, 'the man who saved Irish rugby' through the try he scored against Argentina in 2003 World Cup pool game.)

'Heineken Cup offers chance of *redemption* after French nightmare.' (*Irish Independent*, 5 November, 2007 – reference to resumption of European Rugby Competion and Ireland's involvement in it after the country's failure to come out of the group stage in the World Cup.)

'Wales searching for *redemption.*' (*The Daily Telegraph*, 24 November, 2007 – reference to Wales v. South Africa match which the world champions won easily.)

'Vainikolo *redeemed* by Wasps' generosity.' (*The Observer*, 5 October 2008 – reference to score in Gloucerster's 24-19 victory over Wasps in English Rugby Premiership.)

'Anderson urges Saints to *redeem* themselves.' (*The Daily Telegraph*, 20 February, 2007 – reference to rugby league club St Helens prior to World Club challenge against Brisbane Broncos.)

'"Sinner" Doherty redeemed.' (*The Daily Telegraph*, 25 April, 2006 – reference to snooker player Ken Doherty's victory to put him in the quarter-finals of the World Championship.)

'In the shadow of St Luke's both sides in need of *salvation* in their seasons'. (ITV *The Championship*, 3 March, 2002, with a view of a church from Everton's Goodison Park.)

'Can Bowyer and West Ham *save* each other?' (*The Guardian*, 11 January, 2003)

'Scholes provides cup *salvation* for United.' (*The Sunday Independent*, 4 April, 2004 – reference to FA Cup semi-final result Manchester Utd 1 Arsenal 0.)

'*Salvation* beckons for Bolton Wanderers.' (ITV *Premiership*, 11 May, 2004 – commentator's response to Jay-Jay Okocha's revealing T-shirt with 'Thank You Jesus' after scoring second goal in final match of season requiring victory for survival in the Premiership.)

'Millwall, the *saviours* of English football?' (*The Independent*, 6 April, 2004)

'Self-made *saviour.*' (*The Irish Times*, 22 January, 2005 – reference to Ken Bates, chairman of Chelsea for 22 years.)

'Ronaldo's gem fails to *redeem* the fading stars.' (*The Daily Telegraph*, 21 April, 2005)

'Arsenal's *Saviour*.' (*The Sunday Times*, 22 May 2005 – reference to penalty shoot-out victory by Arsenal over Manchester United in FA Cup Final.)

'Rooney the *saving grace* amid disaster.' (*The Independent*, 18 August, 2005 – reference to goal scored by Wayne Rooney in 4-1 defeat of England by Denmark.)

'The West Ham way can *save* us.' (*The Daily Telegraph*, 25 September, 2005)

'Rattled Ferguson [Manchester United manager] seeks *redemption*.' (*The Daily Telegraph*, 27 September, 2005)

'Das Wunder Von Bern/The Miracle of Berne – Lachrymose [movie] saga using West German football as an analogy for post-war *redemption*.' (*The Guardian*, 1 October, 2005)

'Pressley strikes twice to *redeem* own goal.' (*The Daily Telegraph*, 3 October 2005 – Hearts captain Steven Pressley in 2-2 draw with Falkirk.)

'[Steven] Gerrard goes on the defensive in search of *redemption*.' (*The Times*, 6 October, 2005)

'Youthful gamble offers McLeish possible *salvation*.' (*The Daily Telegraph*, 25 November, 2005 – reference to Glasgow Rangers' manager Alex McLeish.)

'Born-again Fenn has heart set on final *redemption* on Sunday.' (*The Irish Times*, 11 November, 2005 – reference to Cork City striker prior to FAI Cup Final.)

'Saints' redeemer.' (*The Guardian*, 12 December, 2005 – reference to 'wonder goal' scored by 16-year-old Theo Walcott in 1-0 victory over Luton Town.)

'Punters put faith in the Geordie *saviour*.' (*The Racing Post*, 31 August, 2005 – reference to transfer of striker Michael Owen from Real Madrid to Newcastle United.)

'Owen now unable to *save* Souness.' (*The Irish Times*, 2 January, 2006)

'Kewell's *redemption* complete.' (*The Sunday Telegraph*, 15 January 2006 – reference to first goal in thirteen months by Liverpool striker Harry Kewell.)

'Real *redemption* for Cassano as Maradona of Bari goes for a song.' (*The Observer*, 15 January, 2006 – reference to transfer of Antonio Cassano from Italian club Roma to Real Madrid.)

'Yet again Frank Lampard is Chelsea's *saviour*.' (Commentator on BBC Match of the Day, 28 January, 2006 – reference to equaliser scored by Lampard in FA Cup Fourth Round tie versus Everton.)

'There is little point hoping the youth system might deliver *salvation*'. (*The Sunday Telegraph*, 5 February, 2006 – reference to difficulties facing Newcastle United in wake of sacking of manager Graham Souness.)

'Thierry Henry, so often the *saviour*, has by his own admission struggled with the captaincy.' (*The Observer*, 5 February, 2006 – reference to difficulties experienced by Arsenal.)

'For them, as for other weird *religious cults, salvation* is always imminent'. (*The Sunday Telegraph*, 5 February, 2006 – reference to the thirty-seven season wait by Newcastle United fans for a trophy in football.)

'Contrite Barton seeks *redemption*.' (*The Daily Telegraph*, 7 February, 2006 – reference to remorse expressed by Manchester City player after transfer request on eve of end of January transfer window.)

'A filthy-rich *saviour* for long-suffering City?' (*The Guardian*, 22 June, 2007 – reference to former Thai Prime Minister Thaksin Shinawatra's proposed takeover of Manchester City.)

'Haunted Baxter endures a long, slow road to *redemption*.' (*The Guardian*, 7 February, 2006 – reference to British skier Alain Baxter, who was stripped of medal at Salt Lake City Winter Olympics 2002.)

'Robben *redeems* himself as Chelsea stroll to victory.' (*The Times*, 9 February, 2006 – reference to opening goal scored by Arjen Robben in 4-1 victory over Everton.)

'There's also a handy glossary which in itself sheds light on Italian footballing psychology: avoiding relegation is *la salvezza, salvation*.' (*The Independent*, 20 February, 2006 – 'Book of the Week' review of *Calcio: A History of Italian Football*, by John Foot.)

'Ramos makes his fair share of mistakes in the centre of defence but has a formidable combination of speed and strength that means he is nearly always able to *redeem* himself.' (*The Independent*, 21 February, 2006 – reference to 19-year old Real Madrid central defender Sergio Ramos.)

'Toni the *saviour* as Ballack denies move to Chelsea.' (*The Independent*, 1 March, 2006 – reference to Italy's Luca Toni and Germany's Michael Ballack prior to international friendly, which Italy won 4-1.)

'Crouch could be Sven's *saviour* in Germany'. (*Irish Examiner*, 3 March, 2006 – reference to possible England role in World Cup for Liverpool striker Peter Crouch.)

'Given calls for O'Neill to *save* Toon.' (*Irish Independent*, 25 March, 2006 – reference to goalkeeper Shay Given's advocacy for appointment of Martin O' Neill as manager of Newcastle United.)

'*Saviours*' days.' (*The Times*, 31 March, 2006 – title of article about famous goalkeepers, including Gordon Banks, Albert Camus, Che Guevara and Pope John Paul II.)

'The *Saviours*.' (*Irish Independent*, 11 March, 2006 – reference to Arsenal and Liverpool managers Arsene Wenger and Rafael Benitez.)

'Rio's road to *redemption*.' (*The Independent on Sunday*, 1 May, 2006 – reference to England's centre-half Rio Ferdinand prior to World Cup Tournament.)

'Eight people to *save* England's World Cup.' (*The Guardian*, 3 May, 2006 – reference to England team of doctors and physio-therapists.)

'Reina *redeemed* by penalty heroics.' (*The Independent*, 15 May, 2006 – reference to role of Liverpool goalkeeper Jose 'Pepe'

Reina in his club's victory over West Ham Utd in FA Cup Final after penalty shoot-out.)

'Carragher goes from being "not good enough" to Sven's midfield *saviour*.' (*The Independent*, 30 May, 2006 – reference to socalled England midfield holding role for Liverpool defender Jamie Carragher.)

'From Czech To Mate – How Frank Lowy *Saved* Aussie Football.' (*The Observer*, 18 June, 2006 – reference to role of Australia's richest man in rescuing soccer down under.)

'Four years ago Brazil and Ronaldo earned *redemption*.' (Bill O' Herlihy on RTÉ Two, 8 June, 2006, introducing preview of soccer World Cup.)

'Saviour?' (*Irish Examiner*, 8 August, 2006 – reference to 'Midlands Messiah' Martin O' Neill after his appointment as manager of Aston Villa.)

'*Redemption* beckons as brilliant Italy emerge from avalanche of dirt.' (*Irish Independent*, 6 July, 2006 – Columnist James Lawton's reference to Italy's World Cup semi-final victory over Germany in midst of corruption crisis enveloping clubs in Italy's Serie A.)

'Rapid *redemption* for Ronaldo.' (*Irish Independent*, 21 August, 2006 – reference to role of Ronaldo in Machester Utd's 5-1 victory over Fulham in opening game of 2006-7 Premiership in wake of controversy over sending off of team-mate Wayne Rooney in World Cup quarter-final clash between Portugal and England.)

'*Redemption* day for Wenger and Gunners.' (*Irish Independent*, 18 September, 2006 – reference to 1-0 victory over rivals Manchester Utd.)

'England given instant chance for *redemption*.' (*The Independent*, 9 October, 2006 – reference to England's 0-0 draw against Macedonia in Euro 2008 qualifier.)

'Ireland *saves* Ireland'. (*Irish Examiner*, 8 February, 2007 – reference to last-minute goal scored by Manchester City player Stephen Ireland in Republic of Ireland's 2-1 victory over lowly ranked San Marino.)

'Miller is *saviour* for Sunderland.' (*The Daily Telegraph*, 25 February, 2007 – reference to injury-time winning score by Liam Miller against promotion rivals Derby County.)

'Burden of expectation won't hold back Rossoneri as season *salvation* beckons.' (*Irish Independent*, 24 April, 2007 – reference to AC Milan's fortunes in Italy's Serie A and European Champions League competitions.)

'John O'Shea's road to *redemption*.' (*The Daily Telegraph*, 18 May, 2007 – reference to role and reversal of fortune for Manchester United player in the club's capture of the Premiership title.)

'Stokes a late, late *saviour*.' (*Sunday Tribune*, 2 December, 2007 – reference to Anthony Stokes' goal in the third minute of injury time which earned Sunderland a 1-0 victory over Derby County'.)

'*Redemption* realistic for exiled Ireland, but only on Trap's terms.' (*Irish Independent*, 10 October 2008 – reference to Manchester City player Stephen Ireland and his refusal to play for his country.)

'Bulgarian pin-up is the unlikely *saviour* of sumo.' (*The Irish Times*, 28 September 2005 – reference to sumo wrestler Kaloyan Mahlyanov's attempt to win his first major trophy at the Japanese autumn Grand Sumo Tournament.)

'*Deliverance* for Mayweather.' (*Irish Examiner*, 7 May, 2007 – reference to Floyd Maywaether's – 'Boxing's bad boy beat the Golden Boy in one of the richest fights ever' – victory over Oscar De La Hoya for the WBC 154-pound title.)

'New Zealand seek *redemption*.' (*The Daily Telegraph*, 23 June, 2007 – reference to Emirates Team New Zealand in America's Cup sailing competition.)

APPENDIX B

REFERENCES TO ESCHATOLOGY

'Faldo happy to steer clear of the *purgatory* of Pinehurst.' (*Irish Independent*, 31 May, 2005 – reference to golfer Nick Faldo giving US Open a miss.)

'Campbell stuck in *limbo* as Eriksson wavers on line-up.' (*The Times*, 6 September, 2005 – reference to whether English manager would select Arsenal player Sol Campbell to play or not.)

'Leon in *limbo*.' (*Irish Independent*, 27 November, 2007 – reference to Cork City striker Leon McSweeney's contractual situation.)

'England left in limbo by T20 dispute'. (The Independent, 9 October 2008 – reference to Twenty20 cricket game.)

'Liverpool fans in *limbo* after Atletico switch.' (*The Daily Telegraph*, 15 October, 2008 – reference to travel plans and venue for Liverpool versus Atletico Madrid.)

'Newcastle *limbo* risks losing Owen, warns Butt.' (*The Guardian*, 11 November, 2008 – reference to uncertainty over ownership of Newcastle United which could unsettle the future of Michael Owen there.)

'Arsenal reign supreme in football of the *gods*.' (*The Guardian*, 10 November, 2008 – 'Arsenal played *angelic* football and found some hope that they will receive their reward for it long before they get to *heaven*' – opening sentence by Kevin McCarra.)

'Ascension into hurling *heaven*.' (*Irish Examiner*, 13 September, 2005 – reference to Cork's All-Ireland hurling victory over Kilkenny.)

'Cook finds *heaven* after his Ashes *hell*.' (*The Daily Telegraph*, 18 May, 2007 – reference to English cricketer Alastair Cook's century (100) against the West Indies.)

'Armagh unleash *Hell*.' (*The Sunday Tribune*, 21 August, 2005 – reference to Armagh's defeat of Dublin by 2-17 to 1-11.)

'A *Heavenly* Match.' (*Irish Examiner*, 21 June, 2006 – reference to 1978 World Cup Final between Argentina – 3-1 winners after extra time – and Holland.)

'Angel in *heaven* at Oakmont.' (*Herald AM*, 18 June, 2007 – reference to Argentinian golfer Angel Cabrera, winner of 2007 US Open at Oakmont Hills.)

'*Paradise* Regained.' (*Irish Examiner*, 16 January, 2005 – reference to Glasgow Celtic's 4-2 victory over Kilmarnock in Scottish Premier League in home debut for former Manchester United and Irish international player Roy Keane.)

'Ferguson's Blue *Hell*.' (*The Guardian*, 16 2006 – reference to Manchester United manager after his side lost derby game against Manchester City.)

'The greatest of games is heading straight to *hell*.' (*The Independent*, 11 October, 2008 – headline reference in piece by James Lawton on saving of Twenty20 competition.)

'Celtic in *Paradise*.' (*The Daily Telegraph*, 23 November, 2006 – reference to Glasgow Celtic's 1-0 victory against Manchester United to ensure qualification for knockout stage of the Champions League for the first time.)

'Football Heaven.' (*The Racing Post*, 19 May, 2007 – preview of FA Cup Final between Chelsea and Manchester United with picture of renewed Wembley stadium at top and portraits of managers Jose Mourinho and Alex Ferguson beneath.)

'Chelsea in Blue *Heaven*.' (*The Sunday Tribune*, 20 May, 2007 – reference to Chelsea's 1-0 victory over Manchester United in first FA Cup Final at Wembley for seven years.)

'Cole's Blue *Heaven*.' (*The Sunday Times*, 2 January, 2005 – reference to Chelsea player Joe Cole.)

'Demons in heaven as O'Reilly strikes late.' (*Irish Independent*, 30 January, 2006 – reference to UCD Demons 81-79 victory over Limerick Lions in basketball Superleague final.)

'*Heaven* can wait on days like this.' (*Irish Independent*, 17 September, 2007 – reference to Kerry's runaway All-Ireland victory over neighbours and arch-rivals Cork.)

'Rampant Toffeees in seventh *heaven* but it's pure *hell* for Keane's cats.' (*Irish Independent*, 26 November, 2007 – reference to Sunderland's 7-1 'drubbing', defeat by Everton.)

'*Second Coming.*' (*Irish Independent*, 27 August, 2005 – caption for photos of County (Cork, Dublin, Kerry, Tyrone) captains in All-Ireland football championship semi-finals.)

'The *Second Coming* of Tyrone and Armagh.' (*The Sunday Independent*, 4 September, 2005 – reference to replay of Armagh versus Tyrone semi-final.)

'*A Second Coming.*' (*The Sunday Tribune*, 25 September, 2005 – reference to All-Ireland final line-up between Kerry and Tyrone.)

'Paul Broadhurst will be hoping for a *second coming* tomorrow, a week after his world collapsed around him at Wentworth.' (*The Daily Telegraph*, 2 June, 2007 – reference to British golfer Paul Broadhurst.)

'Joker's *second coming.*' (*The Independent*, 14 June, 2007 – reference to career of Peter Chapple-Hyam, trainer of Authorized, the winner of the 2007 Derby.)

'The *second coming* of Kearney.' (*Irish Examiner*, 15 June, 2007 – reference to return of Cork City player Liam Kearney to match against Shelbourne, the club he left at the end of last season.)

'Convert who convinced on his *second coming.*' (*The Irish Times*, 13 November, 2008 – reference to All Black second row forward Brad Thorn.)

'"Bishop" Paddy rewarded with insider's view of two glorious *ascensions.*' (*The Sunday Independent*, 27 May, 2007 – reference to Armagh team kitman Paddy McNamee.)